Sovereign Joy

Sovereign Joy explores the performance of festive Black kings and queens among Afro-Mexicans between 1539 and 1640. This fascinating study illustrates how the first African and Afro-creole people in colonial Mexico transformed their ancestral culture into a shared identity among Afro-Mexicans, with particular focus on how public festival participation expressed their culture and subjectivities, as well as redefined their colonial condition and social standing. By analyzing this hitherto understudied aspect of Afro-Mexican Catholic confraternities in both literary texts and visual culture, Miguel A. Valerio teases out the deeply ambivalent and contradictory meanings behind these public processions and festivities that often reinscribed structures of race and hierarchy. Were they markers of Catholic subjecthood, and what sort of corporate structures did they create to project standing and respectability? *Sovereign Joy* examines many of these possibilities, and in the process highlights the central place occupied by Africans and their descendants in colonial culture. Through performance, Afro-Mexicans affirmed their being: the sovereignty of joy and the joy of sovereignty.

Miguel A. Valerio is Assistant Professor of Spanish at Washington University in St. Louis. His research focuses on the African diaspora in the literatures and cultures of the Iberian world. This is his first monograph.

T0370974

Afro-Latin America

Series editors

George Reid Andrews, *University of Pittsburgh*
Alejandro de la Fuente, *Harvard University*

This series reflects the coming of age of the new, multidisciplinary field of Afro-Latin American Studies, which centers on the histories, cultures, and experiences of people of African descent in Latin America. The series aims to showcase scholarship produced by different disciplines, including history, political science, sociology, ethnomusicology, anthropology, religious studies, art, law, and cultural studies. It covers the full temporal span of the African Diaspora in Latin America, from the early colonial period to the present, and includes continental Latin America, the Caribbean, and other key areas in the region where Africans and their descendants have made a significant impact.

A full list of titles published in the series can be found at:
www.cambridge.org/afro-latin-america

Sovereign Joy

Afro-Mexican Kings and Queens, 1539–1640

MIGUEL A. VALERIO

Washington University in St. Louis

CAMBRIDGE
UNIVERSITY PRESS

CAMBRIDGE
UNIVERSITY PRESS

Shaftesbury Road, Cambridge CB2 8EA, United Kingdom

One Liberty Plaza, 20th Floor, New York, NY 10006, USA

477 Williamstown Road, Port Melbourne, VIC 3207, Australia

314–321, 3rd Floor, Plot 3, Splendor Forum, Jasola District Centre, New Delhi – 110025, India

103 Penang Road, #05–06/07, Visioncrest Commercial, Singapore 238467

Cambridge University Press is part of Cambridge University Press & Assessment, a department of the University of Cambridge.

We share the University's mission to contribute to society through the pursuit of education, learning and research at the highest international levels of excellence.

www.cambridge.org
Information on this title: www.cambridge.org/9781009078207

DOI: 10.1017/9781009086905

First published 2022
First paperback edition 2023

A catalogue record for this publication is available from the British Library

Library of Congress Cataloging-in-Publication data
NAMES: Valerio, Miguel Alejandro, author.
TITLE: Sovereign joy : Afro-Mexican kings and queens, 1539–1640 /Miguel A. Valerio.
OTHER TITLES: Afro-Mexican kings and queens, 1539–1640
DESCRIPTION: Cambridge, United Kingdom : New York : Cambridge University Press, 2022. | Series: Afro-Latin America | Includes bibliographical references and index.
IDENTIFIERS: LCCN 2022010286 (print) | LCCN 2022010287 (ebook) | ISBN 9781316514382 (hardback) | ISBN 9781009086905 (ebook)
SUBJECTS: LCSH: Blacks – Mexico – Mexico City – History – 16th century. | Blacks – Mexico – Mexico City – History – 16th century. | Festivals – Mexico – Mexico City – History – 16th century. | Festivals – Mexico – Mexico City – History – 17th century. | Mexico City (Mexico) – Social life and customs – 16th century. | Mexico City (Mexico) – Social life and customs – 17th century. | BISAC: HISTORY / Latin America / General
CLASSIFICATION: LCC F1386.9.B55 V35 2022 (print) | LCC F1386.9.B55 (ebook) | DDC 972/.53009031–dc23/eng/20220328
LC record available at https://lccn.loc.gov/2022010286
LC ebook record available at https://lccn.loc.gov/2022010287

ISBN   978-1-316-51438-2   Hardback
ISBN   978-1-009-07820-7   Paperback

Cambridge University Press & Assessment has no responsibility for the persistence or accuracy of URLs for external or third-party internet websites referred to in this publication and does not guarantee that any content on such websites is, or will remain, accurate or appropriate.

For all Afro-cofrades
of the past, present, and future

And for my cousin Banni

In memoriam
Jorge Miguel López Valerio
1978–2021

Morena criolla:

Carbón con alma, viviré a la fama.

(Coal with a soul, I will live in fame.)

Torres, Festín

Aquí estoy, vivo y moreno,

 de mi estirpe defensor.

Miguel Hernández

Contents

Figures

Tables

Preface

Joyful Defiance

Blackness is an immense and defiant joy.
Imani Perry[1]

I wrote this book during a turbulent period: between the election of Donald Trump and the COVID-19 pandemic. Black lives continued (and continue) to be wasted – disposed of – by state terror. Thus, from a historical perspective, little had changed in five hundred years. This became ever clearer to me as I wrote Chapter 2. As that chapter explores, in colonial Mexico City, Blacks were summarily executed – hanged and quartered – for their festive practices. The documents at the center of that chapter underscore the longue durée of anti-Black state terror. Like the rest of the book, however, that is not the only story it tells. In 1611, a slave owner beat one of his female slaves to death. (In 1611, slave meant Black, and Black, slave, even when it came to "free/d" Blacks.) In protest, more than forty-five hundred Afro-Mexicans carried the woman's body through Mexico City's streets demanding justice. As they did so, they danced. White audiences could not understand why they would dance for a mournful cause. This remains true today, from New Orleans funerals to Black Lives Matter (BLM) protests. As the Black scholar Imani Perry noted in *The Atlantic* on June 15, 2020: white audiences associate Blackness with tragedy, sorrow, and downtroddenness. As I explore in Chapter 2, and Perry points out, many see Blackness as a curse. As

[1] Perry, "Racism Is Terrible. Blackness Is Not," *The Atlantic*, June 15, 2020.

Perry contends, this is not to see Blackness as Black people see themselves:

> Joy is not found in the absence of pain and suffering. It exists through it. The scourges of racism, poverty, incarceration, medical discrimination, and so much more shape black life. We live with the vestiges of slavery and Jim Crow, and with the new creative tides of antiblackness directed toward us and our children. We know the wail of a dying man calling for his mama, and it echoes into the distant past and cuts into our deepest wounds. The injustice is inescapable. So yes, I want the world to recognize our suffering. But I do not want pity from a single soul. Sin and shame are found in neither my body nor my identity. Blackness is an immense and defiant joy.[2]

As two opinion pieces, one in the *New York Times* and the other in the *Washington Post*, noted a few days before Perry's piece, BLM protesters were seen dancing in the streets of US cities.[3] (I too found myself dancing alongside others as we marched.) Like their Mexican forebears, these protesters were channeling their defiance – of a world built on the principle that Black lives do not matter, are not lives – through their bodies-in-motion. They were joyfully defying the world that denies them ontology – even basic philosophically meaningful Being.[4] Not only that. In 1611, as in other times, Afro-Mexicans, like their counterparts across geographies and time, did not let state terror hamper their festive traditions, going on to replace exiled and deceased festive kings and queens with new ones and making plans for Christmas and Easter. Yet these were expressions not of callousness or cynicism but rather of joyful defiance, affirmations of life. The performances studied in this book express this radical Blackness, and what could be more radical than performing as a sovereign people in a slavocracy?

This book studies the joyful defiance Blacks wrought in Mexico City between 1539 and 1640. It thus documents the first instances of such defiance in the Americas. It studies how that defiance was born and fashioned during its early years and how and why it took roots in the lives of diasporic Afrodescendants. It points to Africa as the source and the diaspora as the cause. Enslaved into a strange new world, not all Africans succumbed to tragedy, sorrow, and

---

[2] Ibid.
[3] Siobhan Burke, "Dancing Bodies That Proclaim: Black Lives Matter," *New York Times*, June 9, 2020; Sarah L. Kauffman, "In Pain and Rage, a Protester Approached Police. And Then He Danced," *Washington Post*, June 6, 2020.
[4] See Fanon, "The Fact of Blackness"; Warren, *Ontological Terror*.

downtroddenness. Instead, they defied the ontology of that world by asserting their humanity through festive customs. They baffled white audiences by being joyful when they were expected to be mournful, by being independent when they were meant to be helpless, and by staging lavish displays that confounded the colonial imagination. This book then is a testament of their joyful defiance, which should serve as an inspiration for those of us still in the struggle. It proclaims that the Black past (and present) is not only one of tragedy – most of all, ontologically – and that to study joy is not to forget pain.

Acknowledgments

This book would not have been possible without Lisa Voigt, who has been with it since its inception in 2013; Kathryn Santner's keen editorial eye; Stephanie Kirk, Diana Taylor, Mariselle Meléndez, and Ximena Gómez – my forever *cofrada* – who read and commented on previous drafts; the anonymous readers; the editors of this series, Alejandro de la Fuente and George Reid Andrews; and Cambridge University Press's team, especially Cecelia Cancellaro and Ruth Boyes. Nor would it have come to fruition without the generous support of The Ohio State University Graduate School, Department of Spanish and Portuguese, Center for Languages, Literatures, and Cultures, Center for Medieval and Renaissance Studies, and Office of Diversity and Inclusion, the Huntington Library, the National Academies, the Andrew W. Mellon Foundation, the Institute for Citizens and Scholars, the Ford Foundation, the Renaissance Society of America, my department at Washington University in St. Louis, the Center for the Humanities, the Center for the Study of Race, Ethnicity, and Equity, and the dean of the Faculty of Arts and Sciences. I am forever grateful to the custodians of the precious sources I was privileged to study in Seville, Lisbon, Mexico City, Salvador, Brazil, Rio de Janeiro, and the Huntington, and to Pamela, Rebeka, and Yolanda for their support.

The book has also benefited from conversations with Lúcia Costigan, Ignacio Corona, Roxann Wheeler, Michelle Wibbelsman, Jean Allman, Sherwin Bryant, Agnes Lugo-Ortiz, Silvia Hunold Lara, Anna More, Nicole von Germeten, Karen Graubart, Herman L. Bennett, Cécile Fromont, Elena Deanda-Camacho, Erin Rowe, Daphne Brooks, Robert Kendrick, Javiera Jaque Hidalgo (my other forever *cofrada*), Larissa Brewer-García, Angélica María Sánchez Barona, Krystle Sweda, Scarlett

McPherson, Adrian Masters, Chloe Ireton, Christina Villareal, Maria Cecilia Ulrickson, Warren Stangl, Nicolás Alejandro González Quintero, Juan Carlos de Orellana Sánchez, Matthew Francis Rarey, Kristie Flannery, Danielle Terrazas Williams, Pablo Miguel Sierra Silva, Fernanda Bretones, Isabela Fraga, Nicolas Jones, Noémie Ndiaye, Allison Bigelow, Jorge Téllez, Daniel Nemser, Joseph Clark, Nathalie Miraval, Carolyn Fornoff, and Xiomara Verenice Cervantes-Gómez, among others.

I was given the opportunity to present my developing ideas at different fora. I thank the organizers and participants of the Symposium on Afro-Christian Festivals in the Americas held at Yale University in February 2015, in the middle of my candidacy exams, Legacies of Conquest at Cambridge University in April 2016, the Americas before 1900 Working Group at Ohio State in March 2017, Slave Subjectivities at the University of Lisbon in July 2018, the Early Modern Reading Group at Washington University in St. Louis in March 2019, Empire and Its Aftermath at the University of Pittsburgh in April 2019, Rethinking Colonialism in Mexico and the Americas at the University of Tulsa in November 2019, the Slavery and Visual Culture Working Group and the Workshop on Latin America and the Caribbean at the University of Chicago in December 2019, Iberian Connections 7.2 at Yale in November 2020, the Cabildo Speaker Series at Oregon State also in November 2020, the Black Studies Symposium at Washington College in February 2021, the conferences where I have presented and the other universities where I was invited to present. Earlier versions of sections from Chapters 1 and 4 appeared in the volume *Afro-Christian Festivals in the Americas* and the journals *Afro-Hispanic Review* and *Confraternitas*.

Mine has been a long journey marked by traumas and promises – it is therefore defiant to write and seek joy, some may say an ontometaphysical impossibility in our anti-Black world. In thanking my family, I do not thank the usual suspects: the doting mother, the stern father who was never there. I thank my grandmother for sacrificing herself for her children and grandchildren, my aunts, Migue and Marcia, and my older sister, Ana, for playing mother to me, my siblings, More, Juanka, and Leo, and my cousins, David, Ricardo, and Nairobi. My older uncle Reyes played father to us all. Many who have been on this journey with me are still caught in its traumas and cannot read this book. I will be silent on them, as this book will be silent to them, speaking no promises. Catholic rituals have always captured my imagination; in my teens, I immersed myself in them, and priests and nuns, especially Father Al and Sister Claudia – who, among other things, lent me the first book of Darío's poetry I read – were instrumental in changing my life's trajectory. I am forever grateful to the Redemptorists, who took a gamble on me and lost, as I immersed myself in literature, not theology. Like my first encounter with Father Al in 2000, my first encounter with Latin American literature changed the course of my life and has brought me here. I would like to name some of my first accomplices at this juncture: Myrna, Eduardo, Alina, Marie-Lise, Carmen, and Toscano were my first teachers of Latin American literature in New York, where after leaving the seminary, my great-aunt, Milagros, gave me a launching pad for my life's new direction. In two years in her house, I went from being this unfamiliar kid from the old country to her children, Lisa, Jessica, Priscilla, and Samantha, to becoming their cousin. It was a joy to be with them as they welcomed new members into the family: Shan, Jonas, Haylie, Logan, Jonathan, Jason, Amaya, and Joel. I thank the Huertas and Lenny and Sally for their generosity, model, and mentorship.

My experience in Columbus, Ohio, where this project more than captured my imagination and first spoke to my roots, would not have been as full as it was without the close bonds a group of us developed. Meghan and Robin – my "church" buddies – Lorena, Celia, Fernando, Aintzane, Lee, Oihane, Laura, Alba, Madeline, John – *la familia* – *sin vosotres, no se hubiere podido. Gracias por todo, con toda el alma.* Patricia, my forever *vecina*, who predated the family, *gracias por su amistad y apoyo continuo en mis tragicomedias.* Thanks also to Omar, Paola, Mónica, Alessandro, Ane, and many others, as well as the professors who welcomed us into their homes. Although I met them in New York, in Dayton, Ohio, I had a family in Mamma, La Ron, and Brittany. In St. Louis, I have benefited immensely from Diana, Christina, Bahia (*mi gente!*), Mayela, Stève, Erik, Fran, Hedy, Ana, Clara, Juan Pablo, Elena, Luna, and Eliza and Caio's friendships. At Washington University, besides the support of my Roman Language and Literatures colleagues, I have enjoyed the collegiality of Leo, Luis, Cynthia, and Rebecca. At home, where I write, and in my private life with its ups and downs and sleepless nights, I have had the reassurance of AJ's unwavering love and faith. Your dedication to occupational therapy has been an inspiring example. Finally, I thank your parents, Dinah, Jim, and Michelle, for their love and generosity.

I dedicate this book to all *Afro-cofrades* of the past, present, and future, who wrought, continue to fashion, and will bring about new forms of joyful defiance, to my cousin Banni – may she find the joyful today she seeks – and to the memory of my brother More, whose Black being was too meagerly dotted with joy. May they forgive me for its shortcomings.

Abbreviations

AASSB	Arquivo da Arquidiocese de São Salvador da Bahia
AGCA	Archivo General de la Corona de Aragón
AGI	Archivo General de Indias
AGN	Archivo General de la Nación, México
AHAM	Archivo Histórico de la Archidiócesis de México
AHDF	Archivo Histórico de la Ciudad de México
AHS	Archivo Histórico de Sevilla
AHU	Arquivo Histórico Ultramarino
AMB	Axiu Municipal de Barcelona
ANB	Arquivo Nacional do Brasil
ANTT	Arquivo Nacional Torre Tombo
APEB	Arquivo Público do Estado de Bahia
AVM	Archivo de la Villa de Madrid
BCC	Biblioteca Civica Centrale, Turin
BNB	Biblioteca Nacional do Brasil
BNE	Biblioteca Nacional de España
BNF	Bibliothèque nationale de France
BNP	Biblioteca Nacional de Portugal
BPR	Biblioteca del Palacio Real, Madrid
HL	The Huntington Library
RNB	Rouen nouvelles bibliothèques
SUB	Göttingen State and University Library

Introduction

Thinking Black Joy, Sovereignty, and Being from Colonial Latin America

In February 1539, Mexico City descended into jubilation to celebrate the Truce of Nice, accorded the previous year between Emperor Charles V and Francis I of France. The celebration constituted New Spain's first major civic ceremony.[1] It is significant therefore that the festivities included a performance (*inbençión*) by "más de çinquenta" (more than fifty) "xinetes hechos de negros y negras *con su rey y reina*" (horseback riders made up of Black men and women *with their king and queen*).[2] The Black performers wore "grandes riquezas ... de oro y piedras ricas y aljófar y argentería" (great riches of gold and precious stones and pearls and silver) as well as a great "diversidad de rostros" (diversity of masks).[3] The Blacks' performance also included a mock battle between the Black actors and a group of Indigenous performers. Described by the conquistador Bernal Díaz del Castillo (ca. 1496–1584) in chapter 201 of his *Historia verdadera de la conquista de la Nueva España* (*True History of the Conquest of New Spain*) (completed ca. 1575), this is also the earliest known American example of a performative genre that became a staple of the African diaspora in the Atlantic: festive Black kings and queens. In Mexico City, there is record of this performance taking place again in 1608, 1610, 1611, 1612, and 1640, in both public ceremonies and communal settings, and as I analyze in this book, it may have been part of an annual celebration among Afro-Mexicans.

[1] See Lopes Don, "Carnivals"; Harris, *Aztecs*, 123–31.
[2] Díaz del Castillo, *Historia verdadera*, 755; my emphasis.   [3] Ibid.

Festive Black kings and queens would be found all over the African diaspora and have been widely studied in Brazil and to a lesser extent in the Iberian Peninsula, the River Plate region, Peru, Panama, Cuba, and even New Orleans, New England, and the Danish Caribbean, but not in Mexico.[4] As the scholarship shows, this performance became a preferred form of festive expression among diasporic Afrodescendants. Through it, Atlantic Blacks sought to recreate parts of their African world as they built a new one. They expressed ancestral and diasporic sovereignty; in sum, they articulated their subjectivities, or how they understood themselves and the world around them. *Sovereign Joy* studies this performative genre among Afro-Mexicans as an expression of their collective agency and selfhood.

In this study, I turn to the only five known texts that describe Afro-Mexican festive kings and queens. Besides Díaz del Castillo's text, I study two other festival accounts. The first is an anonymous "Relación de las fiestas insignes" ("Account of the Great Festival") about Mexico City's 1610 festivities for the beatification of the founder of the Society of Jesus, Ignatius of Loyola. This text describes two performances of Black festive kings (no queens). The second, *Festín hecho por las morenas criollas de la muy noble y muy leal Ciudad de México* (*Dance Performed by the Creole Black Women of the Most Noble and Most Loyal City of Mexico*) (Mexico City, 1640), is unique in many ways. For one, it is the only known colonial festival account solely dedicated to a Black performance. It is also the only text that describes a Black performance for the festivities that normally accompanied the arrival of a new viceroy. Moreover, and perhaps most importantly, it is the only text studied here where women are the sole protagonists.

Besides these celebratory texts, I study two court reports that illustrate how colonial officials could use Afro-Mexicans' festive practices against them. These accusatory texts underscore the anti-Black milieu within which Afro-Mexicans practiced their festive traditions. They demonstrate that while colonial officials welcomed, even sought, Black kings and queens for public festivals, the same authorities were displeased, even

---

[4] Bastide, *African Civilisations*, 182–4; Bettelheim, "Carnaval of Los Congos"; Craft, *When the Devil Knocks*; "*¡Los Gringos Vienen!*"; Mello e Souza, *Reis negros*; Kiddy, *Blacks of the Rosary*; Fromont, "Dancing for the King of Congo"; Walker, "The Queen of *los Congos*; Fogelman and Goldberg, "'*El rey de los congos*'"; Borucki, *From Shipmates to Soldiers*, 99–105; Lund Drolet, *El ritual congo*; Dewulf, *From the Kingdom of Kongo*; Howard, *Changing History*; Piersen, *Black Yankees*, 117–28; Valerio, "The Queen of Sheba's Manifold Body"; "Black Confraternity Members"; "A Mexican *Sangamento?*"

felt threatened by the freedom and autonomy these practices made manifest when staged outside an officially sanctioned festive space.

These accusatory texts have received far more attention than the celebratory ones. For this reason, Afro-Mexican kings and queens have only been studied within the context of colonial Mexico's supposed Black revolts.[5] In other words, scholars have mainly encountered Afro-Mexican kings and queens in these accusatory documents. This has even included the confraternities (or lay Catholic brotherhoods) that often staged festive kings and queens. By focusing on celebratory texts that explicitly describe the performances of Black festive kings and queens among Mexico City's Black confraternities, *Sovereign Joy* attends to this hitherto unstudied aspect of Afro-Mexican sodalities in early colonial Mexico City. It thus steers the discussion about Black kings and queens in colonial Mexico City in a different direction: to a focus on how this performative tradition allowed Afro-Mexicans to express communal sovereignty and their understanding of themselves and of the world around them to themselves and to their host community, Mexico City.

FESTIVE BLACK KINGS AND QUEENS AND THE ARCHIVE AND THE REPERTOIRE

Moving beyond the dichotomy of the archive and the repertoire proposed by Diana Taylor, I read these texts as performance:[6] performance of the performances they describe so ekphrastically, on one hand, and, on the other, of "white" colonial discourse and practices, which often framed the performances they describe within what Peter Mason has called the "exotic genre," which often lacked cultural and geographic specificity.[7] Nonetheless, while the texts studied here are often limited, they are the only repertoire we have of Afro-Mexicans' festive practices. Read critically, they do not just illuminate "white" colonial discourse and practices but, more importantly, give us the only window we have into Afro-Mexicans'

---

[5] Examples include Germeten, *Black Blood Brothers*, 71–103; Bristol, *Christians, Blasphemers, and Witches*, 93–112; Proctor, "Slave Rebellion"; Tardieu, *Resistencia de los negros en el virreinato de México*, 229–76; Palmer, *Slaves*, 110–44; Masferrer León, "Por las ánimas de negros bozales"; Riva Palacio, *Los treinta y tres negros*; Ngou-Mve, *Lucha y victorias*, 137–45; Martínez, "The Black Blood of New Spain"; Nemser, "Triangulating Blackness."

[6] See Taylor, *The Archive and the Repertoire*. I am grateful to Xiomara Verenice Cervantes-Gómez for helping me work through this idea.

[7] See Mason, *Infelicities*.

festive practices, as these practices have not survived in Mexico – as they have elsewhere.

The book casts a wide spatial and temporal diasporic net to supplement the Mexican texts, which more often than not provide scant information. This broad diasporic perspective includes the use of texts and visual material from other times and geographies. The purpose of this approach is to move beyond the text to see, albeit through it, what can be recovered of Afro-Mexicans' festive repertoire. While performance has been traditionally understood as ephemeral, irrecuperable, in performance studies, the absence of live performances of colonial Afro-Mexican festive customs forces us to avail ourselves of the archive to reconstruct them.[8]

Since the texts discussed here – perhaps except for *Festín* – give only brief descriptions of the performances (most are one paragraph at most), a diasporic approach can help us reconstruct the performance from a few lines. This is especially true of Chapter 1, where I discuss Díaz del Castillo's account of the 1539 festival and lay out a genealogy of the performance as a prelude to the remainder of the book. Long in use in diasporic African studies, this approach utilizes similar sources from other geographies and periods of the African diaspora in order to reconstruct a Black diasporic practice that is not given in full in the source under scrutiny but rather supplemented in remarkable ways by one or more sources from a different geography and/or period.[9] Therefore, in order to attempt a relatively full reconstruction of an early modern performance of Black festive kings and queens, I compare Díaz del Castillo's text with the most detailed description of a Black festive king and queen performance to have come down to us, in eighteenth-century Brazil. The continuities in these texts emphasize common – albeit not identical – practices across the African diaspora and, with the first recorded instance of a Black festive king and queen performance in the Americas taking place in Mexico City in 1539, Diaz del Castillo's text marks Mexico as a key early player in the cultural transformations prompted by European expansion into Africa and the Americas.[10] While this approach has its limitations – for one, it does not provide exact parallels, and if not done properly, risks homogenizing the diaspora – it proves useful for reconstructing – however partially – diasporic Black culture from fragmentary sources.

---

[8] I am grateful to Xiomara Verenice Cervantes-Gómez for helping me work through this idea as well.

[9] See, for example, Piersen, *Black Yankees*, 117–28; Chasteen, *National Rhythms*, 170.

[10] Heywood, *Central Africans*; Heywood and Thornton, *Central Africans, Atlantic Creoles*; Thornton, *Africa and Africans*.

This diasporic framework allows me to use both textual and visual sources to supplement the Mexican texts' many lacunae or silences. In many cases, the old adage that a picture is worth a thousand words holds true, for – albeit not without its own limitations – visual art furnishes details that written texts do not. We cannot obtain a full picture of Afro-Mexican festive culture without examining those visual sources, even if they are from other geographies and periods, as there is no visual record of Afro-Mexican festive king and queen performances. (Therefore, this book's cover comes from early nineteenth-century Brazil.) This approach is warranted by the fact that urban colonial Afro-Mexican culture did not exist in isolation, but rather within the broader network of the Black Atlantic, as these supplementary sources show. Moreover, the texts' ekphrastic nature also invites comparison with the visual record.

While the texts may have myriad lacunae, the images I use to illustrate them give us a resonant picture of Afrodescendants' festive lives, even in bondage, or despite it. Thus, through these images I extend Tina M. Campt's invitation "to 'listen' rather than simply 'look at' images," for they reveal an element "that is critical to Black Atlantic cultural formations: sound."[11] In this fashion, we become attuned to what Paul Gilroy has dubbed "the politics of transfiguration" or "the power of music [and performance] in developing black struggles by communicating information, organizing consciousness, and testing out or deploying the forms of subjectivity which are required by political agency."[12] This book seeks to account for the sounds (and colors) of Afro-Mexicans' festive practices, with the help of their counterparts from other localities of the African diaspora in the Atlantic.

ITINERARY

Chapter 1 studies the Black performances for Mexico City's 1539 celebration of the Truce of Nice. This chapter puts into use the diasporic framework perhaps more than any of the others. Using that framework, I reconstruct the performance from Díaz del Castillo's few lines by situating the performance in its broader Atlantic setting. The chapter identifies the origin of the performance in Africa, concretely the Kingdom of Kongo, and documents its diasporic transformations in the Iberian Peninsula, before the first Blacks who accompanied the first Spanish colonizers of New Spain brought it to the Americas. The chapter thus asserts Mexico

---

[11] Campt, *Listening to Images*, 6.　　[12] Gilroy, *The Black Atlantic*, 36–7.

City as a central site of the birth of the Black Atlantic and the cultural transformations set in motion by imperial expansion. The chapter also begins to demonstrate the central role confraternities played in Afrodescendants' diasporic festive practices.

The 1539 performance is surprising for many reasons, not least of which was the fact that it took place less than two years after Blacks in New Spain had been accused of electing a king as part of a plot to "matar a todos los españoles y aserse con la tierra" ("kill all the Spaniards and take over the land").[13] This pattern would repeat itself several times throughout the colonial period. In Chapter 2, through a close reading of two accusatory documents, and the Nahua chronicler Domingo Chimalpahin's (1579–1660) version of those events, however, I question colonial authorities' misrepresentation of Black festive kings and queens. These documents detailed the supposed conspiracies Afro-Mexicans plotted in 1608–9 and 1611–12 to rape and kill all the Spaniards, enslave the Indigenous population, and establish an African kingdom. As in 1537, these plots are said to have begun with the election of kings and, these times, queens. In fact, that, and that Portuguese slave traders supposedly overheard the Blacks plotting in "Angolan," is the only evidence offered for the alleged conspiracies. I contend, however, that the evidence shows that colonial officials, afflicted by an anti-Black racial psychosis or a neurotic fear of Black rebellion, mischaracterized Afro-Mexicans' festive customs, especially when these took place outside the officially sanctioned space of colonial festivals. I situate this psychosis within the broader history of the racialization of Blackness via slavery in the early modern Atlantic to show how Europeans came to conceive of liberty and sovereignty as exclusionary of Black subjects – in other words, how Black subjects became the most-feared objects of colonial psychosis.

Compared with the celebratory texts that make up the bulk of this book, this dynamic presents contradictions that have not been easy to reconcile intellectually. For one, how were Afro-Mexicans able to participate in public festivals so close to being accused of plotting these treasonous conspiracies? What was the colonial thinking that welcomed these subversion-laden performances? Chapters 3 and 4 try to answer these and other questions by showing how Afro-Mexicans were able to leverage this dynamic to their favor, while at the same time presenting it as something that also benefited colonial elites. Chapter 3 concretely studies the

---

[13] "Informe del virrey Antonio de Mendoza," Mexico City, December 10, 1537, AGI, Patronato 184, R. 27, sf.

performances Afro-Mexicans staged for the city's 1610 celebration of the beatification of the founder of the Society of Jesus, Ignatius of Loyola. The text, an anonymous "Relación de las fiestas insignes" ("Account of the Great Festival"), is one of the few sources to directly link confraternities to Afrodescendants' festive practices. While this connection has been assumed in the literature, or deduced from indirect references, this text explicitly connects confraternities to Afrodescendants' festive customs, underscoring the former's centrality to the latter in ways other sources do not. More importantly, however, this chapter explores how Afro-Mexicans engaged with the material culture of baroque festive culture, especially floats. This is demonstrated by the fact that two Black troupes appeared with their kings (no queens) on elegant floats: one shaped like a castle and the other like an elephant. The chapter also explores Afro-Mexican dance and musical practices, as the festivities also included eight Black dances. Yet these are not described in the text. Thus in order to offer some idea of what they may have looked (and sounded) like, I offer an overview of Afro-diasporic dances in the early modern Iberian Atlantic. Finally, from the fact that these performances were staged for a religious celebration, I contend that the Blacks' performances could show how Afro-Mexicans sought the protection of religious orders to guard them from colonial officials' mischaracterization of their festive practices.

Chapter 4 studies the only Mexican text to describe a Black performance for the arrival of a new viceroy, in 1640. The performance is the most complex of all the performances studied in this book. In it, eleven Afro-Mexicanas (women) reenacted the Queen of Sheba's visit to King Solomon. The women multiplied the queen's body to represent different aspects of their creole identity. I contend that the performance constitutes the most mature expression of Afro-Mexican identity analyzed in this book. I show how the women articulated an identity that incorporated their African, European, and Mexican heritages. This, I argue, underscores the women's and by extension Afro-Mexicans' cultural literacy, or keen awareness of their cultural makeup. I close the chapter by positing that the women or the confraternity or confraternities they most likely represented sponsored the publication of *Festín*, making it the earliest known such example in the Iberian world.

I conclude the book by musing why *Festín* is the last source about Afro-Mexicans' festive practices, when most of the sources from other latitudes are posterior. Through the analysis of a 1699–1702 Inquisition case that shows Mexicans of all "especie" (kind) acting in concert, I propose that the case may demonstrate the natural result of creolization: the incorporation of different cultures into a new one. Thus, Afro-Mexicans, who had gone from Africans to Afro-Mexicans, become simply Mexicans. This scenario underscores the kind of cultural intimacies Afro-Mexicans developed with other groups and further complicates Mexican narratives of *mestizaje.*

Afro-Mexican history is a well-established field, and this book owes a great deal to the work of scholars such as Gonzalo Aguirre Beltrán, Maria Elisa Gutiérrez Velázquez, Verónica Cristina Masferrer León, Nicole von Germeten, Joan Cameron Bristol, Laura Lewis, Herman L. Bennett, Nicolás Ngou-Mve, Pablo Miguel Sierra Silva, Norah Gharala, Úrsula Camba Ludlow, Ben Vinson, and Frank Proctor, among others. These scholars have shown that Afro-Mexicans joined confraternities, or lay Catholic associations; owned homes; sold foodstuffs in the city's markets, plazas, and streets; built many of the city's houses and public monuments; worked as domestic servants and wet nurses, laundresses, seamstresses, cooks, carpenters, tailors, masons, blacksmiths, cobblers, tanners, candle-makers, bricklayers, carriage drivers, builders, and water carriers, among other jobs; were artists and artisans; and, among other things, joined colonial militias defending Spanish interests.[14] More importantly, these scholars have demonstrated that Afro-Mexicans built community, safety nets, and the Afro-creole culture to which Afro-Mexican kings and queens belong.

Sovereign Joy, however, is not a history, but rather a work of literary and cultural analysis, though it seeks to close the gap between these two disciplinary outlooks. Where historians would hold back for lack of evidence, this book casts a wide diasporic net in search of answers. For this reason, many will find my conclusions speculative, but in-depth critical analysis is required if we are to account for the myriad silences and lies about Afro-Mexicans in the colonial archive. In this respect, *Sovereign Joy* follows the intrepid work of literary scholars like Paul Gilroy, Kim Hall, Daphne Brooks, Jerome Branche, Nick Jones, Larissa Brewer-García, Noémie Ndiaye, and Daniel Nemser; historians like Danielle Terrazas Williams, Jennifer Morgan, Marisa Fuentes, Jessica Johnson, and Sasha Turner; and art historians like Paul Kaplan, Kate Rowe, Cécile Fromont, and Ximena Gómez. These scholars have nar-rowed the divide between historical and cultural analysis and employed

---

[14] See Bennett, *Africans; Colonial Blackness*; Germeten, *Black Blood Brothers*; Bristol, *Christians, Blasphemers, and Witches*; Sierra Silva, *Urban Slavery*; Vinson, *Bearing Arms*; Palmer, *Slaves*.

creative methodologies to account for the lives and subjectivities of Black people in early modernity.

The book is also indebted to scholars of early modern Black festive culture such as Marina Mello e Souza, Elizabeth Kiddy, Philip A. Howard, Patricia Lund Drolet, Judith Bettelheim, and Jeroen Dewulf, to name a few; scholars of Africa and the African diaspora more broadly, particularly John Thornton, Linda Heywood, James H. Sweet, Carmen Fracchia, Erin Rowe, Erika Edwards, Sherwin Bryant, Carmen Bernand, David Wheat, David Eltis, José Ramón Jouve Martín, Ricardo Raúl Salazar Rey, Alex Borucki, Sarah Rachel O'Toole, Tamara Walker, Michelle McKinley, and Karen Graubart, to name a few; scholars of Black confraternities such as Patricia A. Mulvey, Célia Borges, and Lucilene Reginaldo; historians of race like Robert S. Schwaller, Daniel Nemser, Douglas Cope, María Elena Martínez, Mariselle Meléndez, Geraldine Heng, and Thomas Holt, to name a few; and finally, ethnomusicologists like Peter Fryer and Charles Chasteen. The book then engages with and hopes to contribute to several fields, including Afro-Mexican, literary and cultural, confraternal, festive, critical race, performance, and religious studies as well as art history.

Sovereign Joy studies a varied archive of published and archival sources. As stated earlier in this introduction, only *Festín* was published in its day. Díaz del Castillo's text was published in 1632, but I work with a recent edition of his unpublished draft. "Relación de las fiestas insignes" remained unpublished until 1896 and has not received any attention since then. Moreover, its manuscript version has not survived. Chapter 2 is based on well-known archival sources that have not been studied vis-à-vis Afro-Mexicans' festive practices. As outlined previously, I further rely on a wide range of printed, archival, and visual sources from the Iberian world to supplement the many, inherently violent, silences and falsehoods found in the Mexican sources.

Sovereign Joy seeks to make several interventions. While historians have done remarkable recuperative work, Latin American literary and cultural studies – my home field – has privileged "white" creole lettered culture from its inception, although since the 1980s, the field has paid increasing attention to Indigenous texts and voices.[15] What it has neglected, as the historian María Elena Díaz has lamented, is Black bodies and

---

[15] See, for example, Adorno, *Polemics of Possession*; Bauer and Mazzotti, *Creole Subjects*; Mazzotti, *The Creole Invention of Peru*; Merrim, *The Spectacular City*; More, *Baroque Sovereignty*; Rama, *La ciudad letrada*.

voices as subjects of cultural analysis.[16] And it is not because those bodies and voices are not to be found in the archive. José Ramón Jouve Martín's *Esclavos de la ciudad letrada* – to give an example framed within colonial Latin American literary and cultural studies – shows us that they abound.[17] While the texts studied here do not always account for Black voices, they all provide us a different way to account for Black bodies – and their corporeal or physical subjectivities – other than the quantitative analysis of slavery, for example.

At the heart of the matter of Black royal courts are New Spain's confraternal groups; Black festive kings and queens were typically performed by confraternity members. While this aspect of Black confraternities has been extensively studied in Brazil and to a much lesser extent in colonial Peru and the River Plate region, the scholarship on Afro-Mexican confraternities has not given significant analysis to the festive royal courts of Afro-Mexican confraternal life.[18] Scholars have linked Afro-Mexican confraternities to Black kings via a 1612 report, one of the accusatory texts I study. This anonymous report contends that the *mayordomos* (leaders) of Mexico City's Black confraternities, who were usually crowned kings, led a plot to kill all the Spanish men, rape the women, and enslave the indigenous population in the *monarquia africana* (African kingdom) they would establish after taking over the land. In Chapter 3, I discuss one of the few texts in the Atlantic that directly links Black confraternities and Black festive king and queen performances. My analysis sheds new light on the kind of festival performances Black confraternities staged in the early modern Atlantic and informs my reading of the two court reports.

After coming up with the title, I discovered that "sovereign joy" coincides with a translation of a line from St. Augustine's *Confessions*: "vera tu [domine] et *summa suavitas*" ("you [Lord] who are the true, the sovereign joy").[19] Afro-Mexicans' sovereign joy, then, is also theological

[16] Díaz, "Writing Royal Slaves."

[17] Examples include Sierra Silva, *Urban Slavery*, McKinley, *Fractional Freedoms*, and Walker, *Exquisite Slaves*.

[18] Besides those works listed earlier in this chapter, on Brazil, see Borges, *Escravos e libertos*; Reginaldo, *Os Rosários dos Angolas*. On Afro-Mexican confraternities, see Germeten, *Black Blood Brothers*, "Black Brotherhoods," "Colonial Middle Men?" and "Juan Roque's Donation"; Bristol, *Christians, Blasphemers, and Witches*, 93–112; Masferrer León, "*Por las ánimas de negros bozales.*"

[19] Augustine, *Confessions*, 9.1. English in Piper, *The Legacy of Sovereign Joy*, 40. "Suavitas" is rendered as "delight" in Hammond's translation in the Loeb Classical

(as sovereignty is for Derrida) insofar as Afro-Mexican *cofrades* genuinely embraced Christianity, as I explore in this book.

In founding and joining confraternities, Afro-Mexicans were taking advantages of the new powers the Council of Trent (1545–63) gave the laity.[20] They thus behaved as full members of the Catholic community. Here I propose that confraternities constituted sovereign spaces that allowed Afro-Mexicans to set devotional, charitable, and cultural priorities, and that festive kings and queens symbolically expressed this communal sovereignty. Black confraternal sovereignty took the form of caring for the sick, disabled, and dying; burying and remembering the dead; helping the enslaved escape particularly cruel masters or overseers; supporting Black litigants seeking to keep the family unit together or other relief; and a whole host of other social interventions of this nature in an anti-Black world that made no such provisions. Confraternities thus became Afro-Mexicans' only social safety nets. Therefore, there was a relatively large number of Afro-*cofradías* in Mexico City and at least fifty-nine in the whole viceroyalty by the end of the seventeenth century. This makes Mexico second only to Brazil, which had at least 165 brotherhoods in the eighteenth century. Festive kings and queens then emerge as a jubilant praxis through which Afro-Mexicans articulated discursive and communal sovereignty, both in public festivals and in group practices.

I define discursive sovereignty as that which we allow ourselves to tell our ourselves and others about ourselves – in other words, articulations about a group's corporate self, fashioned by the group and intended to enhance the group's and outsiders' understanding of the group. These articulations are often bold statements that defy outsiders' opinions of the group. The group can also surprise itself by articulating a sovereignty it has not been granted. In the performance of festive Black kings and queens, in both public festivals and communal spaces, Afro-Mexicans proclaimed themselves, to themselves and to others, as a sovereign community with its own identity, social space, and localized culture.

In *African Kings and Black Slaves*, Herman L. Bennett invites us to rethink the African–European encounter beyond that of superior–inferior power dynamics, but rather as one that entailed negotiations on equal terms.[21] Likewise, I invite us to reconsider the African diaspora to give

---

Library and as "sweetness, pleasantness, agreeableness" in Freund's Latin dictionary as rewritten by Lewis (1879).
[20] See, for example, Rubial García, "La formación de una nueva sensibilidad religiosa."
[21] Bennett, *African Kings*, 6.

account for the many ways people of African descendent, and, by extension, all subaltern subjects, exercised sovereignty in their daily lives,
pressing colonial elites and administrators for autonomy, as Bennett
puts it elsewhere.[22] My analysis of this performative genre then interro-
gates questions of Black sovereignty, expanding the concept of sovereignty beyond its classical conception of (European/white) royal or
territorial sovereignty. I demonstrate that, despite what has become the
norm in the literature, armed revolt was not the only avenue to sovereignty available to people of African descent during the age of slavery. I
further contend that this performance sought to recreate an African space
of sovereignty, one that existed in the horizon of the actors' collective
memory.

Furthermore, *Sovereign Joy* expands the growing corpus on colonial
Afro-Mexicans, which has thus far paid little attention to the role of
festive culture.[23] The book also joins a growing bibliography on the
urban Black experience in colonial Latin America, such as Tamara J.
Walker's research on dress and honor in colonial Lima. Most of those
works, however, have framed the urban Black experience from the perspective of slavery.[24] *Sovereign Joy*, on the other hand, asserts the actors'
freedom and believes therefore that the performers – even if only for the
duration of the performance – *are* free. Indeed, many of the performers
may have been freepersons as Mexico City had a large free population and
liberty would have afforded the organizers and performers the mobility
needed to stage the performances.[25] Yet this freedom is not to be taken
lightly, for any liberty Afro-Mexicans achieved was hard won and tenu-
ous, as Chapter 2 shows.

Additionally, in Chapter 2, by focusing on how and why senior
colonial officials attempted to curtail Afro-Mexican culture,
Sovereign Joy contributes to our growing understanding of racial
ideology in the early modern Iberian world. Finally, this study
expands the approach to the Black Atlantic in literary studies.
Mexico has been largely excluded from literary debates about the
cultural formation of the Black Atlantic, which have primarily
focused on the eighteenth- and nineteenth-century Anglophone
Caribbean since the publication of Paul Gilroy's seminal *The Black*

[22] Bennett, *Africans*, 2.   [23] See notes 6 and 7.
[24] Examples include Bernand, *Negros esclavos*; Jouve Martín, *Esclavos de la ciudad letrada*;
Sierra Silva, *Urban Slavery*; Walker, *Exquisite Slaves*.
[25] See Bennett, *Africans*.

Atlantic (1995).[26] Like other works on Afro-Mexico, the texts and performances I study in this book position Mexico City as a central site of the Black Atlantic. Thus, incorporating New Spain and colonial Latin America as a whole into literary debates on the Black Atlantic expands this framework and its utility for conceptualizing early modernity. This approach also shifts these discussions temporally, as it centers the Black Atlantic culture of the Iberian empires that emerged in the sixteenth century. It thus "reperiodizes" the processes of creolization Gilroy identified in his book. In this sense my study builds on the works of historians like John K. Thornton, Lynda Heywood, and others.[27] These scholars have focused on the role Central African culture played in the formation of the Black Atlantic, which was dominated by the Iberian empires in its early stages.

Philosophically, *Sovereign Joy* seeks to provoke and probe thinking about the sovereignty of subaltern joy, the joy of subaltern sovereignty, and Black joy and Black being. If, according to Fanon, Black ~~being~~ is nonbeing, are Black sovereignty and Black joy possible?[28] With Imani Perry (see Preface), Frances Negrón-Muntaner, Diana Taylor, and others, I hope to answer these questions affirmatively, and in doing so, also affirm Black being.[29]

The book, in fine, invites scholars to think about the joy people of African descent sought and wrought in early modernity. I define this joy along Spinozan lines: "Spinoza's concept of joy is not an emotion at all but an increase in one's power to affect and be affected. It is the capacity to do and feel more. As such, it is connected to creativity and the embrace of uncertainty."[30] As the critical thinkers Nick Montgomery and carla bergman have observed: "Bubbling up in the cracks of Empire, joy remakes people through combat with forces of subjection. Joy is a *desubjectifying* process, an unfixing, an intensification of life itself."[31] The texts studied

---

[26] Examples of this scholarship include Chiles, *Transformable Race*; Dillon, *New World Drama*; Gilroy, *The Black Atlantic*; Jordan, *White Over Black*; Gruesser, *Confluences*; J. W. Sweet, *Bodies Politics*; Walters, *Archives of the Black Atlantic*; Wheeler, *The Complexion of Race*.

[27] See, for example, J. H. Sweet, *Recreating Africa*; Heywood, *Central Africans*; Thornton, *Africa and Africans*.

[28] Fanon, "The Fact of Blackness." See also Warren, *Ontological Terror*.

[29] Perry, "Racism Is Terrible"; Negrón-Muntaner, "Decolonial Joy"; Taylor, *¡Presente!*

[30] Montgomery and bergman, *Joyful Militancy*, 29–30.

[31] Ibid., 59–60; emphasis in the original.

here show how Afro-Mexicans took advantage of the interstices of imperial rule to articulate joyful sovereignty.

Finally, in questioning archival silences, I seek to gesture to the role nonarchival forms of knowledge transfer, especially performance (i.e., body language), played in Afro-Mexicans' lives. Diana Taylor understands performance as a nonarchival form of knowledge transfer.[32] What, then, are Afro-Mexicans telling us about what they knew and thought of themselves and their world through their festive performances? I propose that they were communicating a great deal about their self-understanding and knowledge of colonial society, the diaspora, and the broader world.

BLACK FESTIVE KINGS AND QUEENS AND THE EARLY MODERN URBAN AFRO-IBERIAN EXPERIENCE

The texts and performances can be grouped into three specific moments in the history of Mexico City: early colonization, a turbulent period at the onset of the seventeenth century, and the consolidation of colonial rule by the mid-1600s. Díaz del Castillo's text speaks to the – later unfulfilled – promises of cultural intimacies, or conditions for symmetrical or quasi-symmetrical intercultural relations the encounter of European, African, and Amerindian cultures (viewed from an optimistic outlook) held as a promise. Chapters 2 and 3 examine texts produced between 1609 and 1612, a period generally perceived by historians as one of Mexico City's most turbulent moments, marked by stark political instability. The texts and performances studied in these two chapters reveal that while senior colonial officials became hyper-vigilant of Mexico City's subaltern subjects (Chapter 2), Afro-Mexicans could still find ways to insert themselves in colonial festivals (Chapter 3). *Festín* at once suggests that the Renaissance promises of cultural intimacies were still alive or perhaps even taking concrete form in 1640 and brings those promises to an abrupt end as the last text that describes a performance of Black festive queens – without kings – in colonial Mexico City.

By documenting urban Afro-Mexican festive culture from 1539 to 1640, *Sovereign Joy* also accounts for Mexico City's physical and demographic growth from a new Spanish city built on the ruins of Tenochtitlan to the largest urban space in the Americas.[33] In 1539, Blacks most likely performed in a muddy field (see Figure I.1). By the early 1600s, that field

[32] Taylor, *The Archive and the Repertoire*, xvii.
[33] See Mundy, *The Death of Tenochtitlan*.

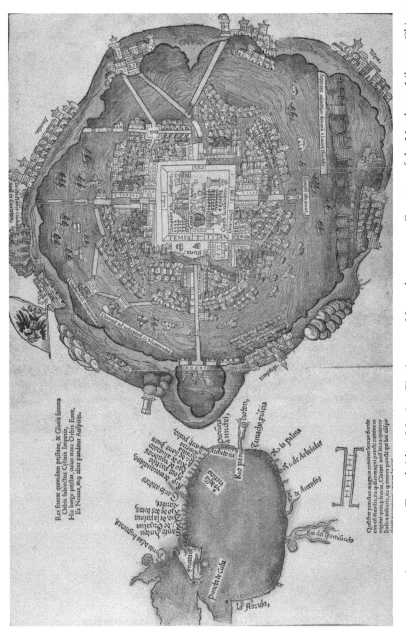

FIGURE 1.1 Anonymous, Tenochtitlan–Mexico City in 1524. Nuremberg, 1524. Courtesy of the Newberry Library, Chicago

15

was an impressive public space flanked by imposing civic buildings such as the cathedral, the *ayuntamiento* or palace of the city council, the palace of the archbishop, and, most imposing of all, the viceregal palace (see Figure I.2). Afrodescendants played an important role in that growth from the early 1500s to the early 1600s, as builders, artists and artisans, masons, and bricklayers, for example. Afro-Mexicans no doubt worked on the construction of those public buildings. According to Bennett, the capital grew so fast that "by 1570, Mexico City was home to the largest African population in the Americas."[34] Mexico City was to retain that status at least until 1640.[35]

These years also include the period 1580–1640, during the unification of the Spanish and Portuguese crowns, when the largest number of enslaved Africans, about 110,000, were imported into New Spain.[36] Kidnapped mainly by Portuguese traders, most of these Africans were captured in Angola and the Kongo, where the Portuguese had established slaving posts.[37] Thus, as Bennett and Nicolás Ngou-Mve have observed, in the first decades of the seventeenth century (1595–1640), most Afro-Mexicans had Central African roots.[38] As the historian Joseph C. Miller noted, Angola and the Kongo formed a common cultural space.[39] In this book, especially in Chapter 1, I demonstrate how Afro-Mexicans' festive culture was linked to this Central African cultural space.

This book focuses on the performative festive culture of the descendants of those Central Africans enslaved in Mexico City. According to Bennett, in 1646, the earliest date for which such numbers exist, "the creole population, largely free and comprised of mulattos, numbered 116,529, whereas the predominantly African slave population totaled 35,089."[40] About 50 percent of these Africans and Afro-Mexicans lived in or near Mexico City.[41] This book studies the period when this population and its Afro-creole culture were forming. Free Afro-Mexicans were the main agents of Mexico City's Afro-creole festive culture.

Religious confraternities, or lay Catholic associations, were instrumental in facilitating Afro-Mexican festive culture. Confraternities emerged in

[34] Bennett, *Colonial Blackness*, 4.   [35] See Sierra Silva, *Urban Slavery*.

[36] Bennett, *Africans*, 1. See also Vinson, *Bearing Arms*, 1.

[37] See Aguirre Beltrán, *La población negra*, 33–48; Sierra Silva, "The Slave Trade to Colonial Mexico"; *Urban Slavery*, 107–43.

[38] Bennett, *Colonial Blackness*, 4; Ngou-Mve, *El África Bantú*.

[39] Miller, "Central Africa," 22. See also Thompson, *Flash of the Spirit*, 103–4.

[40] Bennett, *Africans*, 27.   [41] Bennett, *Colonial Blackness*, 5.

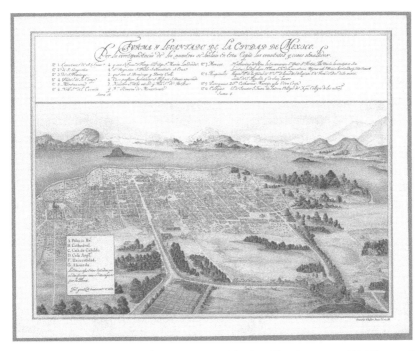

FIGURE I.2 Juan Gómez de Trasmonte, Mexico City in 1628. (A) Viceregal palace. (B) Cathedral. AGI. 1920 reproduction of lost original. Courtesy of the David Rumsey Map Collection

the high Middle Ages as cities grew, not just as devotional and charitable institutions but also as ways of preserving and celebrating kinship.[42] As different groups from far-flung towns and kingdoms found themselves in medieval cities like Paris or Rome, they formed confraternities as both safety nets and social spaces. In the Iberian Peninsula, Blacks began to establish their own confraternities in the mid-fifteenth century; some argue earlier (see Chapter 1). While both the Church and Crown saw baptism and conversion as ways of assimilating Blacks into Iberian society, Blacks began to exercise their agency by forming confraternities.[43] Both the pious and social elements of confraternities became very important for Iberian Blacks: one allowed them to articulate their devotion and Afro-Catholic identity; the other permitted them to care for each other in

---

[42] See Vincent, *Les confréries médiévales*, 31–9.
[43] See Graubart, "*So color de una cofradía*."

time of need, illness, and death, to form community, kinship networks, and group cohesion, and to develop their festive traditions. As the historians Nicole von Germeten, Elizabeth W. Kiddy, and Patricia A. Mulvey argue, Blacks were attracted to confraternities because medieval views on death and other elements of medieval culture – which, like sub-Saharan culture, was community centered – resonated with sub-Saharan cosmologies, where funeral rites formed an important cultural component.[44]

Confraternities provided Blacks other important benefits such as autonomy. Thus, while some scholars argue that confraternities were another means of European domination, I contend that by giving them an Afro-creole hue, Blacks used these corporate groups to exercise social and cultural agency and express their Afro-Catholic subjectivities.[45] In other words, Afrodescendants availed themselves of confraternities as institutions that allowed them to continue and adapt their African-derived festive practices within a Christian context. This is not to say that confraternity members were not genuinely Christian, even if as Afro-Christians they practiced a syncretism of Catholic and African beliefs and practices.[46] Moreover, Blacks' colonial-era religious practices, which have survived, though not unchanged, in Afro-Catholicism, Candomblé, Santería, Vudú, and other forms, show how they exerted agency in adapting African religious beliefs to Christianity, beliefs that were inseparable from their ritualistic practices.

The Afro-Iberians who accompanied the first Spanish colonizers brought the practice of confraternities and Afro-Iberian festive culture to Mexico in the 1520s.[47] These Afro-Iberians in Mexico City may have joined mixed confraternities as early as the 1530s (see Chapter 1). By the 1570s, Afro-Mexicans – creole Blacks, mulattos, and Afro-mestizos – had founded their own confraternities (see Chapter 1). Like their Iberian predecessors, Afro-Mexicans availed themselves of confraternities to fulfill important social and cultural functions. This book focuses on the

---

[44] Germeten, *Black Blood Brothers*; Kiddy, *Blacks of the Rosary*, 15–63; Mulvey, "Black Lay Brotherhoods," 16.

[45] See, for example, Boschi, *Os leigos e o poder*. See also Ngou-Mve, "El cimarronaje." See also Scarano, "Black Brotherhoods" and *Devoção e escravidão*, esp. 9–48; Russell-Wood, "Black and Mulatto Brotherhoods" and "Aspectos"; *Black Man in Colonial Brazil*, esp. 128–60; Mulvey, "Black Brothers and Sisters"; "Slave Confraternities." For summaries of these arguments, see, for example, Germeten *Black Blood Brothers*, 4, and Voigt, *Spectacular Wealth*, 122–3.

[46] See Mello e Souza, "The Construction of a Black Catholic Identity."

[47] See, for example, Garofalo, "The Shape of a Diaspora"; Valerio, "That There Be No Black Brotherhood."

cultural functions that confraternities helped Afro-Mexicans carry out, particularly their festive traditions. This connection has been assumed or inferred in the scholarship, but I study texts that make it more explicit. *Sovereign Joy* demonstrates how this tradition differed from other Iberian geographies in Mexico, taking on a uniquely Afro-Mexican character.

IBERIAN BEGINNINGS

Afro-Iberians led a vibrant festive social life in the early modern Iberian Mediterranean.[48] One may wonder how this was possible. Iberian authorities had their reasons for allowing Afro-Iberians to engage in their festive practices. As a seventeenth-century Sevillian alderman, Diego Ortiz de Zuñiga (1636–80), puts it:

[E]ran en Sevilla los Negros tratados con gran benignidad desde el tiempo de el Rey Don Henrique Tercero, permitiendoseles juntarse à sus bayles, y fiestas, en los días feriados, con que acudian mas gustosos al trabajo, y tolerauan mejor el captiuerio.[49]

[I]n Seville, the Blacks have been treated with great benignity since the time of King Henry III of Castile (r. 1390–1406), being allowed to gather for their dances and fiestas on holidays, which made them work with greater joy and better bear their captivity.

We find the same argument in the Italo-Portuguese Jesuit missionary to Brazil André João Antonil's (1649–1716) *Cultura e opulencia do Brasil* (*Culture and Opulence of Brazil*) (Lisbon, 1711). Arguing against those who opposed Black festive practices, especially colonial authorities, Father Antonil contends that not only was it necessary to allow Blacks, especially confraternities, to have their fiestas, but that masters should fund them:

Negarlhes totalmente os seus folguedos, que saõ o unico alivio do seu cativerio, he querrellos descosolados, & melancolicos, de pouca vida, & saude. Por tanto naõ estranhem os Senhores o crearem seus Reys, cantar, & bailar por algumas horas honestamente em alguns dias do anno, & o alegraremse innocentemente a tarde depois de terem feito pela manhãa suas festas de Nossa Senhora do Rosario, de Saõ Benedito, & di Orago da Capella do Engenho, sem gasto dos Escravos, acudindo o Senhor com sua liberalidade aos Juizes, & dandolhes algum premio do seu continuado trabalho. Porque se os Juizes, & Juizas da Festa houverem de gastar do

---

[48] See Earle and Lowe, *Black Africans*; Jordan and Lowe, *The Global City*.
[49] Ortiz de Zuñiga, *Anales eclesiásticos y seculares*, 374.

seu, será causa de muitos inconvenientes, & offensas de Deos, por serem poucos os
que o podem licitamente ajuntar.[50]

To wholly deny them their merriment, which is the only relief they have in their
captivity, is to want them desolate, and melancholy, depressed, and ill. Therefore,
the masters should not bar them from having their kings and queens, singing, and
dancing honestly for some hours some days of the year, and innocently rejoicing on
the afternoon after celebrating, in the morning, the feast of Our Lady of the Rosary,
St. Benedict of Palermo, and the patron of the plantation's chapel, without cost to
the slaves, but rather the master rewarding all their work with his generosity. For if
the grand marshals have to spend their own, it would be a great inconvenience, and
offense to God, since very few can honestly come up with the money.

From the point of view of church and city authorities, this permissive
practice constituted what has become known in the social sciences as the
safety release valve theory of containment, which is precisely what Ortiz
de Zuñiga and Antonil espouse in these excerpts, namely that such allow-
ances permitted Blacks to get much-needed rest from their oppressive
labor so that "acudian mas gustosos al trabajo, y tolerauan mejor el
captiuerio" ("they would work with greater joy and better bear their
captivity").

In other words, from the point of view of Iberian and colonial officials,
allowing Blacks to engage in merriment every now and then reduced
discontent and, therefore, the likelihood of rebellion. Antonil, for
example, calls for masters to fund Black celebrations so that they will
not turn to crime in order to pay for the festivities. However, performance
anthropologists offer a different theory, contending that communal festive performances constitute transformative practices through which subaltern groups form community and collective identity.[51] So, while Iberian
authorities may have allowed Blacks to engage in merriment to provide
them a safety release valve, these festive practices were also the catalyst of
Afro-Iberian identity and culture formation as well as creolization.
Continued in Mexico, these practices laid the foundation upon which
Afro-Mexican creole culture could form.

CREOLIZATION AND COLONIAL SPACES OF CORRELATION

In Mexican scholarship and society, the process through which Mexican
society emerged from the encounter with Europe has come to be called
mestizaje. Scholars of Afro-Mexico have sought to problematize this idea,

---

[50] Antonil, *Cultura e opulencia*, fol. 28.   [51] Turino and Lea, *Identity and the Arts*, 8–10.

which often reduces the Black past to slavery and erases Blackness from Mexicanness. As Theodore W. Cohen puts it, "mestizaje becomes nothing more than a euphemism for black disappearance."[52] For this reason, like Bennett and others, I prefer the term *creolization*, which centers Mexicanness from a Black perspective.

While the term "creole" (*criollo* in Spanish) has been mainly used in (Hispanic) colonial Latin American literary studies for those persons of "pure" Spanish descent born in the Americas and their culture, I use it here in its original and broader meaning: "born or developed in the New World."[53] In fact, the historian James Lockhart noted in 1968 that before 1560, the term *criollo* was only used for Afrodescendants.[54] This reflects the word's Portuguese origin, where *crioulo* (diminutive of *criar*, to rear a child) originally meant (Black) child house slave (*criado* in modern Spanish and Portuguese). This meaning then expanded to include all Afrodescendants born in the Americas and was the one borrowed by the French, in whose American colonies *creole* meant a person of "pure" African descent born in the Americas.

The process through which the term *criollo* acquired its broader meaning in Spanish America is the same one through which Afro-Mexican creole culture formed: *creolization*. While white *criollos* have occupied (Hispanic) colonial Latin American literary studies since the field's inception – in such a way that it could be said that the field created white *criollos* – the process of creolization is hardly ever discussed, thus making invisible the role of subaltern subjects, be it passive or active, in the formation of dominant culture. In *African Mexicans*, Marco Polo Hernández Cuevas argues that the postrevolutionary Mexican state erased "the Africanness of Mexican *mestizaje* ... from national memory and identity."[55] Hernández Cuevas also claims that "national African ethnic contributions were plagiarized by the *criollo* elite."[56] It could be said that colonial Latin America literary studies has done something similar by assuming that colonial Blacks did not contribute anything significant to the formation of creole culture. *Sovereign Joy* makes visible colonial Afro-Mexicans' active role in the formation of Novohispanic (or New Spain's) dominant culture at three key moments, as detailed earlier in this introduction.

---

[52] Cohen, *Finding Afro-Mexico*, 11. See also Hernández Cuevas, *African Mexicans*; Ramsay, *Afro-Mexican Constructions*.

[53] Buisseret, *Creolization in the Americas*, 6. See also Gutiérrez Rodríguez and Tate, *Creolizing Europe*; Restall, *Beyond Black and Red*.

[54] Lockhart, *Spanish Peru*, 175. [55] Hernández Cuevas, *African Mexicans*, ix. [56] Ibid.

Creolization is a process of transculturation or cultural transfer.[57] Take, for example, the fact that Spanish creoles laid claim to the term *criollo* to define their own class and American culture, transferring the concept from Blacks unto themselves. The transfer, however, did not end the original use; it only broadened it. This is what creolization does: it broadens cultural practices. Stuart Hall has articulated the best definition of creolization, understanding it as a process that

occurs in such a way as to produce, as it were, a "third space" – a "native" or Indigenous vernacular space, marked by the fusion of cultural elements drawn from all originating cultures, but resulting in a configuration on which these elements, though never equal, can no longer be disaggregated or restored to their originary forms, since they no longer exist in a "pure" state but have been permanently "translated."[58]

We may compare the third space created by creolization to what the art historian Cécile Fromont calls "spaces of correlation" in her study of how Central Africans adapted Christian culture in early modernity. Fromont defines these spaces of correlation as "cultural creations such as narratives, artworks, or performances that offer a yet-unspecified domain in which their creators can bring together ideas and forms belonging to radically different realms, confront them, and eventually turn them into interrelated parts of a new system of thought and expression."[59]

Viewing the performance of festive Black kings and queens as "spaces of correlations," I propose to show how Africans translated their ancestral culture into (creole) Afro-Mexican culture and used public festival participation as a space of negotiation where they could redefine their colonial condition. My analysis also identifies colonial festivals as a third space where colonial identities and practices were correlated into cultural intimacies. In other words, I also position Afro-Mexican cultural becoming within the broader process of Latin American becoming.

CULTURAL AGENCY

This book joins the great recuperative work on Black cultural agency by historians of Afro-Mexico and the African diaspora in the rest of Latin America. As these scholars have shown, studying this cultural agency is crucial for understanding Black subjectivities in colonial Latin America, for people express themselves through their cultural practices. Concretely

[57] See Ortiz, *Contrapunteo.*   [58] Hall, "*Creolité*," 15.
[59] Fromont, *Art of Conversion*, 15.

here I seek to study what Afro-Mexicans sought to communicate about themselves and their notions of sovereignty through festive kings and queens.

I use the term *cultural agency* to mean the "effectual activity" through which Afro-Mexicans *formed* and *performed* their festive culture.[60] I contend that this cultural agency arises from collective agency. As the cultural psychologist Carl Ratner has observed, "agency always operates within and through a social structure. Agency does not precede society and create it as a voluntary agreement of independent individuals. Individuals are always socially related. Therefore, any action that individual agency initiates (including action to transform society) always takes place from a social basis."[61] Or as Martin Hewson puts it, agency arises "[w]hen individuals collaborate" and "engage in effectual activity."[62] In other words, collective agency results whenever collectives engage in social action. It is through this perspective that I look at Afro-Mexicans' festive culture. I see the performances I study in this book as social action oriented not only toward improving Afro-Mexicans' colonial conditions but, more importantly, toward building and sustaining a meaningful social existence – as opposed to the social death Orlando Patterson sees in slavery.[63]

Furthermore, as Doris Sommer posits in the introduction to *Cultural Agency in the Americas*, "Culture enables agency. Where structures or conditions can seem intractable, creative practices add dangerous supplements that add angles for intervention and locate room for maneuver."[64] The texts and performances explored in the following chapters illustrate how festive culture enabled agency, and more importantly, how Afro-Mexicans maneuvered within colonial structures – in spite of colonial society's reluctance to allow Black autonomy – through their creole consciousness to *form* and *perform* agency. The specific form of agency I look at in this book is cultural agency. As Ratner asserts,

Agency is cultural in several ways. Not only is it intentionally oriented toward objectifying itself in social relations. Agency is also cultural in that its quality or character is a function of the quality and character of social relations in which an individual participates. An individual deprived of social stimulation and support would not develop agency just as she would not develop psychological functions. Agency has heterogeneous forms which correspond to the heterogeneity of social

---

[60] Hewson, "Agency," 13.   [61] Ratner, "Agency and Culture."
[62] Hewson, "Agency," 13.   [63] Patterson, *Slavery and Social Death*.
[64] Sommer, "Wiggle Room," 3.

relations within a social division of labor. Capitalists have different social relations from workers, and workers themselves have different kinds of social relations depending on their particular line of work. Each pattern of social relations fosters different characteristics in agency.[65]

While for Ratner all agency is cultural, I specifically look at the agency embodied in Afro-Mexicans' festival culture. As I demonstrate in Chapter 2, for colonial authorities, this agency was dangerous because, as Julita Scarano has argued in her study of Black confraternities in Brazil, it created "breaks" in the system through which Afro-Mexicans could express themselves publicly, enter the colonial archive, bring about changes to their colonial conditions, and, more importantly, forge a meaningful social existence.[66] Through this agency, moreover, Afro-Mexicans answered Gayatri Spivak's famed question ("Can the subaltern speak?") affirmatively. In other words, Afro-Mexicans used their bodies to actively insert themselves into the colonial archive, to have a voice. While the bulk of the archive on the African diaspora was produced by the oppressor, Afrodescendants' effectual activity means that they indirectly and sometimes directly produced that archive (see Chapter 4). Finally, as Chasteen shows in his study of Latin American national rhythms, through this agency Afro-Mexicans contributed rhythms and dances that still mark Latin American music to this day.[67]

As the scholarship has shown, Afro-Mexicans' social and cultural agency was intersectional. That is to say that it did not rely on only one locus of agency, but rather different loci were combined to strengthen agency. Confraternities were used to facilitate social and cultural functions.[68] Marriage was used to keep the family unit together.[69] The courts were used to curtail abuses.[70] Confraternities paid for legal fees and purchased freedom and protested en masse when the courts ignored Afro-Mexicans' rights (see Chapter 2). Clothing was used to "express ideas about masculinity and femininity," "attend to conceptions of belonging," and blur socioracial differences.[71] Military service was used to attain certain privileges, such as tribute relief and *fuero*, or legal immunity.[72] Soldiers were also confraternity members. Freedom – whether permanent or temporary – was used to accumulate

---

[65] Ratner, "Agency and Culture."   [66] Scarano, "Black Brotherhoods," 13.
[67] Chasteen, *National Rhythms*.   [68] See Germeten, *Black Blood Brothers*.
[69] See Bennett, *Colonial Blackness*.
[70] See Bennett, *Africans*; Jouve Martín, *Esclavos de la ciudad letrada*.
[71] Walker, *Exquisite Slaves*, 19.   [72] See Vinson, *Bearing Arms*.

capital and sustain kinship networks. Capital was used to support confraternal activities and fund private fiestas and public performances. Contributions to public festivals were used to negotiate status and challenge colonial racial categories (see Chapter 2).

I would like to offer one final note on language and translation. I have transcribed words as they appear in the original, be it an archival source or printed text. I have relied on Sebastián de Covarrubias' *Tesoro de la lengua castellana* (1611) for meaning, the *Diccionario de Autoridades* (1726–39) when the term is not given by Covarrubias, and Joan Coromines' *Diccionaro crítico etimológico* (1991) for the etymology of terms of significant interpretative value. Thus I have also adapted a transhistorical approach to language, while at the same time acknowledging its historic specificity. In this spirit, I have translated certain terms to their modern meaning. For example, *Et(h)iopia* and *Guinea* were among some names given to the African continent in the Iberian world in early modernity. Therefore, when texts used these terms, I have translated them as Africa. Likewise, I have translated *etiope/guineo* as African.

My aim is that the original serves as the evidence. The translation is only meant to help those unfamiliar with Latin, early modern Spanish, Portuguese, or Italian. Moreover, the original keeps me accountable for my argument. Too often translations provoke questions that go unanswered without access to the original. This is more important for archival sources that are often inaccessible to most readers. Thus I prioritize here the original as a true reflection of what Iberian intellectuals thought about Africans and Afrodescendants and their confraternal and festive practices.

"With Their King and Queen"

Early Colonial Mexico, the Origins of Festive Black Kings and Queens, and the Birth of the Black Atlantic

In February 1539, Mexico City was consumed by a series of extravagant public displays. These festivities, intended to commemorate the Truce of Nice, signed the previous year between Emperor Charles V (r. 1516–56) and King Francis I of France (r. 1515–47) at Aigues-Mortes near Nice, represented an end to a long period of economic instability for New Spain. Trade with Spain had ground to a halt, no ships had arrived with news or goods for six months, and a prominent friar began to darkly predict the end of Spanish rule, which unnerved the city's small Spanish population.[1] Amidst local political disruptions, an alleged Black rebellion plot in 1537 had been blamed on the war.[2] So, when the news of the peace accord arrived in Mexico City in September 1538, Viceroy Antonio de Mendoza (r. 1535–50) and the Audiencia, the two government authorities most closely linked to the victorious monarch, ordered the staging of great festivities whose planning took more than four months.[3] The celebrations in Mexico City mirrored those held at Aigues-Mortes and other parts of the empire, which included banquets, mock battles, and jousting, among other festive acts, with one notable addition: surprisingly, given the Black rebellion plot supposedly thwarted in 1537, the festivities in Mexico included a procession of "más de çinquenta" (more than fifty) "negros" (Blacks) wearing "grandes riquezas ... de oro y piedras ricas y aljófar y

---

[1] "Informe del virrey Antonio de Mendoza," sf.   [2] Ibid.
[3] Díaz del Castillo, *Historia verdadera*, 754. See Lopes Don, "Carnivals," 17–18.

argentería" (great riches … of gold and precious stones and pearls and silver).[4]

Bernal Díaz del Castillo (ca. 1496–1584), who had come to Mexico with Hernán Cortés (1485–1547), witnessed the festival. Writing some thirty years later, Díaz del Castillo described these celebrations in chapter 201 of his *Historia verdadera de la conquista de la Nueva España* (*True History of the Conquest of New Spain*) (ca. 1575).[5] According to Díaz del Castillo, the two-day festivities consisted of mock stag hunts, a *moros y cristianos* (Moors and Christians) choreography, a mock naval battle reenacting the Siege of Rhodes, a mock battle between Black and Indigenous performers, plays, banquets at the end of each day – one hosted by Mendoza at the viceregal palace and the other by Cortés in his own palace – jousting tournaments, speeches by significant personages, and the procession of the more than fifty Blacks, "todos a cavallo" (all on horseback).[6]

The mock battles shared a common theme of the triumph of Christendom over its infidel enemies. The reenactment of the Siege of Rhodes, either in 1480 or 1522, both of which took place against the Ottoman Empire, was itself a restaging of Cortés' offensive against Tenochtitlan in 1521. Cortés, who had fallen out of royal favor and had been dismissed from his post of governor of New Spain, was elected to perform the prominent role of Captain General, symbolically returning to his former post.[7] On both occasions (1480 and 1522), the Europeans lost to the Ottomans.[8] The reenactment in Mexico City then was a reinvention of that loss as victory in light of what had happened in Tenochtitlan in 1521. The *moros y cristianos* choreography was also significant, dramatizing the Reconquista (780–1492), or the war to expel the Moors from the Iberian Peninsula.[9] These various mock and restaged battles were

---

[4] Díaz del Castillo, *Historia verdadera*, 755. Aigues-Mortes' festival is narrated in the anonymous *Relación muy verdadera* (1538). For analysis of other commemorations of the truce in the viceroyalty of New Spain, see Harris, *Aztecs*, 123–47.

[5] Published posthumously in 1632 in Madrid, Spain. That edition was based on what became known as the "Madrid" manuscript, which is a clean copy of the "Guatemala" manuscript, believed to be Díaz del Castillo's first draft and from where I cite. The "Guatemala" manuscript contains Díaz del Castillo's redactions. For example, he had originally written that there were "çiento y çinquenta" (150) Blacks in the festival, later crossing out "çiento y" and leaving just "çinquenta" (50) (755n5).

[6] Díaz del Castillo, *Historia verdadera*, 753–60.

[7] The viceroyalty of New Spain, Spain's first in the Americas, was created in 1535 and Mendoza was appointed its first viceroy.

[8] The Knights Hospitaller colonized Rhodes at the onset of the fourteenth century. The Ottomans had tried unsuccessfully to expel them in 1444: see Nicholson, *The Knights Hospitaller*.

[9] See Harris, *Aztecs*.

intended to signify conquest, the triumph of Christianity, and the military superiority of the Spanish Empire. The battle staged between the Black and Indigenous actors, however, stands apart as a festive performance with a different genealogy, albeit this is one of its earliest known iterations.

The Blacks' performance took place on the first day in a life-size forest set up in the city's main square: "amanesçió hecho un bosque en la plaça mayor de México, con tanta diversidad de árboles tan natural como si allí oviera[n] nasçido" (in the morning there was a forest in Mexico [City]'s plaza mayor, with such a diversity of trees, which look so natural, as if they had grown there).[10] The forest had been the setting of the mock hunt, wherein Indigenous performers stalked Mesoamerican animals to the delight of onlookers, but Díaz del Castillo writes that the spectacle

no fue nada para la inbençión que ovo de xinetes hechos de negros y negras con su rey y reina, y todos a cavallo, que eran más de çinquenta, y de las grandes riquezas que traían sobre sí, de oro y piedras ricas y aljófar y argentería; y luego van contra los salvajes y tienen otra quistión sobre la caça, que cosa era de ver la diversidad de rostros que llevavan las máscaras que traían, y cómo las negras daban de mamar a sus negritos y cómo hacían fiestas a la reina.[11]

was nothing compared to the performance of horseback riders made up of Black men and women who were there with their king and queen, and all on horses, they were more than fifty, wearing great riches of gold and precious stones and pearls and silver; and then they went against the savages [in battle] and they had another hunt, and it was something to be seen the diversity of their faces, of the masks they were wearing, and how the Black women breastfed their little children and how they paid homage to the queen.

Scholars such as the historian Jerry Williams and the folklorist Max Harris have struggled to explain this performance. Williams, unable to account for the Blacks' performance, wondered whether – and Harris concurs – their rich regalia and diversity of masks were a parody or an imitation of the Spaniards' own ostentatious clothing, for, according to Díaz del Castillo, the Spanish women were richly dressed in "sedas y damascos" (silk and damask dresses) and wearing "oro y plata y pedrería" (gold and silver jewelry with precious stones).[12] I contend that this assessment a priori underplays the Blacks' agency and propose instead in this chapter a line of inquiry that attends to their previously ignored role in the festivities.

Díaz del Castillo's text leaves open several major questions about the performance. Was this a particular type of (festival) performance? Who

---

[10] Díaz del Castillo, *Historia verdadera*, 754.   [11] Ibid., 755.
[12] Williams, *Teatro*, 65; Harris, *Aztecs*, 130; Díaz del Castillo, *Historia verdadera*, 755.

were the performers? That is, what ethnocultural group did they represent? If the 1537 rebellion plot had really transpired, how were they able
to perform in a public festivity only two years later, and what would that
participation mean? In this chapter, I pursue possible and thus far unex-
plored avenues for answering these questions. First, I address the question
of the identity of the performers. To do so, I explore the demography of
New Spain's Black population at the time, which consisted of two groups:
ladinos and *boçales*. *Ladinos* were Christianized, Spanish-speaking,
mostly free Blacks, while *boçales* (or *bozales* in later Spanish) were slaves
newly arrived from the African continent itself. I contend here that the
performers were *ladinos* and that the 1537 plot, if it took place, would
have been led by *boçales*. I then move on to identify the performance itself,
tracing *ladinos'* journey from Africa to New Spain via the Iberian
Peninsula. I then consider the possibility that this performance could be
the first American instance of or at least a precedent for the Central
African–derived festival performance of kings and queens that became
widespread in the African diaspora in the Atlantic.[13] As this book contends, this performance was central to Afro-Mexicans' festive culture.
Finally, I consider the possibility that the Black performers represented a
confraternity, or lay Catholic brotherhood, since these performances were
normally staged by Black confraternities in the Iberian Atlantic.

Critically, I also attempt a full reconstruction of the 1539 performance
of Black kings and queens in order to trace the development of this genre
in public, official ceremonies. Since Díaz del Castillo's account reveals few
details of the performance, it is therefore necessary to situate this performance within a festive tradition that took place across the early modern
Atlantic. Using a diasporic framework, I discuss the performance's
African origins and Iberian transformations and link them to colonial
iterations. Finally, I compare Díaz del Castillo's text to the most detailed
description of festive Black kings and queens in the early modern Atlantic,
staged in Brazil in 1760. Through it all, I seek to apply to the Mexican
context what scholars have discovered about this practice in the Atlantic,
while attending to the specificity of early colonial Mexico.

Examining this performance from an Afro-centric perspective (in the
broadest meaning of the term) foregrounds cultural continuity in the
diaspora. In other words, it demonstrates how Africans took and adapted
their culture to their new Iberian lives. In the case of Latin America, as

---

[13] See Dewulf, *From the Kingdom of Kongo*; Fromont, "Dancing for the King of Congo";
Kiddy, *Blacks of the Rosary*; Mello e Souza, *Reis negros*.

advocated by the historian Herman L. Bennett, this approach allows us to tell the story of the African diaspora from a perspective other than that of the institution of slavery.[14] The work of historians such as Linda A. Heywood, John H. Thornton, and James H. Sweet demonstrates the value of this paradigm for understanding the African diaspora from the perspective of Afrodescendants.[15] More related to this book's topic, Marina Mello e Souza's *Reis negros no Brasil escravista* (2002) and Jeroen Dewulf's *From the Kingdom of Kongo* (2017) demonstrate how adapting this approach is useful to account accurately for the fragmentary evidence Europeans and Afrodescendants alike left of their colonial lives.

Scholars who have studied Díaz del Castillo's text have struggled to understand the Blacks' performance because they have not looked to Africa or the African-derived festive practices of colonial Latin America. Although those practices are only recorded in later sources, a range of details amply warrant an evaluation of their connection with the performance Díaz del Castillo describes. Starting in the 1570s, for example, the *actas* (minutes) of Mexico City's *cabildo* (city council) record payments for Black performances for some of the city's major annual celebrations, such as Corpus Christi.[16] Because of the dearth of scholarship on Afro-colonial festivals available to them at the time that these scholars wrote about Díaz del Castillo's text, it is easy to understand why they may have overlooked this aspect of the performance. Moreover, the Black performance was not the focus of their analysis, and it is precisely because they viewed the Black performance through the lens of the European performance (i.e., the reenactment of the Siege of Rhodes and the *moros y cristianos* choreography) that previous analyses offered a Eurocentric explanation for its staging. My approach, by contrast, analyzes the fragmentary descriptions of Black festive performances by bringing them together with other examples of this performative genre in the African diaspora. This broad comparative method brings to the fore new possibilities to interpret Afro-Mexican festive traditions heretofore overlooked or misunderstood.

While the paucity of sources means that my analysis remains speculative, pursuing this line of inquiry has significant implications for the scholarship on Afro-colonial festivals and, more generally, on the

---

[14] Bennett, *Colonial Blackness*, 5–7.
[15] J. H. Sweet, *Recreating Africa*; Heywood, *Central Africans*; Thornton, *Africa and Africans*.
[16] See *Actas del cabildo*, 17:180, 335, 18:79, 296.

diaspora. For one thing, it invites scholars to probe further into the often-overlooked sixteenth century, and thus push back the timeline of research on expressions of Black social and religious life in the Americas. An examination of New Spain is key in any attempt to write a full history of Black festive tradition in the Americas, even if it has not received substantial scholarly attention to date. Not only did New Spain's Afro-colonial festive history begin the earliest but it also had arguably the most vibrant festive culture of early modern America, one that regularly incorporated Black festive practices.[17] While most scholarship on the topic of Afro-colonial festivals has focused on Brazil in the eighteenth and nineteenth centuries, attending to New Spain in the sixteenth and seventeenth centuries, as recorded in many manuscript and printed volumes (especially post-1570), can help us construct a clearer history of Afro-colonial festivals in the Americas and their unique Mexican iterations.[18] This approach, moreover, helps us further inscribe New Spain within the Black Atlantic, in whose debate it has not featured prominently, and at the same time expands our understanding of this cultural space.

In this chapter, by comparing the 1539 performance with later, similar performances from the Iberian Atlantic, I propose that the former stands at the threshold of the cultural transformations that ushered in the modern Black Atlantic. In order to illustrate this proposition, I begin using the diasporic framework outlined in the Introduction. My main goal in this chapter is to emphasize early Afro-Mexicans' place in the formation of the Black Atlantic. Simply put, Díaz del Castillo's text and the others analyzed in this book put Mexico City at the forefront of the cultural transformations set in motion by imperial expansion, particularly the slave trade, as well as mark Mexico City as a central locus in the formation of the Black Atlantic as a cultural space.

The chapter is divided into four sections. The first section looks at New Spain's Black population in the 1530s in order to identify why *ladinos* were better poised to stage this performance. The following section discusses Kongolese court pageantry to investigate how it may have inspired festive Black kings and queens in the Atlantic, as scholars contend. The third section looks at the development of Black confraternities in the Iberian World and specifically in Mexico City. Given confraternities'

[17] See Curcio-Nagy, *The Great Festivals*, 58–63.

[18] For the scholarship on Afro-Brazilians' festive practices, see, for example, Mello e Souza, *Reis negros*; Kiddy, *Blacks of the Rosary*; Fromont, "Dancing for the King of Congo"; Voigt, *Spectacular Wealth*, 121–50.

historic association with festive Black kings and queens and the possibility that Afro-Mexicans may have been admitted to a brotherhood as early as 1538, I propose that the Blacks who performed in 1539 may have already belonged to a Mexican sodality. The last section discusses a 1762 text that describes a performance of festive Black kings and queens in Brazil. This text, the best description of this performance we have, and despite its temporal and geographical separation from Mexico City, bears striking similarities to Díaz del Castillo's text, especially in its description of a mock battle between Blacks and "Indians." I propose that these similarities underscore continuities in the African diaspora and allow us to make sense of the performance Díaz del Castillo describes. The aim of the chapter then is to discuss the origins and continuities of this tradition in the Atlantic and Mexico's place and role in it.

THE BLACK POPULATION OF NEW SPAIN IN 1539

As noted earlier in this chapter, on December 10, 1537, less than two years before the festival, Viceroy Mendoza had written in his annual report that he had been informed by "un negro" (a certain Black man) that "los negros tenian helegido un rrey y concertado entrellos de matar a todos los españoles y aserse con la tierra" (the Blacks had elected a king and plotted to kill all the Spaniards and take over the land).[19] Mendoza also wrote that, because the informant was Black, he did not give it much weight at first, but that after doing the "proper" investigations, he was convinced of the plot and had hanged "al que tenian helegido por rrey y a los mas principales que se pudieron aver" (the one they had elected as king and the leaders that could be apprehended). Mendoza's report is the first instance of what would become a fairly common trope in the colonial archive: rebel Black king (and sometimes queen), as I explore in the next chapter.[20] Yet, without any other source, it is difficult to verify if what Mendoza was informed of was indeed a Black conspiracy seeking to undermine Spanish rule or the first record of festive Black kings and queens in Mexico and possibly the Americas. This background makes the inclusion of the Black group in the 1539 festival surprising. Were they included to make them demonstrate a certain submission to Spanish rule or did they represent a different group, that given the alleged plot sought

---

[19] "Informe del virrey Antonio de Mendoza," sf.
[20] See, for example, Tardieu, *Resistencia de los negros en el virreinato de México*; *Cimarrones de Panamá*.

to distance itself from another Black group by showcasing their allegiance to the Spanish crown? The evidence supports the latter. Nonetheless, the choice to perform "with their king and queen" is significant.

The inclusion of Blacks in the festival could be explained by New Spain's two different Black groups at the time. As noted earlier in this chapter, in the early colonial period, two groups of Africans populated Mexico City: *boçales* and *ladinos*. *Boçales* were mostly West Africans (i.e., from regions between Senegambia and the Bight of Biafra) brought as slaves to the Americas starting in 1501.[21] Colin Palmer estimated in the 1970s that there were ten thousand *boçales* in New Spain in 1537, an estimate that has since been called into question.[22] Indeed, the Trans-Atlantic Slave Trade Database, the authoritative source for Middle Passage demography, records fewer than one thousand enslaved Africans in New Spain in 1537. Nonetheless, this is still a significant number of West Africans (*boçales*) in the former Mexica (Aztec) capital only recently seized by Spain. Newly arrived from West Africa, *boçales* had little exposure to European culture, religion, and language. Indeed, *boçal* came to denote the languages spoken by enslaved Africans.[23]

Ladinos, on the other hand, were free Africans or Afrodescendants who had lived in the Iberian Peninsula or the Caribbean, where they had been Christianized before coming to New Spain. Many of these *ladinos* may have been Central Africans who had traveled to or been taken to Iberia after the Portuguese reached the region south of the Congo River in the 1480s. Others may have been second- or third-generation *ladinos*, descended from sub-Saharan Africans brought to the Iberian Peninsula through the trans-Saharan slave trade (700–1500 CE). *Ladinos* came to the Americas as personal servants (*negros de acompañamiento*) of the invading Spaniards; Cortés himself is said to have had at least three *ladinos* in his service.[24] Those *ladinos* who fought alongside their Spanish employers were rewarded for the part they took in the colonization of Mexico and gained a considerable degree of social and economic agency in the new Spanish territory. Working in the service of Spaniards gave *ladinos* a high degree of Iberian cultural literacy and the economic

---

[21] On the early years of the slave trade to Spanish America, see, for example, Borcuki, Eltis, and Wheat, *From the Galleons to the Highlands*; Vila Vilar, "The Large-Scale Introduction"; Mendes, "The Foundation of the System"; Borucki, Eltis, and Wheat, "Atlantic History," in *From the Galleons to the Highlands*, 1–14. *Boçal* refers to the muzzle first used for animals and later on enslaved Africans.

[22] Palmer, *Slaves*, 133.   [23] See Lipski, *A History of Afro-Hispanic Language*.

[24] See Restall, "Black Conquistadors."

rewards reaped from their role in the conquest gave *ladinos* a stake in the colonial project and Novohispanic society.

This allows us to differentiate between two very distinct groups of Afrodescendants in Mexico City at the time of the performance Díaz del Castillo describes. While both groups possessed and sought cultural literacy and cultural capital, *ladinos* were better poised to build the alliances that would have allowed them to stage the performance at the municipal festivities. Newly enslaved in a foreign land, *boçales*, on the other hand, would have been keener to resist their European oppressors. Indeed, Joan Cameron Bristol contends that "African-born slaves may have been more likely to be involved in acts of resistance, in part because many of them had been warriors taken prisoner in Africa."[25]

Narratives of the Spanish colonization of Mexico give some indication of *ladinos'* status in early colonial society. The Azcatitlan Codex, created in the mid-sixteenth century, recounts the history of the Mexica or Aztec people from their migration from their ancestral home, Aztlán, to the Spanish colonization of Mexico from an Indigenous perspective. One of its images chronicling the early colonial period depicts Juan Cortés, one of Hernán Cortés' Black servants, in Spanish clothing (Figure 1.1).[26] In the case of the Codex Durán (ca. 1581), a literary narrative of the colonization of Mexico authored by the Spanish Dominican friar Diego Durán (ca. 1537–88) with illustrations by Indigenous artists, there is no mention of *ladinos*; yet Juan Cortés appears in two illustrations. In the illustration of Hernán Cortés meeting the Lords of Tlaxcala, Juan Cortés stands behind the Spaniard as richly dressed as he appeared in the Codex Azcatitlan (Figure 1.2). These depictions of Juan Cortés suggest that *ladinos* enjoyed some degree of social status in early colonial society. His attire, especially in the Azcatitlan Codex, is comparable to that of a Spanish *señor* or gentleman.

That *ladinos* could attain such status is also recorded in the story of Juan Garrido, who, for his role in the colonization of Mexico, was given a plot of land outside the city. He later became the porter of the city council, for which he was awarded a lot within the city's *traça*, limits, making him a *veçino*, a resident, a privilege normally reserved for Spaniards.[27] This information comes from the *probança de méritos y servicios*, or account

[25] Bristol, *Christians, Blasphemers, and Witches*, 98.
[26] On these images, see Sifford, "Mexican Manuscripts."
[27] Restall, "Black Conquistadors," 177. See also Alegría, *Juan Garrido*; Gerhard, "A Black Conquistador."

FIGURE 1.1 Anonymous, Black conquistador in the Codex Azcatitlan, Mexico, sixteenth century, fol. 22v. Bibliothèque nationale de France, MS Mexicain 59–64. Courtesy of the Bibliothèque nationale de France, Paris, France

FIGURE 1.2 Anonymous, Black conquistador in the Codex Durán, Mexico, sixteenth century, fol. 207 r, detail. Biblioteca Nacional de España, Mss/1980-Mss1982. Courtesy of the Biblioteca Nacional de España, Madrid, Spain

of services to the crown, Garrido made in 1538, requesting a royal pension in his old age. Garrido had been born in West Africa, taken to Lisbon as a child, and subsequently sold to a Spaniard, Pedro Garrido, who took him to the Caribbean, where, as a freed man, he entered Cortés' expedition as a *negro de acompañamiento* of one of Cortés' companions. As stated earlier in this chapter, after the conquest, Garrido was given a lot outside the city's *traça*, where – by his own account – he was the first person to plant wheat in the Americas and where he built a house and a chapel (*ermita*). In his *probança*, Garrido presents himself as a self-sufficient and dutiful subject of the Spanish crown who has not received the reward he deserved for his service to the crown:

Juan Garrido de color negro veçino desta çibdad paresco ante v. m. e digo que yo tengo nescesidad de hazer una provança a perpetuad rey memoria de como e servydo a V. M. en la conquista e pasificaçiçion desta Nueva España desde que paso a ella el Marques del Valle y en su compañia me halle presente a todas las entradas e conquista e pacificaciones que se an hecho siempre con el dicho Marques todo lo qual he hecho a mi costa sym me dar salaryo ny repartimiento de indios ni otra cosa siendo como soy casado e veçino desta çibdad que siempre e ressedido en ella.[28]

I, Juan Garrido, Black resident of this city [of Mexico], appear before Your Mercy and state that I am in need of making a *provança* for perpetual memory, on how I served Your Majesty in the conquest and pacification of this New Spain, from the time when the Marquis of the Valley [i.e., Hernán Cortés] entered it; and in his company I was present at all the invasions and conquests and pacifications which were carried out, always with the said Marquis, all of which I did at my own expense without being given either salary or allotment of natives or anything else though I am married and a resident of this city, where I have always lived.

Garrido emphasizes how he financed his participation in the conquest. He also emphasizes that he is a *veçino* of Mexico City, which was tantamount to saying he was a freeman, like any Spaniard. In his view, Garrido thought that, like other conquistadors, he deserved an *encomienda*, or allotment of land and free Indigenous labor, for his part in the conquest. Garrido's petition demonstrates how *negros ladinos* saw themselves, as Christian conquistadors entitled to the same rewards and privileges as their white counterparts. Six witnesses backed Garrido's claims; however, he never received his pension.[29]

---

[28] "Probanza de Juan Garrido," AGI, Mexico 240, n. 3, fol. 1. See Alegría, *Juan Garrido*, 126–38.
[29] "Probanza de Juan Garrido." See Icaza, *Conquistadores y pobladores*, 1:98.

An anonymous sixteenth-century Dutch painting of Lisbon also illustrates the high social standing some *ladinos* were able to achieve in the Iberian Peninsula.[30] The painting shows daily life in one of Lisbon's central squares, the Chafariz d'El-Rey, or the King's Fountain (Figure 1.3). Prominently featured in the right foreground is a Black knight on horseback, wearing a black cape emblazoned with the cross of the knightly order of Saint James. Two Black figures, perhaps knights themselves or the knight's pages, walk in front of him. To his left, there may be another Black knight, also on horseback; however, as his back is to us, we cannot discern his race. The rest of the painting shows many other Africans of varying social groups engaged in a range of activities, from playing the tambourine in a boat on the Tagus to dancing with a European.[31] Another Black man is hauled away by police officers. The painting demonstrates the wide range of social roles available to Afro-Portuguese in the sixteenth

FIGURE 1.3 Anonymous, *Chafariz d'El-Rey*, Netherlandish, sixteenth century. Private collection. Courtesy of The Berardo Collection, Lisbon, Portugal

[30] See Lowe, "The Lives of African Slaves"; Castro Henriques, *Os africanos em Portugal*, 25–36.
[31] See Lowe, "The Global Population."

century, from the highly decorated knight of St. James to street musicians, water carriers, and slaves. According to Didier Lahon, around 1550, Lisbon had a Black population of ten thousand, or 10 percent of the total population of one hundred thousand;[32] and according to historian Leo Garofalo, there were thirty-five thousand Afrodescendants in the Iberian Peninsula by 1492, which means that most were in Spain.[33] This population would only increase, and as it did so, Afro-Iberians transformed and adapted their African culture to their new Iberian lives and in turn brought that new Afro-Iberian culture to the Americas with them as they accompanied the first Spanish colonizers.[34]

The Dutch painting of Lisbon also bears witness to Afro-Iberians' festive practices in its depiction of music playing and dancing as central components of Iberian life. As the scholarship on these early Afro-Iberians has established, these subjects preserved and developed festive customs and were regularly included in public festivities and ceremonies.[35] Indeed, Afro-Iberians held their own communal celebrations and were included in public festivities in both Portugal and Spain starting in the fourteenth century.[36] In Lisbon, in 1451, for example, Afro-Iberians performed dances for the wedding of Leonor of Portugal and Holy Roman Emperor Frederick III.[37] Though the documents leave no explicit description, these dances were presumably African-inflected.

This Iberian precedent of Black knights could explain why the performers in Mexico City appeared as a cavalry. If that is the case, it will begin to illustrate how Afrodescendants adapted European elements to their festive practices, as I further show in what follows. Horses were a rare commodity in New Spain in 1539; Mendoza himself reported in 1537 that there were only 620 horses in the whole viceroyalty, 450 of which were in good health.[38] Given this scarcity, we can imagine the significance of seeing *ladinos* on horseback. Since the horses were likely borrowed from the city's elite, the Black actors would have had to coordinate with the city's elites to enable their performance. This already begins to

---

[32] Lahon, "Da redução," 54.
[33] Garofalo, "The Shape of a Diaspora," 28; Franco Silva, *La esclavitud en Sevilla*; Cortés, *La esclavitud en Valencia*; Fonseca, *Escravos e senhores*; Cortés López, *La esclavitud en la España peninsular*; Saunders, *Social History of Black Slaves*; Phillips, *Slavery*; González Díaz, *La esclavitud en Ayamonte*; Armenteros Martínez, *La esclavitud en Barcelona*.
[34] See the works cited in the previous note.
[35] See Lowe, "The Global Population"; Moreno, "Plurietnicidad"; Trambaioli, "Apuntes."
[36] See Lahon, "Da redução" and "Esclavage"; Moreno, "Plurietnicidad."
[37] Lowe, "The Global Population," 58.
[38] "Informe del virrey Antonio de Mendoza," sf.

illustrate the *cultural intimacies*, or conditions for symmetrical or quasi-symmetrical relations sometimes created by cultural contact. In this performance, these intimacies imply the collaboration of Black, Indigenous, and Spanish actors for its staging. This collaboration in turn suspended the colonial hierarchy, however briefly, and may have gained the groups involved more lasting leverage. Mary Louise Pratt has called the spaces where creolization takes form "contact zones," or "social spaces where disparate cultures meet, clash, and grapple with each other, often in highly asymmetrical relations of domination and subordination."[39] However, the texts studied in this chapter and the remainder of this book, especially in Chapters 3 and 4, demonstrate that those relations were not always "highly asymmetrical"; and not just for the duration of the preparation and execution of colonial festivals, but beyond, as festival coordination required and produced less asymmetrical relations.

Several elements in Díaz del Castillo's text (the Black performers' rich regalia, the fact that they are portrayed as Black knights, and their masks) have led scholars to see the Blacks' performance as carnivalesque mockery à la Rabelais.[40] And indeed we cannot exclude the carnivalesque from these performances. As Cécile Fromont has proposed and as I discuss later in this chapter, festive Black kings and queens were added to an African martial dance in the Iberian Peninsula; or alternatively, an African martial dance (which in Díaz del Castillo's text may have taken the form of the mock battle between the Black and Indigenous actors) was added to Afro-Iberian festive kings and queens. Thus, besides filling in for absent African monarchs, this practice may have been inspired by European carnival customs of mock courts. Moreover, as with confraternities (see Introduction), Afrodescendants may have found a parallel between African masks and European carnival masks. As we have already seen and will see again later in this chapter and in Chapter 3, masks were staples of these performances. Furthermore, in the next chapter, we will see how carnivalesque play of inversion may have been central to this performance.[41] Thus this performance can truly be seen as a "space of correlations" (see Introduction), where European and African practices were correlated to create creole culture. This is further borne out by the fact that many of the elements of this tradition were later incorporated

---

[39] Pratt, *Imperial Eyes*, 4. See my discussion of creolization in the Introduction.
[40] See Harris, *Aztecs*, 123–31; Lopes Don, "Carnivals."
[41] See Bakhtin, *Rabelais and His World*.

into carnival, especially in Brazil, the River Plate region, Panama, and New Orleans.[42]

Finally, in her analysis of this festival, Lopes Don demonstrates how the Indigenous actors' performance was informed by Nahua culture. According to Lopes Don, the comparison of what she calls "the Indian festival of 1539" with ethnographic information collected by the likes of friar Bernardino de Sahagún (ca. 1499–1590) in the Florentine Codex – the most extensive record of preinvasion Nahua culture – demonstrates that "all festival ceremonial behaviors were related to pre-Hispanic worship."[43] For example, Lopes Don notes that "the artificial forest of decorated trees, flowers, live animals, and birds on the plaza was typical of [Nahua] monthly festivals and intermittent festivals, most of all those related to the ancient rain god Tlaloc."[44] Lopes Don concludes that "the aesthetic and symbolic characteristics of the Renaissance triumphal festival as it developed in the sixteenth century corresponded very well to the Indian festival mode."[45] By showing how African culture also informed this mock battle, I triangulate Díaz del Castillo's text, accounting for the three cultures – African, American, and European – that gave the performance and the festival as a whole its shape. More importantly, in doing so, I emphasize the cultural intimacies this performance put into play. While the colonial encounter of Europe, Africa, and the Americas has been rightly portrayed as one of unimaginable catastrophic human, cultural, and environmental consequences, Díaz del Castillo's text attests to the possibilities for cultural intimacies that encounter held. This is perhaps borne out by the fact after the mock battle, the Indigenous and Black performers staged another stag hunt. Creole culture forms through cultural intimacies.

BLACK KINGS AND QUEENS IN THE ATLANTIC WORLD

While it is shy on details, Díaz del Castillo's account may very well be the earliest textual evidence we have of a Black festive tradition that became commonplace in the Atlantic: Afrodescendants performing with "their king and queen." This tradition has been the subject of a few scholarly

---

[42] See Fryer, *Rhythms of Resistance*; Dewulf, *From the Kingdom of Kongo*; Atkins, *New Orleans Carnival Balls*; Borucki, *From Shipmates to Soldiers*, 99–105; Mello e Souza, *Reis negros*; Cunha, *Ecos da folia*; Bettelheim, "Carnaval of Los Congos"; Craft, *When the Devil Knocks* and "*¡Los Gringos Vienen!*"; Lund Drolet, *El ritual congo*.
[43] Lopes Don, "Carnivals," 24.   [44] Ibid., 24–5.   [45] Ibid., 34.

works, notably Mello e Souza's *Reis negros*, Elizabeth Kiddy's *Blacks of the Rosary*, and Fromont's "Dancing for the King of Congo," all focusing on this tradition in Brazil.[46] These works highlight two different aspects of the king and queen tradition that seems to be present in Díaz del Castillo's text: royal regalia (Mello e Souza and Kiddy) and a ritual battle (Fromont). In what follows, I locate the African origins of these two elements and attempt to identify their Afro-Iberian diasporic transformations, situating the 1539 performance within a wider Atlantic tradition. The line of inquiry I pursue through this diasporic framework allows us to see New Spain's importance for understanding the formation of the Black Atlantic.

Then I draw a wide temporal and geographic diasporic net in search of answers to the many lacunae in Díaz del Castillo's text. The connections I make bear on this chapter and those to come. These connections seek to highlight spatial and temporal continuities in the diaspora. This global view of the diaspora is not intended to erase local specificities but rather to underscore similarities that may provide answers to questions where the local context offers limited clues. In the case of the performance Díaz del Castillo describes, only such a broad view allows us to make sense of it. This section specifically looks at Kongolese royal culture to investigate to what extent it may have influenced this tradition, as scholars have argued. In the last section, I look at a Kongolese martial dance that has been identified as a constituent part of this tradition and that seems to explain the mock battle between the Black and Native actors in Díaz del Castillo's text. My discussion then builds on Fromont, Kiddy, and Mello e Souza's work on this tradition by adding Mexico to the discussion.

In Brazil, where the tradition persists, the performance of Black kings and queens became known as *congados* (translatable as "Kongolese kingdoms").[47] This name indicates the tradition's African, specifically Kongolese, origins. I argue that while of Kongolese origin, this tradition was adapted by Afro-Iberians and colonial Afro-Latin Americans regardless of African origin, although it was primarily the descendants of Central Africans who practiced this performance.[48] Mello e Souza and others claim that *congados* originated in the diaspora as an imitation of

---

[46] For studies of this performance in other Atlantic geographies, see Dewulf, *From the Kingdom of Kongo*; Piersen, *Black Yankees*, 117–42; Bastide, *African Civilisations*, 182–4; Bettelheim, "Carnaval of Los Congos"; Craft, *When the Devil Knocks*; "*¡Los Gringos Vienen!*"; Walker, "The Queen of Los Congos; Fogelman and Goldberg, "El rey de los congos"; Borucki, *From Shipmates to Soldiers*, 99–105; Lund Drolet, *El ritual congo*; Howard, *Changing History*.

[47] See Kiddy, *Blacks of the Rosary*.   [48] See Fromont, "Dancing for the King of Congo."

Kongolese royal pageantry.⁴⁹ These scholars point to the description offered by the Italian Franciscan missionary Giannantonio Cavazzi da Montecuccolo (1621–78) in his *Istorica descrizione de' tre regni Congo, Matamba et Angola* (*Historical Description of the Three Kingdoms of Congo, Matamba, and Angola*) (Bologna, 1687). In Book II of *Istorica descrizione*, Cavazzi da Montecuccolo describes how the Kongolese ruler was chosen in early modernity as well as the displays of pageantry he made on a regular basis. These elements do indeed resonate with what we know about *congados*, where the king and queen were elected annually and made ostentatious public displays, as witnessed by the Italo-Portuguese traveling soldier Carlos Julião (1740–1811) in late eighteenth-century Rio de Janeiro (Figures 1.4–7).⁵⁰ At the time Cavazzi da Montecuccolo wrote

FIGURES 1.4–7 Carlos Julião, "Black Kings and Queens," ca. 1775. In *Riscos illuminados de figurinhos de brancos e negros dos uzos do Rio de Janeiro e Serro do Frio*, fols. 70–3, Iconografia C.I.2.8 in the collections of the Fundação Biblioteca Nacional, Rio de Janeiro, Brazil. Courtesy of the Biblioteca Nacional

---

⁴⁹ Mello e Souza, *Reis negros*, 85–95; Lara, *Fragmentos*, 176–9.
⁵⁰ On these images, see Fromont, "Dancing for the King of Congo."

FIGURES 1.4–7 (cont.)

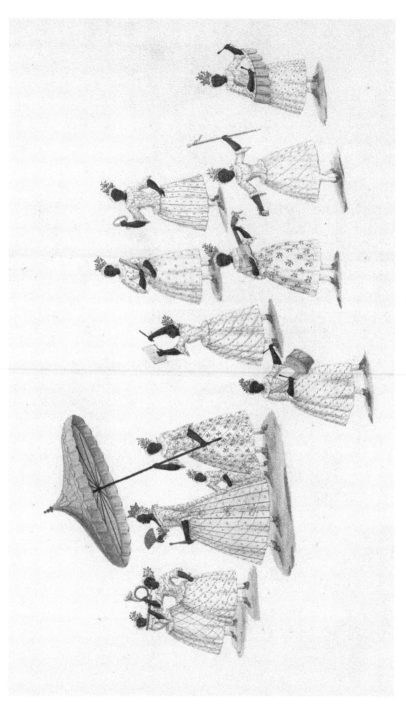

FIGURES 1.4–7 (cont.)

FIGURES 1.4–7 (cont.)

about the Kongo, its culture had already been heavily influenced by European, especially Portuguese practices, as we will see.

    This imitation of Kongolese royal pageantry is also connected to the elections and coronations of Afro-Mexican kings and queens and elucidates their origins. In the Kingdom of Kongo (ca. 1390–1914; Figure 1.8), royal succession was not determined by primogeniture, but rather new rulers were elected by the kingdom's regional governors.[51] According to Cavazzi da Montecuccolo, akin to the election of a new pope or Holy Roman Emperor, in the Kingdom of Kongo the election of a new ruler began with the gathering of the electors after the death of the preceding ruler: "Nella elettione vonvengono necessariamente trè principali Signori del Regno, cioè i Mani-enffunda, il Matti Batta, & il Conte di Sogno" (For the election, the

FIGURE 1.8 Kingdom of Kongo in the seventeenth century. Pierre Duval, 1682. Courtesy of the David Rumsey Map Collection

---

[51] See Fromont, *Art of Conversion*, 27.

three main lords of the kingdom, Efunda, Mbata, and Soyo, necessarily gathered).[52] This triumvirate included the three main leaders of the Kongo: the high priest (Efunda) and the governors of the two provinces (Mbata and Soyo).[53] This is an essentially Kongolese component of the ceremony, governed by pre-Christian tradition.

As it happens in St. Peter's Square in the Vatican during a conclave, in the Kongo, the expectant people gathered in the main square in the capital, Salvador: "Divulgatasi la fama, convengono i principali del Regno con infintà di Popolo nella Città Metropoli detta S. Salvatore sù la Piazza, che'ssi chiamano il Terreno, affine di publicare solennemente quale sia l'Eletto" (As the word spread, the lords of the kingdom, with an infinitude of people, gathered in the square, which they call the Ground, in the city of Salvador, waiting for the new king to be solemnly announced).[54] Though this tradition predated the arrival of Christianity to the Kongo, the second part of the ceremony demonstrates how Africans incorporated Christian elements into the new king's coronation:

Al sentirsi quel tale proclamato per nuovo Rè, immediatamente si postra davanti al Prelato, e nelle mani di lui promete di vivere Cattolico, e di spargere il sangue in difesa della vere Fede ... Il Prelato dopoi presolo per la mano, e condottolo a sedere sù'l Trono, gli consegna le Insegne reali, e l'incorona; intanto che tutto il Popolo secondo il suo costume prosteso al suolo, come vero Rè, lo riconosce, e l'adora.[55]

Upon hearing that he had been elected, the new king immediately prostrated himself before the bishop, and promised to live a Catholic life, and to spill his blood in defense of the true faith ... The bishop then took him by the hand and guided him to the throne, where he [i.e., the bishop] crowned him and gave him the royal insignias, while the people, prostrated on the ground, as per their custom, recognized and paid homage to him as true king.

In the period before the Christianization of the Kongo in 1491, the king may have been proclaimed and crowned by the Effunda, or high priest, but here he is crowned by the Catholic bishop.[56] This illustrates, as John K. Thornton has argued, that from the start of European contact, Central Africans "were quick to adapt elements of European culture, including religion and aspects of material culture."[57] Indeed, we can see this

---

[52] Cavazzi da Montecuccolo, *Istorica descrizione*, fol. 251. *Mani* is the Kikongo term for lord.

[53] Mello e Souza, *Reis negros*, 88.

[54] Cavazzi da Montecuccolo, *Istorica descrizione*, fol. 252.

[55] Cavazzi da Montecuccolo, *Istorica descrizione*, fols. 252–3.

[56] On the early modern Christian Kongo, see Fromont, *Art of Conversion*.

[57] Thornton, "Central Africa," 84. See also his *Africa and Africans*, 206–34.

propensity in the first European text about the Kongo, Filippo Pigafetta's
Relatione del Reame di Congo (*Description of the Kingdom of Congo*)
(Rome, 1591), which influenced subsequent early modern writings on the
Kongo, including Cavazzi da Montecuccolo's *Istorica descrizione*.
Pigafetta's text is not a firsthand account but rather based on an account
he heard from a Portuguese emissary, Duarte Lopes, who accompanied a
Kongolese embassy to Rome in 1583.[58]

In his chapter on the Kongolese court (Book II, Chapter 7), Pigafetta
describes how the Kongolese king and his court promptly adopted
European customs.

Ma poiche quel regno ha ricevuto la Chriftiana fede, li grandi della Corte han
cominciato à vestirsi all'usanza de Portoghesi portando mantelli, cappe, tabarri di
scarlatto, & di drappi di seta ciascheduno secondo la sua possibilità, & in testa
capelli, & berrete, & in pie pianelle di velluto & di cuoio, & stivaletti al modo
Portogheso, con le sue spade à canto, & i popolani, che non possono farsi gli habiti
al modo de' Portoghesi, ritengono la pristina consuetudine. Le femine etiandio
vanno alla Portoghese, fuorche non hanno il manto, ma ben nel capo veli, & sopra
loro vna beretta di velluto nero, ornata di gioie, & al collo catene d'oro assai: ma le
povere al modo antico, peroche solamente le donne di corte alla guisa predetta
s'adornano. I oscia che il Re si conuertì alla Chriftiana fede confermò etiandio la
sua Corte in certo modo alla somigliãza del Re di Portogallo, & prima in quanto al
servitio della tavola, quando mangia in publico, s'erge un solio di tre scaglioni,
coperto di tapeti d'India, & sopra vi si colloca la mensa con la sedia di velluto
cremesi, con li chiodi d'oro, & sempre mangia solo ne gia mai alcuno siede con
esso lui à tavola, stando li prencipi coperti. Hà li vaselli della credenza d'oro, &
d'argento, & gli si fa la credenza nel mangiare, & del bere. Tiene la guardia degli
Anzichi, & d'altre nationi, che ftà d'intorno al suo palazzo ornata dell'arme
sudette, & quando vuole uscire suonano le nacchere, che s'odono lunge cinque ò
sei miglia, cõcio intendendosi il Re volere andar fuori.[59]

Since that kingdom received the Christian faith, its courtiers began to dress in the
manner of the Portuguese, with red silk capes, hats, velvet and leather shoes and
boots, with his sword on his side, each according to his means. The women too,
but not capes, but rather a veil on their heads, and on top of it a velvet hat adorned
with jewels, and gold chains on their necks. The poor, who cannot afford these
things, keep their old customs. Since the King converted to the Christian faith, he
arranged his court in the fashion of the King of Portugal. First, when he eats in
public, a platform, with three steps, covered with an Oriental rug, is erected. On
this platform, a table with a chair is placed. This chair has a velvet seat and gold
arms. The king always eats alone. He eats and drinks from gold and silver vessels
and cups. He is guarded by members of the Anzichi nation and of other

---

[58] See Pigafetta and Lopes, *Le royaume de Congo*, esp. 9–16.
[59] Pigafetta and Lopes, *Relatione*, fols. 67–8.

neighboring nations. When he wishes to go out, drums are beat. These drums can be heard for five or six miles. When they are heard it is understood that the King wishes to go out.

This phenomenon also points to how quickly Central Africans adapted Christian/European customs in Africa and the diaspora. While Pigafetta is mostly silent on the pomp that accompanies the king when he goes out, stating only that "Tutti i Signori l'accompagnano" (he is accompanied by his courtiers), we do not have to wonder about it, for Cavazzi da Montecuccolo provides a detailed description.[60] First, however, these luxury items – silk, gold, Oriental rugs, swords – are examples of the kinds of foreign objects the Portuguese brought, especially from India, to the Kongo as trading goods. More importantly, however, this fragment underscores how the precedent for Black kings and queens in the diaspora was set in Africa itself. There are, for example, some similarities between this text and a 1609 description of the ceremony in Mexico City (see Chapter 2). For example, in 1609, the festive king also sat on a throne set up on a dais. A banquet was also a central part of the Mexican performance. Moreover, as Reginaldo Lucilene argues, when Central Africans arrived in Europe and the Americas, they already had these practices – Afro-Christian confraternities and celebratory rituals – in their cultural repertoire.[61] Furthermore, in Europe and the Americas, Africans and their descendants acted on this propensity to adapt new cultural elements – European and American – into older traditions, as may be suggested by the cavalry and mock battle between the Black and Indigenous performers in Díaz del Castillo's text. It was through this adaptability that Afrodescendants built their own creole culture in the diaspora, not only as forms of survival, but as concrete social practices that gave meaning to their existence beyond mere survival.[62]

One recurring ceremony Cavazzi da Montecuccolo describes may best resemble Black confraternal kings and queens' cultural practices:

Una cerimonia molto riguardevole, principalmente per la stima, con cui vedesi praticata, usano i Rè del Congo, e volgarmente chiamasi benedire i suoi Sudditi. A certi tempi determinati, ò quando affronta il giorno di qualche straordinaria, e publica allegrezza, cõgregasi tutto il Poppolo sù'l Terreno maggiore della Città, attendendo dalla benignità del suo Sovrano questa, ch'essi reputano pregiatissima grazia. Esce egli con tutto l'imaginabile decoro, e postosi in luogo rilevato,

---

[60] Cavazzi da Montecuccolo, *Istorica descrizione*, fol. 68.
[61] Reginaldo, *Os Rosários dos Angolas*, 51–64.
[62] See J. H. Sweet, *Recreating Africa*, 2; Hall, "Creolité."

distintamente osserva, se vi sia qualche immeritevole, e non veggendone, ò non essendo avvisato in contrario ... con la mano destra alzata, movendola à guise di paralitico, senza proferire parola, torce le dita or quà, or là sopra gli astanti.[63]

A very remarkable ceremony, more for how much they value it, which the kings of the Congo have, is that which they commonly call the blessing of his subjects. At a determined time, or before a day of extraordinary public joy, they all gather in the city's main square, to wait for their sovereign's blessing, which they consider a great favor. He comes out with all the imaginable pomp, stands on a high place, attentively observes, and if there is no one unworthy, or he is not informed of it ... with his hand raised, moving it like a paraplegic, without saying a word, he bends his fingers here and there above the attendants.

This ostentatious display foreshadowed what Afrodescendants would seek to reenact in the performance "with their king and queen" in the diaspora. The foregoing examples make explicit that Afrodescendants were not merely imitating European markers of status in the performance of festive kings and queens. Instead, they were seeking to recreate their African world in the diaspora. Indeed, as discussed in what follows, Afrodescendants in the diaspora added festive kings and queens to their festive practices because many of them stemmed from dances normally performed before African rulers.

While Díaz del Castillo does not describe the Black king and queen, the examples from Brazil I discuss next may illustrate what that pomp may have looked like, as do those I discuss in the next chapters. The images I use to supplement these texts underscore the importance of visual records to fully understand this performative genre; though, as with the texts studied here, we cannot accept them prima facie. Indeed, we must be cautious of both as many of them participate in the exotic genre, or exoticization of the non-European Other.[64]

The final ceremonial element Cavazzi da Montecuccolo describes may best resemble what *congados* looked like:

Il Rè hà una Corte, che non uguaglia quelle de' Principi Europei, tuttavia vi è fasto, e nobilità proportinata alle alter cōdizioni del Regno. Quando egli esce in publico, le Guardie, armate di archi, li lancie, e di moschetti, inordinatamente sanno la scorta: dietro ad essi vanno I Sonatori, toccando i loro barbari stromenti, & e anche i Pisseri, havendone da Portughese appreso l'uso, col quale festevole, benche non armonioso concerto, accordano sovente musicali encomij intorno alle prodezze, & alla magnificenza del Rè presente, e de' suoi Aui; & in questa sorte di componimenti, sommamente adulatorij, sono aiutati da certi Araldi, che maneggiando Mazze di ferro con alcuni Campanelli, si fanno senitre

---

[63] Cavazzi da Montecuccolo, *Istorica descrizione*, fol. 254.   [64] See Mason, *Infelicities*.

ben da lontano: dopo questi la Corte bassa ... poscia i Paggi, gli Ufficiali, e
grande numero di Cavalieri detti della Croce di Christo, Ordine molto nobile,
instituito da Primi Rè Conghesi Cattolici, e fino al giorno di hoggi sostenuto in
molta riputazione: finalmente comparisce il Rè, servito da due Scudieri giovanetti, di sangue illustre, uno de' quali porta una Targa coperta di pelle di Tigre, &
una Scimmitarra gioiellata, l'altro tiene in mano un bastone coperto di velluro
rosso, guernito d'oro con un Pomo di argento massicio: a' fianchi l'assistono due,
che sventollano code di Cavalli, quasi in atto di cacciare le Mosche; e queata trà
le Cariche familiari, stimasi la più riguardevole. Un Caviliere de' più favoriti
porta il Parasole di damasco cremesino trinato d'oro sempre aperto sopra del suo
Signore.[65]

The king has a court which, although it does not equal those of the princes of
Europe, still has pomp and nobility proportionate to the other conditions of the
kingdom. When he goes out in public, guards armed with bows, lances, and
muskets make up his escort. Behind them go the musicians playing their barbarous
instruments and fifes, which they have learned to play from the Portuguese,
disturbing, with their dissonant noise, the king's valor and magnificence, as well
as his ancestors. In this kind of composition, they are aided by some heralds who
make themselves heard from afar with metal clubs and small bells. Then follows
the lower court ... the pages, the officials, and a great number of knights of the
Cross, a very noble order instituted by the first Christian kings of the Congo and
still held in high esteem. The king comes in last, attended by two young squires of
noble blood. One carries a shield covered in tiger hide and a bejeweled cutlass. The
other carries a staff covered with red velvet, adorned with gold and solid silver.
Two pages accompany the king swinging horse's tails to keep away flies. This task
is the most esteemed of all. Then one of the king's favorites carries a parasol, which
is always open on the king.

In the mid-eighteenth century, the Capuchin missionary Bernardino d'Asti
depicted this pageantry in a watercolor of a meeting with the governor of
Soyo (Figure 1.9).[66] In the image, the missionary and the Kongolese ruler,
both shaded by a parasol, meet as equals, their respective retinues behind
them. The ruler's costume communicates his elevated status through
elements borrowed from both European and African aristocratic traditions.[67] Afro-Iberians appeared in a similar fashion – albeit on a float – in
Braga, Portugal, in 1731. The performance was part of the city's Corpus
Christi festivities. Intended to show the rest of the Iberian world how the
city of Braga celebrated Corpus Christi – through the a priori publication

---

[65] Cavazzi da Montecuccolo, *Istorica descrizione*, fol. 257.
[66] Elsewhere in the manuscript D'Asti appears saying mass under a parasol. Cavazzi da
Montecuccolo, Julão, and D'Asti were all from Turin, Italy.
[67] Fromont, "Dancing for the King of Congo," 188–90.

FIGURE 1.9 Bernardino D'Asti, "Franciscan Missionary Meets the Governor of Soyo, ca. 1750, fol. 9 r." In *Missione in prattica: Padri cappuccini ne Regni di Congo, Angola, et adiacenti*, Biblioteca Civica Centrale, Turin, Italy, MS 457. Courtesy of Biblioteca Civica Centrale

of the festivities' components (hence the future tense) – the Black performance was meant as one of the festival's main attractions:

> Formarse-ha hum vistoso Carro, ou Carroça, pela qual hiraõ puxando dous Leões, no frontespicio, do Carro se veraõ duas Aguais, e no fim se levantarà huma gruta, dentro da qual hiraõ sentados Rey, Rainha, sobre a gruta se verà hum pavilhaõ, ou guardasol de penas, o qual sustentarà un Negro vestido à Ethiopeza.[68]

There will be an elegant carriage drawn by two lions, there will be two eagles in the front of the carriage, and on the back there will a cave, inside which will travel the king and queen. On top of the cave there will be a parasol held by a Black person dressed in African custom.

This performance was most likely staged by one of Braga's Black confraternities. Furthermore, the king and queen in Julião's images appear under a parasol – to highlight a recurring element – illustrating that Black confraternities imitated this European practice first adopted in Africa

---

[68] Anonymous, *Breve extracto*, fol. 2.

throughout the Atlantic in their festive performances. The parasol was an important symbol of status in European culture, and here we see Afrodescendants using it to denote prestige.[69]

We do not know when this tradition began to take root on Iberian soil. Isidoro Moreno posits that Black confraternities may have held elections and coronations of festive kings and queens in Seville as early as 1477.[70] In the nineteenth century, João Ribeiro Guimarães suggested that Blacks performed "with their king and queen" in Lisbon in 1484.[71] As for the Americas, writing in the early 1540s, the Italian "conquistador" Girolamo Benzoni (1519–72) wrote that "ogni natione" (every [Black] nation) in Hispaniola "tiene il suo Re, o Governatore" (has its king or governor).[72] Indeed, in the Iberian Peninsula, Black communities were assigned a "governor" who saw to the community's affairs and resolved disputes.[73] In 1475, for example, Queen Isabella named the Afro-Iberian Juan de Valladolid (not to be confused with the *converso* Juan de Valladolid also known as Juan Poeta) "mayoral e juez" (overseer and judge) of the Blacks of Seville, instructing "que no puedan fazer, ni fagan los dichos Negros, y Negras, y Loros, y Loras, ningunas fiestas, nin juzgados de entre ellos, salvo ante vos" (that the said Black and mulatto men and women, may not, and cannot, have fiestas nor meetings, unless it is in your presence).[74]

A common office among Afro-Iberians, the mayor acted as justice of the peace in the community and was sometimes referred to by a royal title, as was Juan de Valladolid, who was known as the "conde negro" (Black count).[75] According to Moreno and other scholars, these "governors" would perform as kings in Afro-Iberians' festivities.[76] While Benzoni's text seems to suggest that this practice continued in the Americas, if it did, it was only initially, for by the 1600s Afrodescendants had been assimilated into the *república de españoles* (commonwealth of Spaniards) and, thus, were deprived of an officially recognized form of political

---

[69] See my discussion of *Trujillo del Perú* in Chapter 3.

[70] Moreno, "Plurietnicidad," 176.   [71] Guimarães, *Summario de varia historia*, 5:148.

[72] Benzoni, *Historia*, fol. 64; see W. H. Smyth's translation in *History of the New World*, 92; Thornton, *Africa and Africans*, 202.

[73] Fracchia, *"Black but Human,"* 48–54; Moreno, "Plurietnicidad"; Phillips, *Slavery*, 93–4. This practice was even common in eighteenth-century New England (see Piersen, *Black Yankees*, chap. 10).

[74] In Ortiz de Zuñiga, *Anales*, 374.

[75] Germeten, *Black Blood Brothers*, 81; Moreno, *La antigua hermandad*, 43; "Plurietnicidad," 176.

[76] Moreno, "Plurietnicidad."

organization. While they were technically members of the republic of Spaniards, Afro-Latin Americans saw their nominal rights mostly neglected by colonial authorities (see Chapter 2). It was perhaps to redress this lack of a state-recognized form of political existence that Afrodescendants elected ceremonial kings and queens in an effort to thereby exercise some semblance of sovereignty.

Confraternities, the main hosts of festive Black kings and queens, offered Afrodescendants some degree of political authority, as they allowed members to have some power over their own lives as well as helped them form their creole performative culture. This contrasts with José Ramón Jouve Martín's argument that "la inexistencia de una comunidad negra colonial entendida como una unidad social ideológica, jerárquica y políticamente cohesionada, en la que los individuos tuvieran una fuerte conciancia de pertenencia al grupo, hizo que ésta tampoco se pueda encontrar textual y discursivamente" (the inexistence of a colonial Black community understood as an ideologically, hierarchically, and politically cohesive unit, where the individuals had a strong sense of belonging, means that this community cannot be found in colonial texts or discourse).[77] I contend, on the contrary, that Black confraternities and Afrodescendants' festive culture speak to their communal activities and "strong sense of belonging."[78] This is borne out by the fact that, as Jouve Martín points out, *cofrades* stipulated in their wills that they wanted to be buried in their parish church and that their *cofrades* attend their funeral mass and burial and annual masses for their soul.[79] As stated previously, confraternities were the closest thing colonial Afro-Latin Americans had to a political organization; through them they forged and expressed a strong sense of community and belonging, both to their confraternal and to the broader community.

THE DEVELOPMENT OF BLACK CONFRATERNITIES

Although sub-Saharan Africans have been present in the Iberian Peninsula since antiquity, they began arriving in larger numbers in the late medieval period through the Muslim slave trade.[80] Christian Iberians also took part

---

[77] Jouve Martín, *Esclavos*, 183.

[78] Ibid., 183; Bennett, *Africans*, 2. Jouve Martín's book in fact demonstrates the opposite of what he argues in the cited text.

[79] See also Jouve Martín, "Death, Gender, and Writing."

[80] See Phillips, *Slavery*; Fonseca, *Escravos e senhores*; Silva, *La esclavitud en Sevilla*; Cortés, *La esclavitud en Valencia*; Armenteros Martínez, *La esclavitud en Barcelona*.

in this enterprise. Lisbon, Seville, Valencia, and Barcelona became the main slave ports of the Peninsula. It was in these cities that a free Black population began to emerge, and with this population, Black confraternities developed at the end of the fifteenth century (see Table 1.1).[81] Seville, for example, was home to what is considered the oldest Black confraternity, Our Lady of the Angels, known as "Los Negritos," believed to have been founded for infirm Blacks toward the end of the fourteenth century by the city's archbishop.[82] In 1455, a group of free Blacks in Barcelona received royal approval for their confraternity's charter:

Nos Iohannes etc. caritatis zelus et ingens devocio quos nec sine cordis puritate vigere comprehendimus in vos christianos nigros libertate donatos et qui in civitae Barchinone habitatis instituendi seu faciendi confratriam inter vos et alios christianos ex gente vestra nigra libertate donatos et qui in futurum ipsa libertate donabuntur sub invocacione et ecclesia parrochiali Jacobi.[83]

TABLE 1.1 *Afro-Iberian confraternities, fifteenth and sixteenth centuries*

CONFRATERNITY	CITY
Our Lady of the Angels	Seville
Our Lady of the Rosary	Seville
Saint Idelfonso	Seville
Saint Jaume	Barcelona
Our Lady of Mercy	Valencia
Our Lady of the Rosary	Lisbon

SOURCES: AGCA; BNP; Blumenthal, *"La casa dels negres"*; Camacho Martínez, *La hermandad de los mulatos*; Fonseca, *Religião e liberdade*; Moreno, *La antigua hermandad*; Mulvey, "Black Lay Brotherhoods," 283–6

[81] Moreno, *La antigua hermandad*, 25–56. On Afro-Iberian confraternities, see Brásio, *Os prêtos em Portugal*; Camacho Martínez, *La hermandad de los mulatos*; Fonseca, *Religião e liberdade*; Armenteros Martínez, "De hermandades y procesiones"; Blumenthal, "La Casa dels Negres"; Martín Casares, "Free and Freed Black Africans"; Lahon, "Da redução and "Esclavage"; Phillips, *Slavery*, 94–7. For a relatively comprehensive list of early modern Afro-Iberian confraternities, see Mulvey, "Black Lay Brotherhoods," 283–6.

[82] Moreno, *La antigua hermandad*, 25–56; Fracchia, *"Black but Human,"* 48–55. Karen Graubart contests this narrative, arguing that there were too few sub-Saharans in Seville at the time to support the existence of this confraternity before the sixteenth century (in conversation, July 2015).

[83] Bofarull y Mascaré, *Documentos inéditos de la corona de Aragón*, 8:466.

We John etc. understand that you, freed Black Christians residing in the city of Barcelona, moved by the zeal for charity and devotion that emanates from pure hearts, seek to establish among yourselves and other freed Blacks, and other Blacks who will be freed in the future, a confraternity under the invocation and in the parish church of St. James.

In 1472, a group of free Blacks in Valencia received the same royal approval.[84] In Lisbon, Blacks were admitted to the city's Rosary confraternity in 1460 and "soon formed an independent entity that outsiders could already recognize in the last decades of the fourteen hundreds."[85]

The origins of these Afro-Iberian confraternities highlight the different means by which Black confraternities in the Iberian world first came about. First, Los Negritos' origins point to the fact that some Black confraternities were established by non-Black Europeans, through paternalistic gestures, to minister to Blacks. In the port cities of the Iberian Peninsula, there were many of these confraternities, particularly those ministering to enslaved Africans passing through the Peninsula on their way to the Americas.[86] Los Negritos' path in this sense is unique, for they appear to be the only such confraternity to eventually come under Black leadership.[87] This points to the social development Afro-Iberians engineered for themselves in Iberia, from newly arrived Africans in the fourteenth century to semiautonomous communities in the fifteenth.

Second, the admittance of Afro-Portuguese into Lisbon's originally white Rosary confraternity points to another means by which Black confraternities came into existence. In this case, Blacks were first admitted to an existing confraternity. For whatever reason, most likely because they did not enjoy the same privileges as their non-Black fellow *irmãos* (confraternity members in Portuguese), the Blacks in Lisbon established their own branch in 1565 (Figure 1.10).[88]

---

[84] Gual Camarena, "Una cofradía de negros."

[85] Fromont, "Dancing for the King of Congo," 185. See also Fonseca, *Religião e liberdade*, 23–37; Saunders, *A Social History*, 150–6.

[86] See Graubart, "*So color de una cofradía.*'"

[87] In the eighteenth century, however, white Spaniards took over the confraternity, and this is the one that survives today, still known as Los Negritos.

[88] "Compromisso da irmandade de Nossa Senhora do Rosário dos homens pretos," Lisbon, 1565, BNP, MS 151, fols. 9v–10r; Fonseca, *Religião e liberdade*, 23–37.

FIGURE 1.10 Anonymous, Compromisso da Irmandade do Rosário dos Homens Pretros, Lisbon, 1565, Biblioteca Nacional de Portugal, MS 150. Courtesy of the Biblioteca Nacional de Portugal

The origins of Lisbon's Black Rosary confraternity also point to the role religious orders played in urging Blacks to establish confraternities, something missionaries like Alonso de Sandoval (Seville, 1576–Cartagena de Indias, 1652), known for his work with Blacks, did in their ministry.[89] In New Spain, it was primarily the mendicant orders, particularly the Dominicans, Franciscans, Augustinians, and Mercedarians, that encouraged Afro-Mexicans to establish confraternities and defended them from secular authorities (see Table 1.2).[90] Finally, the origins of Barcelona and Valencia's Black confraternities point to the crucial fact that Blacks also founded confraternities on their own initiative, recognizing the valuable social and cultural functions, such as caring for the sick, burying the dead, and allowing them to maintain kinship networks, these corporate groups allowed them to fulfill.

As avenues for self-governance and the expression of collective identity, confraternities helped Afrodescendants negotiate their status within Mexican society and thus develop their own creole culture. Pertinent to our discussion is the festive culture of Afro-Iberian confraternities. These groups held their own celebrations and participated in public performances in the Iberian Peninsula, where they elected Black royalty and performed in city streets with "their king and queen."[91] Indeed, the 1565 charter of Lisbon's Black Rosary brotherhood called for the election of "principe, reys, duque, condes, marquezes, cardeal & quaes quer outras dignidades" (kings and queens, princes and princesses, dukes and duchesses, counts and countesses, marquises and marchionesses, cardinals, and other royal titles).[92] This provision became the norm among Black confraternities. Didier Lahon, for example, cites an undated election by a Black confraternity from the city of Vila Viçosa, Évora, Portugal, indicating that it took place before 1639.[93] Afrodescendants brought this tradition to the Americas, where it reached its full potential, becoming an integral part of Novohispanic festive culture. Díaz del Castillo's text shows how early this tradition crossed the Atlantic, within twenty years of the conquest of Mexico. While Afro-Mexican confraternal statutes have not survived, the festive traditions studied in this book show that Afro-Mexicans built on this Iberian precedent.

A year before the festival chronicled by Díaz del Castillo, two confraternities were founded in Mexico City. One, that of the Most Blessed Sacrament, was founded by Cortés himself, supposedly for "conquistadors," although the founding document does not state anything to that

---

[89] See Sandoval, *Un tratado*; Germeten, *Black Blood Brothers*, 1.
[90] See Valerio, "That There Be No Black Brotherhood."
[91] See Fromont, "Envisioning Brazil's Afro-Christian *Congados*."
[92] "Compromisso," fols. 9v–10r.   [93] Lahon, "Esclavage," 142–3.

effect.[94] Even so, "Black conquistadors" such as Juan Garrido and Juan Cortés may have been admitted to this confraternity. In fact, Garrido's house in Mexico City was on Calle Tacuba, which still bears this name to this day, very close to the Cathedral, where the Confraternity of the Most Blessed Sacrament had its chapel. Garrido's status and location in the city's *traza* may have given him access to this confraternity, and certainly to the second one founded in 1538: that of the Rosary.[95] Moreover, in a 1699–1702 Inquisition case, this confraternity appears along some Black sodalities, including one of Mexico City's oldest, Saint Nicholas of Toletino, accused of processing through the streets of Mexico City without ecclesiastical approval (see Conclusion).[96] This case shows the Blessed Sacrament *cofradía* forming part of a broader, interethnic community.[97]

The Rosary confraternity was founded by the Dominican fathers, who arrived in Mexico in 1526.[98] The Order of Preachers (Ordo Pedicatorum) had been founded by the Spaniard Domingo of Guzmán (1170–1221), known as Saint Dominic, in 1216 to teach Christian doctrine to the poor. One means by which they did this was by promoting devotion to the Rosary, which until that point had only been used by cloistered men and women. To this end, the Dominicans began establishing Rosary confraternities, where the members would meet regularly to pray the abbreviated five-decade Rosary in use today.[99]

As we have seen, in the Iberian Mediterranean, Dominicans were the first to admit Blacks into their Rosary confraternities; these members established their own chapters in turn, as they did in Lisbon in 1565.[100] Moreover, two Afro-Sevillian sodalities – Our Lady of the Rosary and St. Idelfonso – were founded with the Dominicans' aid. Unsurprisingly, then, one of the first actions the Dominicans took in Mexico City was establishing a confraternity dedicated to their patroness, the Virgin of the Rosary. According to Fray Agustín Dávila y Padilla, the first chronicler of the

---

[94] "Copia de la fundación de la Ylustre Archicofradía del Santísimo Sacramento," Mexico City, 1538, AGN, Cofradías, vol. 10, exp. 1, fols. 1–39. See Larkin, "Confraternities," 194.

[95] Dávila y Padilla, *Historia*, 354–7; Méndez, *Crónica*, 80–1.

[96] "El señor fiscal del Santo Oficio contra Ysidro de Peralta, mulato, por fundar a su modo una religion de san Agustin," Mexico City, 1699, HL, Mexican Inquisition Papers, Series II, Box 6, HM35168 and HM35169.

[97] See Farman Sweda, "Black Catholicism"; Bristol, "Afro-Mexican Saintly Devotion."

[98] Rivera Cambas, *México pintoresco*, 2:7.

[99] See, for example, Kiddy, "Congados" and *Blacks of the Rosary*, chapters 1 and 2; Mello e Souza, *Reis negros*, 160–3. The full Rosary worn by religious persons had fifteen decades.

[100] "Compromisso."

Dominican order in Mexico, "en pocos días" (within a few days) after
Mexico City's Rosary confraternity was founded, "casi no huvo en toda
ella hombre ni muger que no lo estuviese" (there was hardly any man or
woman in the city who was not a member).[101] While the next chapter
shows that later definitions of personhood may have not included Blacks,
at least not as free persons, the Dominicans' Iberian practices indicate that
they may have let Afro-Mexicans, especially *ladinos*, into this sodality.
(For this period, however, Chloe Ireton has shown that *ladinos* could
affirm themselves as free persons through the Spanish legal system.[102])
Moreover, the founding document does not state who was welcomed into
or barred from the confraternity.[103] Indeed, Clara García Ayluardo and
Nicole von Germeten have proposed that "membership was open to
all."[104]

If that was the case, the Blacks in the 1539 festival may have belonged
to the Rosary confraternity. This would have better positioned the performers to stage the performance and collectively procure the necessary
resources. The Dominicans, for example, may have aided them in these
efforts. Eventually, there came to be a Black confraternity in Mexico
City's Dominican convent, which performed with their king in the 1610
festival I analyze in Chapter 3. It could be that, as in Lisbon, this confraternity emerged from a group of Black members of the original Rosary
confraternity, changing their name to Holy Christ of the Expiration and
the Holy Burial when they branched off.[105] Moreover, several Afro-
confraternities date to the sixteenth century, albeit we do not know their
year of foundation (Table 1.2).[106] The oldest is believed to have been
Exaltation of the Cross and Tears of Saint Peter in the parish of Santa
Veracruz, Mexico's oldest, known for its Black *ladino* parishioners.[107]
While research on Afro-Mexican sodalities has focused on the seventeenth
and eighteenth centuries, Table 1.2 shows Black brotherhoods that were
active in Mexico City in the sixteenth century.

---

[101] Dávila y Padilla, *Historia*, fol. 357.   [102] Ireton, "They Are Blacks."
[103] "Reglas de la cofradía del Rosario," Mexico City, 1538; in Bautista Méndez, *Crónica*,
    80–1.
[104] Quote: Germeten, *Black Blood Brothers*, 22; García Ayluardo, "Confraternity," 132–9.
[105] "Memorial de todas las cofradías de españoles, mulatos e indios," Mexico City, 1706,
    AGN, BN, vol. 574, exp. 2, sf. This is the earliest surviving census of Mexico City's
    confraternities. See Germeten, *Black Blood Brothers*, 83.
[106] See Valerio, "That There Be No Black Brotherhood."
[107] See Germeten, *Black Blood Brothers*, 82–3; Valerio, "That There Be No Black
    Brotherhood."

TABLE 1.2 *Afro-Mexican confraternities founded in the sixteenth century*

CONFRATERNITY	LOCATION
Exaltation of the Cross and Tears of Saint Peter	Parish of Santa Veracruz
Holy Christ of the Expiration and Holy Burial	Dominican convent
St. Nicholas of Mount Calvary	Augustinian convent
St. Iphigenia	Mercedarian convent
Saint Benedict and Coronation of Christ	Franciscan convent
Our Lady of the Conception	Hospital of Our Lady of the Conception
Our Lady of the Helpless	Hospital of Our Lady of the Helpless

SOURCES: "Carta del virrey Martín Enríquez," Mexico City, April 28, 1572, AGI, México R. 19, N. 82, f. 1v; *Actas del cabildo*, 14:115, 227; "Contra algunos mulatos que han fundado cofradia y salido en procesion sin licencia," Mexico City, 1600, AGN, Bienes Nacionales, vol. 810, exp. 28; Franco, *Segunda parte de la historia de la Provincia de Santiago*, 546; Ojea, *Libro tercero*, 10

As Table 1.2 shows, Afro-Mexican confraternities were linked to religious orders, especially the mendicant orders (Augustinian, Dominican, Franciscan, Mercedarian). This was true even of Exaltation of the Cross and Tears of Saint Peter, for Franciscans ran the parish church of Santa Veracruz where they were based.[108] As Karen B. Graubart and others have noted, "the Catholic Church had long mistrusted all *cofradías*."[109] Yet missionaries relied on them to evangelize Black and Indigenous populations. This is borne out by the fact that the situation was similar in Lima, where most Black confraternities were linked to the religious orders in the city.[110] Indeed, a 1578 Dominican document states that the friars "se ocupan todos los dias en confesiones de españoles é indios é indias, negros y Negras y mestizos y mestizas y mulatos y mulatas" (dedicate their days to hearing the confessions of Spaniards, Indians, Blacks, mestizos, and mulattos).[111] Moreover, in his chronicle of the Dominicans in Mexico, Fray Hernando Ojea (d. 1577) singled out Fray Juan de Contreras, who "en especial gustaua mucho de

[108] Germeten, *Black Blood Brothers*, 19–20, 84.
[109] Graubart, "*So color de una cofradía*," 48.   [110] See Bowser, *The African Slave*, 249.
[111] Anonymous, "Información apologética de los dominicos en México en 1578," in Ojea, *Libro tercero de la historia religiosa*, 4.

confessor á gente pobre y humilde como son indios, negros y otros de desta manera" (delighted in confessing the poor, such as Indians, Blacks, and others).[112] These sources invite further investigation into the mendicant orders' work with urban Black populations in colonial Latin America.

Table 1.2 also speaks to another important aspect of Afro-Mexican confraternities: their devotion to Black saints. Initially promoted by missionaries, as scholars have noted, Black brotherhoods eventually embraced Black saints as their own.[113] Saints and biblical figures like the Queen of Sheba; the Black magus Balthazar (or sometimes Caspar); Iphigenia, a legendary first-century Aksumite (Ethiopian) princess said to have been converted to Christianity by the Apostle Matthew; and another sixth-century Aksumite royal convert, Kaleb of Axum, inscribed Blacks in the story of salvation from antiquity and allowed Afro-Mexicans to make claims to Old Christian blood in a world that saw them as "the quintessential foreign element that, like 'Jewishness,' could not be fully assimilated into Spanish colonial society," as María Elena Martínez observed.[114] For missionaries, more contemporary saints like St. Nicholas of Mount Calvary (ca. 1246–1305), a supposed mulatto, and the sixteenth-century Afro-Sicilian lay Franciscan friars St. Benedict the Moor (1526–89) and Anthony of Carthage (d. 1549) served as models of the kind of piety they wished to instill in Afro-Mexicans. Afro-Mexicans, like other Blacks in the Iberian world, formed devotion to these latter two saints decades before they were officially canonized by Rome.[115]

Yet Afrodescendants' main aim in founding or joining confraternities was to form community in the diaspora, pool their meager resources to care for each other in times of need, and express their Afro-Catholic identity through devotional and festive practices.[116] Indeed, caring for ill members and poor Blacks was a major tenet of Black sodalities. This

---

[112] Ojea, *Libro tercero de la historia religiosa*, 68. For Jesuit examples, see *Monumenta mexicana*, 1:296, 437, 529.

[113] See Brewer-García, "Hierarchy and Holiness"; Rowe, *Black Saints*, "Visualizing Black Sanctity," and "After Death Her Face Turned White."

[114] Martínez, "The Black Blood of New Spain," 515. On Blacks claiming Old Christian blood, see Ireton, "They Are Blacks."

[115] See Rowe, *Black Saints*; Castañeda García, "Santos negros."

[116] See Germeten, *Black Blood Brothers*, 1–10; Kiddy, *Blacks of the Rosary*, 15–38; Mulvey, "Black Lay Brotherhoods," 1–37.

principle can be seen in the oldest surviving confraternity constitution, that of Barcelona (1455):

Item sia ordinacio de la confraria que si algun confrare o confraressa vendra a pobressa o fretura per malaties o perdues o en altra qualsevol manera que los prohomens de la dita confraria e caxa segons llur bon vijares a aquell o aquella la dita fretura sostendra axi en provisio de son menjar com en necessitats de metges et de medecines com en totes alters coses a ell o a ella necesaries.[117]

It shall be a statute of this confraternity that if any member falls into poverty through illness or loss of goods or any other manner, the board shall provide for their sustenance, medicine, or any other need.

While Afro-Mexican confraternal statutes have not survived, Afro-Mexican confraternities must have been guided by this principle, found in most Black brotherhood charters. Indeed, as Table 1.2 shows, two Afro-Mexican sodalities – Our Lady of the Conception and Our Lady of the Helpless – were directly involved in the care of the sick in Mexico City. These brotherhoods cared for ill Afro-Mexicans when these were admitted to the hospitals from where they took their names. But Afro-Mexican *cofrades*, and mainly *cofradas* (female members), cared for ill Afro-Mexicans in other settings as well, especially in domestic ones. Moreover, in 1568, a group of Mexican mulattos tried unsuccessfully to establish a hospital "aviendo cofradía" (with a confraternity) to care for their own, because, as they put it in their petition, "pues los que hay en [en la ciudad de] México son para españoles o para los indios" (those in the city only serve Spaniards and Indians).[118] A 1572 viceregal report states that another Black sodality (another name for a confraternity) also tried to found a hospital around the same time.[119] In this respect, Afro-Mexican

---

[117] "Ordenanzas de la cofradía de los cristianos negros de Barcelona," March 20, 1455, AGCA, R. 3298, fol. 3v.

[118] "Memorial de vecinos mulatos de la Nueva España," Mexico City, March 5, 1568, AGI, México 98, s/f; "Carta del virrey Martín Enríquez," fol. 1v. See Valerio, "That There Be No Black Brotherhood" and "The Spanish Petition System."

[119] "Carta del virrey Martín Enríquez," fol. 2r. See also "Real cédula a la Audiencia y a el arzobispo de México para que en la solicitud de los mulatos de Nueva España, hijos de negros e indias o de españoles y negras, que piden licencia y ayuda para hacer un hospital donde sean curados y fundarlo junto a la iglesia de San Hipólito, en unos solares al lado de la ermita de los Mártires, les proporcionen sitio en dichos solares sin perjuicio de tercero y el favor y ayuda necesarios," El Escorial, November 4, 1568; AGI, Mexico N.1089, R.5, ff. 260; "Real cédula a Martín Enríquez, virrey de Nueva España, y a la Audiencia de México para que provean lo que convenga en la solicitud de los mulatos de México que piden un sitio, con estancias y propios, para fundar un hospital, pues los que hay en México son para españoles o para los indios," El Escorial, June 2, 1569, AGI,

confraternities resembled the others in the city and through the Iberian world. It was indeed their festive practices and predilection for Black saints that set them apart.

While Afro-Mexican confraternities were not allowed to establish their own health-care institutions, Afro-Peruvians, by comparison, were in fact forced to do so. While in Mexico City Blacks were allowed to minister to infirm Blacks in the city's hospital for the Indigenous population – which was run by a religious order – and later in the hospital for Blacks, mulattos, and mestizos founded by the Castilian Doctor Pedro López in 1582 – which was administered by the Dominicans – in Lima, Blacks were excluded from the city's health-care institutions for Spaniards and the Indigenous population.[120] In Lima, two hospitals located outside the city's wall were dedicated to the care of infirm Blacks: San Lázaro, for enslaved Africans, and San Bartolomé, initially established for free Afro-Limeños but eventually available to all Afro-Limeños.[121] These hospitals were founded and staffed by members of the city's Black confraternities, especially their female members.[122] As Germeten has noted, in Afro-Mexican confraternities, women too were principally responsible for Afro-Mexicans' medical care.[123]

Another pivotal activity of Black confraternities was the burial of members and poor Blacks. In a world that disposed of deceased slaves' bodies in "dung heaps or open fields" – as Dom Manuel I of Portugal (r. 1469–1521) put it in 1515 – this confraternal function was so important to Afrodescendants, for whom proper burial was crucial, that in the 1970s, Patricia A. Mulvey argued that Black brotherhoods emerged as a "form of death insurance."[124] In Mexico City, Holy Christ of the

Mexico N.1089, R.5, ff. 347v–348v; "Real cédula al virrey de Nueva España y presidente de la Audiencia de México para que informen sobre la solicitud de los mulatos de Nueva España que piden ayuda para la fundación y edificación de un hospital," El Escorial, November 3, 1570, AGI, Mexico N.1090, R.6, f. 180; "Carta del virrey Martín Enríquez," f. 1v; Valerio, "That There Be No Black Brotherhood."

[120] "Testamento del fundador Dr. Pedro López," AGN, Tierras, vol. 3556, exp. 4, f. 38r; Dávila y Padilla, *Historia*, 446; *Actas del cabildo*, 7:548, 572; Martínez Ferrer, "Pedro López"; Mondragón Barrios, *Esclavos africanos*, 57; Jouve Martín, *The Black Doctors*, 10–11.

[121] Jouve Martín, *The Black Doctors*, 13–14. See also Deusen, "The 'Alienated' Body."

[122] Ibid.   [123] Germeten, *Black Blood Brothers*, 41–70.

[124] See Mulvey, "Black Lay Brotherhoods," 15. On the importance of proper burial to Afrodescendants, see Kiddy, *Blacks of the Rosary*; Reis, *Death Is a Festival*. For another example of Europeans' neglect of deceased slaves' bodies, see Sandoval, *Treatise on Slavery*, 70–1.

Expiration and Holy Burial was particularly dedicated to this mission.[125]

Thus it is clear that in the sixteenth century, Afro-Mexicans had access to Mexico City's confraternal life and were keen to establish confraternities from the colony's earliest years. Like their Afro-Iberian predecessors, Afro-Mexicans recognized confraternities' valuable social and cultural instrumentality. This is not meant to suggest in the least that Afro-Mexicans, or Afro-Iberians for that matter, only founded confraternities for their usefulness. Afrodescendants in the Iberian world were truly devout Catholics, but they imbued their popular form of Catholicism with African-inflected elements, practicing a syncretic Afro-Catholicism that has survived to this day, particularly in Brazil and the Caribbean. Of course, as we will see in the next chapter, both secular and religious colonial authorities found this worrisome and even threatening to colonial rule. Finally, Afro-Mexican confraternities of the sixteenth century have not been studied, and the 1539 performance and other sources could gesture to how early New Spain's Black population sought to join or start confraternities. Confraternities indeed would have been ideal sites for community formation, mutual aid, and expressions of group cohesion, kinship, and festive practices. Díaz del Castillo's text may show the first Afro-Mexican confraternity engaging in these customs.

A MEXICAN SANGAMENTO?

Perhaps the best available description of Black festival kings and queens in the Americas is the Luso-Brazilian Francisco Calmon's *Relação das fautíssimas festas* (*Account of the Most August Festivities*) (Lisbon, 1762). Calmon's text narrates the festivities held in Santo Amaro, a major sugar production hub a few miles from Salvador, the capital of colonial Brazil between 1550 and 1763, in honor of the nuptials of the heir to the Portuguese throne, Princess Maria, the future Dona Maria I, in October 1760. The festivities that took place in Santo Amaro bear striking similarities to the performance described by Díaz del Castillo. The performers appear on horseback, wear masks, the king and queen don rich regalia, and there is a ritual battle. These remarkable parallels put Díaz del Castillo's text in dialogue with Calmon's and, more importantly, point to a continuum – neither static nor unchanging – of this practice from Africa to the Americas, from the sixteenth century to the eighteenth.

---

[125] Ojea, *Libro tercero de la historia religiosa*, 10.

The *congado* in Santo Amaro was performed in two parts. First there was an *embaixada* (embassy) announcing the main performance with the king and queen to follow:

O dia quatorze foi singularmente plausível pela dança dos Congos, que apresentaram os Ourives em forma de embaixada, para sair o Reinado o dia dezesseis. Vinha adiante um estado de dezesseis cavalos ricamente ajaezados, cobertas as selas de preciosos pelizes, trazidos por fiadores pelas mãos de dezesseis pajens.[126]

The fourteenth day was singularly praiseworthy because of the Congo dance which the goldsmiths presented in the form of an embassy, announcing the ceremony of the sixteenth. This embassy was led by sixteen richly mounted horses, the saddles covered in precious leather, guided by sixteen pages.

This was followed by "vinte criados custosamente vestidos, e montados em soberbos cavalos" (twenty servants richly dressed and riding majestic horses).[127] Then came the *embaixador do rei* (the king's ambassador),

magníficamente ornado de seda azul, com uma bordadura formada de cordões de ouro, e peças de luzidos diamantes, e na cabeça levava um chapéu da mesma fábrica com cocar de plumas brancas matizadas de encarnado: descia-lhe pelos ombros uma capa de veludo carmesi agaloado de ouro.[128]

magnificently dressed in blue silk, with an embroidery made of golden cords, and precious stones. He was wearing a hat of the same style with a cockade of white feathers. From his shoulders descended a red cape with gold trimmings.

As Fromont points out, the cape and other European elements were adopted by Africans in the Kongo in the original ceremony that *congados* imitated, *sanagmento*, discussed in what follows.[129] The ambassador's horse was no less elegant: "O cavalo, em que vinha montado, correspondia ao demais ornato, e preciosidade, e se fazia admirar pelo ajustado da marcha, com que ao som de muitos instrumentos acompanhava as mãos, e os festejos" (The horse on which he traveled corresponded with the rest in ornament and gallantry, and caused admiration with its march, to the rhythm of many instruments and dancing).[130] As in Díaz del Castillo's account, here we find many of the performers on horseback; this may point to Afrodescendants' use of horses as markers of status. Upon arriving before the city council, the ambassador "anunciou ao Senado, que a vinda do Rei estava destinada para o dia dezesseis" (announced to the council that the king's arrival was set for the sixteenth).[131]

---

[126] Calmon, *Relação*, fol. 6.   [127] Ibid.   [128] Ibid.
[129] Fromont, *Art of Conversion*, 47.   [130] Calmon, *Relação*, fol. 6.   [131] Ibid., fol. 7.

These *embaixadas* were a unique component of the Afro-Bahian version of festival kings and queens and reflect historical African embassies to
Brazil. In 1642, for example, the ruler of Soyo, one of the three provinces
of the Kingdom of Kongo, sent an embassy to Recife, at that time the
capital of Dutch Brazil (1630–54).[132] It was in the context of this embassy
that the first *sangamento* (ritual fight) was recorded in Brazil by the official
chronicler of Dutch Brazil, Gaspar van Baerle (1584–1648). According to
Baerle's chronicle of Dutch Brazil, *Rerum per octennium in Brasilia* (*Eight
Years in Brazil*) (Amsterdam, 1647),

Mira eorum tripudia, saltus, gladorium vibrationes terribiles, oculus irae in hos-
tem simulation scintillantes, coram vedimos. etiam scenam sedentism in solio
Regis sui & majestatem pertinaci silentio testantis. inde Lagatorum peregrè
venientium & Regem ritibus gentium suarum adoratium, habitum & sicta obse-
quie ac veneratinem. quae recreandis nostratibus post pocula hilariores
exhibebant.[133]

I saw with my own eyes as I watched their dances which were marvelous to see, the
way they leapt, the fearful flourishing of their swords, their eyes flashing as they
pretended an attack on their enemy. We also witnessed a scene of the king sitting
on his throne, maintaining an absolute silence as testimony of his majesty. Also,
how foreign envoys, coming from far, pay homage to the king according to the
rituals of their country; they showed us their fawning behavior and pretended
honor, which they reenacted to our great hilarity after bouts of drinking.[134]

Baerle's text points to the fact that Afro-Brazilian king and queen performances drew on actual African embassies to Brazil. In Chapter 3, we
will see how European festive motifs inspired by African embassies to
Europe made it to Mexico. For this reason, it is worthwhile to look at
other African embassies to Brazil and consider their possible connections
to Afro-Mexican festive practices.

Albert Eckhout, painter to the Dutch court in Recife, also left us images
of the five envoys.[135] The principal ambassador, whom Fromont has
identified as Miguel de Castro, wears a hat resembling a papal tiara, but
is in fact what is known in the Kongo as a mpu cap (Figure 1.11). He has
on a voluminous black cape over a black tunic, with a white sash at his

---

[132] The Dutch invaded Salvador, Bahia, in 1624, then under the Iberian Union, but the
Spanish retook the city the next year. The Dutch then invaded Pernambuco in 1630 and
occupied the captaincy until 1654. See Baerle, *The History of Brazil*; Boxer, *The Dutch in
Brazil*; Ferrão et al., *Dutch Brazil*.
[133] Baerle, *Rerum*, fol. 245.   [134] Baerle, *The History of Brazil*, 238.
[135] See Fromont, *Art of Conversion*, 215–23.

FIGURES I.11–12 Albert Eckhout, *Portraits of a Kongo Ambassador to Recife, Brazil*, ca. 1642. Jagiellonian Library, Krakow, Poland. Courtesy of the Jagiellonian Library

waist and a red sash across his chest. According to Cavazzi da Montecuccolo, black silk was the most prized fabric in the Kongo.[136] In one image, the ambassador wears a gold chain with a heart pendant and in another, a chain with a cross. In both, he has a long red bead collar wrapped twice around his neck and descending to his waist (Figures I.11–12). This display of wealth underscores the kind of material culture African elites deployed to impress foreigners. As Díaz del Castillo's text

[136] Cavazzi da Montecuccolo, *Istorica descrizione*, fol. 116.

FIGURES I.II–I2 (cont.)

suggests, Afrodescendants in the diaspora likewise mobilized similar material wealth in their festive practices, seeking to impress white audiences.

In 1750, moreover, after his forces attacked the Portuguese fort of Ajuda on the Minas Coast, the king of Dahomey sent an embassy to the Portuguese governor in Salvador to ease the tensions between the two nations the incident had caused.[137] José Freire Monterroio de Mascarenha describes the ambassador in his *Relaçam da embayxada* (*Account of the Embassy*) (Lisbon, 1751). According to Monterroio de Mascarenha,

Estava o Embayxador vestido com hum sayal de tela carmesi, todo guarnecido de rendas de ouro crespas, com huma especie de saya como de mulher, sem coz, a que elles dão o nome de *Malaya*, tambem do mesmo estofo, todo guarnecido de franjas de seda, hum sendal curto con bordas pendentes, e huma capa com um grande cauda, como roupa Real, de tela furta-cores, forrada de setim branco com listas de cores differentes.[138]

The ambassador was wearing a red petticoat, with curled gold tassels, and a short seamless skirt, like a woman's, which they call "malaya," and a shirt of the same fabric, with silk borders, as well as a large, royal cape of iridescent fabric, lined with white satin and strips of different colors.

These embassies elucidate Afro-Brazilians' firsthand knowledge of African ambassadors, Brazil's close relations with Africa, and, finally, an element – the embassy – of the performance not present in other geographies. Yet the fact that some Afro-Mexican festive practices drew from Renaissance and baroque motifs inspired by African embassies invites to consider to what extent Afro-Mexicans were aware of these embassies and acted as "African" ambassadors in their festive performances. It is worth asking, therefore, to what extent were Afro-Mexicans inspired by these displays of material wealth in the Atlantic?

The similarities among (the real and ceremonial) ambassadors' regalia, such as the cape and gold accents, also show how much of Africa remained in these ceremonies across the Atlantic, even though the Dahomean ambassador hailed from a different region than most Afro-Brazilians, who, like Afro-Mexicans, came mostly from Central Africa, specifically Angola and the Kongo, particularly before the nineteenth century.[139] As Silvia Hunold Lara has concluded by comparing these two types of performances – *congados* and the actual African embassy – "podiam rememorar outros reis negros, na longíqua África ou bem mais próximos, líderes de muitos irmãos e confrades pretos" (they could have recalled other Black kings, in faraway Africa or much closer, leaders of many brothers in the Black confraternities).[140] Thus, both the embassy

---

[137] See Lara, "Uma embaixada africana."   [138] Mascarenha, *Relaçam*, fol. 8.
[139] On the slave trade to Brazil, see Klein and Luna, *Slavery*; Alencastro, *O trato dos viventes*, esp. 155–326; Vieira Ribeiro, "The Transatlantic Slave Trade"; Florentino, "Slave Trading."
[140] Lara, *Fragmentos*, 217–18. Voigt, *Spectacular Wealth*, 131.

and *congados* functioned as bridges between Africa and the Americas. This points to one of the main raisons d'être of Black performances in the Americas: to recall, to keep Africa alive in the collective memory, and, in so doing, to honor their ancestors. Black performances in the Atlantic, moreover, did not merely evoke the past but projected themselves onto the present, not only as performances of a desired sovereignty but also of social and cultural agency – a self-fashioned sovereignty that allowed Afrodescendants to preserve community and rituals in the diaspora, as well as make statements about their dignity to a wider colonial audience.

Like no other text, Calmon's account of the festivities that took place in Santo Amaro allows us to see the opulence the regalia worn by festive Black kings and queens could reach:

Na tarde do dia dezesseis saiu o Reinado dos Congos, que se compunha de mais de oitenta máscaras, com farsas ao seu modo de trajar, riquíssimas pelo muito ouro, e diamantes, de que se ornavam, sobressaindo a todos e Rei, e a Rainha.[141]

In the afternoon of the sixteenth the Reinado dos Congos came out, which was composed of more than eighty masked figures, with costumes in their manner of dress, the king and the queen foremost among them.

As in Díaz del Castillo's text, masks are a central component of the performance, though neither chronicler describes them. There are two interpretative possibilities for these masks that have significant implications for how we understand the performance of festive Black kings and queens. A Eurocentric interpretation would see these masks as European carnival masks. This would signal the performance as an imitation of European practices and give the performance a Rabelaisian nature.[142] But if we consider that masks are central to West and Central African ritualistic practices, we could also see these masks as African. This would give other layers of meaning to the performance. First, African masks were a common feature of colonial Afro-Latin American festive practices.[143] Second, Afrodescendants managed to use these African masks in public ceremonies, and colonial authorities at the very least allowed them.[144] This gives Afrodescendants great autonomy in shaping their own public performances in colonial festivals.

[141] Calmon, *Relação*, fol. 11. Voigt, *Spectacular Wealth*, 129.
[142] See Bakhtin, *Rabelais*.
[143] See Carvajal y Robles, *Fiestas de Lima*; Jouve Martín, "Public Ceremonies."
[144] We also see this in the watercolors from *Trujillo del Perú* I discuss in Chapter 3.

As was to be expected, the king's and queen's costumes were far more ornate than their ambassador's:

Vinha o Rei preciosíssimamente vestido de uma rica bordadura de cordões de ouro matizada de luzidas peças de diamantes. Trazia pendente do cinto um formoso lagarto dos mesmos cordões, com tal artifício, que parecia natural: na cabeça coroa e ouro na mão direita cetro, e na esquerda o chapéu guarnecido de plumas, e pernas manilhas de ouro batido, nos sapatos bordaduras de cordões, e matizes de luzidos diamantes. A capa, que lhe descia pelos ombros, era de veludo carmesim agaloada de ouro, e forrada de tela branca com agradáveis florões. Pelo ornato do Rei se pode medir o da Rainha, que em nada era inferior.[145]

The king was dressed most ornately with rich gold embroidery and golden cords with bright gemstones. About his waist was a beautiful alligator made of the same cords and in such a fashion that it seemed real. On his head, a gold crown, and on his right hand, a gold scepter. On his left, a hat adorned with feathers. His shoes were of gold embroidery with bright gemstones. The cape, which fell from his shoulders, was of red velvet with gold borders, and lined with white fabric with beautiful roses embroidered on it. The queen's costume, which was in no way inferior, can be measured from the king's.

While it may be impossible to determine what it meant for the actors from an African perspective, the alligator often stood for Africa in Renaissance allegories of the four continents. If this is the meaning invoked here, it would underscore how creole, American-born Afrodescendants sometimes "Africanized" themselves in their performance of African culture. Where the alligator could evoke barbarism, its description as "beautiful" (*formoso*) negates these connotations. Finally, the account's claim that the costume was made in such a "fashion that it seemed real" (*artifício que parecia natural*) could underscore how the actors self-fashioned their regalia and performance to imitate and compete with Europeans, to make claims about their dignity and status, and to proclaim the quality of their craftsmanship or the wealth they mobilized to commission others.

Even though the monarchs are more richly attired than their ambassador, there are many parallels between the two components of the performance, making the first part a true foreshadowing of the second. In other words, the embassy's regalia accorded with the "monarchy" it represented. Moreover, while the queen is only referred to as being attired in a similar manner as the king, Carlos Julião's watercolors allow us to see what these costumes might have looked like. While Calmon does not describe the queen, Julião dedicates two additional illustrations to her

---

[145] Calmon, *Relação*, fols. 11–12.

(see Figures 1.6–7).[146] And while in the Brazilian iteration, the king has been understood as wielding more or the same power as the queen,[147] evidence from Peru and elsewhere in the diaspora demonstrates that the queen wielded more power.[148] Moreover, in the form this tradition has taken in Panama, the king is also secondary to the queen.[149] Perhaps Díaz's text alludes to this dynamics when it states that the Black performers "[les] hacían fiestas a la reina" (paid homage to the queen).[150]

Similar to the festivities in Mexico City two centuries earlier, the *congado* in Santo Amaro included a battle between the king's guard and Black performers dressed as Indigenous people, which Calmon describes in terms similar to Díaz del Castillo:

Não foi de menor recreção para os circumstantes hum ataque, que por ultimo fizerão os da guarda do Rei com seus alfanjes contra hum troço de Indios, que sahírão de emboscada, vestidos de pennas, e armados de arco, e frecha, com tal ardor de ambas naçaoes, que com muita naturalidade representárão ao seu modo huma viva imagem da guerra.[151]

Those in attendance were no less entertained by an attack, which, as the last act, the king's guard, with their swords, charged against a group of Indians, who, dressed in feathers and armed with bows and arrows, ambushed the guard. There was such ardor between the two nations that they easily represented a vivid image of war.

Like the performers' royal regalia, this component is of African origin. As a matter of fact, Fromont has argued that this ritual battle, known as *sangamento*, was the original African performance and that Black confraternities added ceremonial royalty to it in the diaspora.[152] Although *sangamentos* do not appear in the other performances studied in the book, they can help us understand the Blacks' performance Díaz del Castillo describes.

---

[146] See Fromont, "Dancing for the King of Congo."

[147] See ibid. See also Kiddy, *Blacks of the Rosary*; Dewulf, *From the Kingdom of Kongo*; Mello e Souza, *Reis negros*.

[148] See Walker, "The Queen of *los Congos*."

[149] See Lund Drolet, *El ritual congo*; Craft, *When the Devil Knocks*, "¡Los Gringos Vienen!"; Bettelheim, "Carnaval of Los Congos."

[150] While Chapter 3 discusses a text that only features kings, the final chapter studies a text where women – performing as the Queen of Sheba – are the protagonists.

[151] Calmon, *Relação*, fol. 12. This component of the performance became known as *quicumbis* in Brazil: see Fryer, *Rhythms of Resistance*, 72–3, and Voigt, *Spectacular Wealth*, 130.

[152] Fromont, "Dancing for the King of Congo," 185.

According to Fromont, this ritual fight developed in the Kongo after the arrival of Portuguese traders in 1483.[153] The ritual battle staged in Mexico City bears many similarities with the form *sangamento* took in the diaspora. Thus I propose looking at this dance as the second stage of this tradition as evidenced in Díaz del Castillo's text. As Fromont points out, in the Christian Kongo *sangamento* consisted of two acts:

In the first act, the dancers dressed "in the way of the country," wearing feathered headdresses and using bows and arrows as weapons. In the second act, the men changed their outfits, donning feathered European hats, golden crosses, necklace chains, knee-length strings of corals, and red coats embroidered with gold thread.[154]

This description already illustrates how the dance had incorporated European elements in Africa. As Fromont notes, the two parts of *sangamento* reenacted the two foundations of the Kongo, one mythological and the other Christian.[155] The first act of the dance reenacted the founding of the Kongo by Lukeni in the region's creation myth.[156] The second act of the dance reenacted the founding of the Christian Kongo by King Afonso I Mvemba a Nzinga (r. 1509–42) in 1509. As Fromont asserts, Afonso "imposed Christianity as the kingdom's state religion and integrated it into the symbolic and historical fabric of the Kongo."[157]

After rising to power, through several letters to the kingdom's elite, Afonso recast his victory over his main challenger, his brother Mpanzu a Kitima, as a Christian miracle. As Fromont points out, while the Portuguese recognized Afonso as his father's legitimate successor as the firstborn son of the deceased king, Kongo law only recognized him "as one of several eligible successors."[158] Mpanzu opposed his brother's rule because he did not want to convert to Christianity. He led an army of followers who also rejected Christianity. According to the legend, during what seemed the final battle, greatly outnumbered and about to be defeated, Alfonso's soldiers began shouting the name of St. James, the saint Iberians called upon in their battles against the Moors during the Reconquista (711–1492). The shouting of Afonso's army caused Mpanzu's men to panic, costing them the battle and the war. According to the narrative formulated by Afonso in his letters, those who survived from Mpanzu's army later said that – in Fromont's words – "an army of horsemen led by Saint James himself appeared in the sky under a

---

[153] On the meaning of *sangamento*, see Fromont, *Art of Conversion*, 21. [154] Ibid., 23.
[155] See ibid., 23–53. [156] Ibid., 24. [157] Ibid., 4. [158] Ibid., 27.

resplendent white cross and struck scores dead."[159] After this, *sangamento* developed as a martial dance that reenacted this decisive battle, especially on royal occasions (Figure 1.13).[160]

According to Fromont, *sangamento*'s next transformation was the addition of ceremonial kings and queens in the Iberian Peninsula in the late fifteenth century.[161] As stated earlier in this chapter, Afro-Iberians may have elected ceremonial royalty as early as the 1470s. The Kongolese practice therefore found and joined an existing festive tradition in the peninsula – one that allowed it to fill in for now absent African sovereigns. This transformation may have been brought about by the presence of Kongolese nobles in the Iberian Peninsula. We can see these Kongo elites on horseback in the anonymous sixteenth-century Dutch painting of

FIGURE 1.13 Bernardino D'Asti, "Franciscan Missionary Blesses Warriors before a Sangamento," ca. 1750, fol. 18 r. In *Missione in prattica: Padri cappuccini ne Regni di Congo, Angola, et adiacenti*, Biblioteca Civica Centrale, Turin, Italy, MS 457. Courtesy of Biblioteca Civica Centrale

[159] Ibid. Not only was *sangamento* a Kongolese tradition brought to the Americas by slaves, but it was also performed on American soil by Kongolese envoys, as in Recife, Brazil, in 1642, while under Dutch rule (1630–54). See ibid., 114–21.

[160] Ibid., 23.   [161] Fromont, "Dancing for the King of Congo," 185.

Lisbon's central square discussed earlier (Figure 1.3). These Black knights and those in Afonso's narrative of his victory could account for those in Díaz del Castillo's text. *Ladinos* like Garrido could have learned about this practice during their time in Lisbon. Díaz del Castillo's text, therefore, may show how this practice was brought to the Americas by the Afro-Iberians who accompanied the first Spanish colonizers. So, even though *sangamentos* do not appear in the other performances studied in the book, they can help us understand the Blacks' performance in Mexico City in 1539.

Santo Amaro's *congado* was sponsored by the town's goldsmiths. This has caused some controversy since the guild of goldsmiths did not admit Blacks.[162] Some historians have argued that the performers in the *congado* were the goldsmiths themselves imitating an Afro-Brazilian practice. José Ramos Tinhorão, for example, contends that a close reading of Calmon's text leaves no confusion that the goldsmiths were also the performers.[163] Silva Hunold Lara, citing imitations of "uma dança de ... americanos pretos" (a dance of ... Black Americans) by non-Black Europeans in Porto, Portugal, in 1793, and *congados* by *pardos* or mulattos in Rio de Janeiro, in 1762, argues that the goldsmiths performed all the components.[164] On this basis, she concludes that Santo Amaro's goldsmiths were merely taking part in a long tradition of white, non-Black actors imitating Afrodescendants' festive practices.[165] Others contend, as I do, that the performers were Blacks who were hired by the goldsmiths.[166] Mello e Souza, for example, argues that only those who knew the tradition to the fullest – that is, Blacks – could perform it. Indeed, as the author asserts,

[A]s embaixadas com danças e versos africanos, e o reinado festivo ... tinham que ser realizadas por quem conhecesse as tradições, os gestos a serem executados, os passos de cada coreografia e os versos dos episódios representados. O rei, a rainha, a corte, os músicos e os dançarinos tinham que ser negros habituados a tais tradições.[167]

The embassies with African dances and songs, the festive royalty ... had to be performed by those who knew these traditions, the gestures to be executed, the steps of each dance and the song of each element. The king, the queen, the court, the musicians and the dancers had to be Blacks familiar with these traditions.

---

[162] Alves, *Mestres ourives*, 7.   [163] Tinhorão, *As festas*, 127n14.
[164] Lara, *Fragmentos*, 787–9.   [165] Ibid., 188.
[166] Mello e Souza, *Reis negros*, 263; Fromont, "Dancing for the King of Congo," 196.
[167] Mello e Souza, *Reis negros*, 263. Fromont also argues that it is more likely that the performers were Black: "Dancing for the King of Congo," 196.

Thus, as Mello e Souza concludes, the goldsmiths sponsored but did not perform Santo Amaro's *congado*. The goldsmiths' access to gold may have made this one of the most lavishly attired Black performances of the Iberian Atlantic. So, while *pardos* may have performed *congados*, as Lara contends, it is unlikely that Europeans did.

In the absence of details in Díaz del Castillo's text, Calmon's text and Julão's images – albeit temporally and geographically removed – could suggest how the king and queen at the 1539 celebration may have been attired. In this fashion, the diasporic framework adopted in this book can help supplement the many intentional, racialized silences about Afro-Mexicans' performative culture in so many colonial texts. Beyond this, the performance's rich fanfare underscores how Afrodescendants mobilized African and European symbols of prestige to perform symbolic, if not real sovereignty. Their customs recalled European monarchs as well as African rulers. This amalgamation speaks to the cultural intimacies that characterize the process of creolization.

The *congado* in eighteenth-century Santo Amaro, Brazil, illustrates how the original African practice was transformed in the Americas. Acquainted with feathered headdresses and bows and arrows in the African context – as Fromont's text attests – Africans found in Amerindian attire and weapons familiar components. Díaz del Castillo's account could be the first evidence of this cultural transformation in the Atlantic, placing Mexico squarely at the center of the cultural changes ushered in by early modern imperial expansion.[168]

When we consider this tradition's African origins, we can see, as Mello e Souza points out apropos the election of ceremonial royalty among Afro-Brazilian confraternities, "[a]s raízes africanas eram visíveis no processo de escolha dos reis e se manisfetavam na comemoração festiva da eleição e coroação, com ritmos própios, ao som de instrumentos de origem africana, acompanhando danças" (its African roots were clearly visible in the process of choosing the king and queen and manifested themselves in the celebration of the election and coronation, with African rhythms and instruments accompanying dances).[169] And while Díaz del Castillo's text does not state if the Blacks performed with music in 1539, we will see in Chapter 3 how music was central to Afro-Mexicans' festive practices, as it was and remains for all Afrodescendants.

---

[168] See Heywood and Thornton, *Central Africans*; Thornton, *Africa and Africans*.
[169] Mello e Souza, *Reis negros*, 181.

CONCLUSION

While scholars have struggled to explain the performance, its true nature may come to light when viewed from the perspective of a *sangamento*, as delineated earlier in this chapter. Newly arrived from the Iberian Peninsula (either Seville or Lisbon), *ladinos* could have brought the festive practice to New Spain.[170] If that is the case, as I have indicated, this would be the first performance of *sangamento* in the Americas, many years before it was recorded in Brazil.[171] Even if that were not the case, the events still formed a significant precedent against the backdrop of which Afro-colonial festivals would later develop in Mexico and elsewhere in the Americas.[172]

The *sangamento* dimension would also add another layer of meaning to the battle between the Black and Indigenous performers. In his analysis of the festival, Harris argues that this mock battle came from the European tradition of battles of wild men.[173] However, when viewed from the perspective of a *sangamento*, this battle gains a new significance. As Fromont points out, in the Christian Kongo, the second part of *sangamento* was formulated as a battle between Christian victors and defeated heathens.[174] In the Americas, Indigenous people took the place of the heathens in the performance.[175] Viewed from this standpoint, the battle between the Black and Indigenous performers could suggest that the Black performers coordinated the battle with the Indigenous performers. This would indicate the agency of Black performers in the planning of the festivities, which previous analyses of the festival have neglected.[176] Viewed from this viewpoint, the Blacks' performance stands on its own and is not dependent on the Spaniards' performance and attire for meaning. Nevertheless, it fits within a well-established European genre of theatrical performances of Christianity triumphing over Islam. That fact is significant to our interpretation of the cultural adaptability of Afro-Mexicans.

In the current state of knowledge, it is unclear whether the Black performers in Díaz del Castillo's text performed a *sangamento* or belonged to a confraternity. Nor can we ascertain who they were

---

[170] On Blacks' trajectory from Africa to the Iberian Peninsula and the Americas, see Graubart, "*So color de una cofradía.*'"

[171] See Fromont, "Dancing for the King of Congo."   [172] See Mello e Souza, *Reis negros.*

[173] Harris, *Aztecs*, 128.   [174] Fromont, "Dancing for the King of Congo," 188.

[175] Ibid., 196–200.

[176] Lopes Don, "Carnivals"; Williams, *Teatro*, 64–5; Harris, *Aztecs*, 123–31.

individually. Strong evidence, however, indicates that they were *ladinos* who had lived as members of African and Afrodescendant communities in the Iberian Peninsula. There they had the opportunity to join confraternities and to take part in festive celebrations independently or on broader civic or religious occasions. The performance described in Díaz del Castillo's text is the earliest reference to the participation of Africans in festival celebrations in the Americas. As such, it could be the earliest evidence of a *sangamento* in the diaspora, and in any case, it provides us the background against which the American versions of the Kongo martial dance should be considered. Considered as an African-derived event rather than an act of mimicry, the 1539 Black performance provides an important demonstration of uninterrupted – but neither simple nor unchanging – cultural continuity between African and diasporic celebrations, even with a detour through the Iberian Peninsula. It underscores how Africans and their descendants took and adapted their culture to their new lives. At a minimum, this performance remains an important early moment in the archive of Afro-colonial festivals in the Atlantic. It constitutes an important early example of Africans using European Christian rituals as a medium to express their identity. We will see in the next chapters how Díaz del Castillo's account, though brief, marked the beginning of a performative tradition that would characterize the Afro-Mexican colonial experience, even if colonial officials mischaracterized them, as studied in the next chapter. Finally, Díaz del Castillo's text shows that this tradition made forays into the Americas earlier than scholars have suggested, and that it was present in Spanish America as much as it was in Portuguese America.

Through a diasporic framework, we were able to situate this performance and Mexico City at the heart of the early cultural formation of the Black Atlantic. In the following chapters, we will have the opportunity to see how Afro-Mexican festival kings and queens continued to be permanent fixtures of Mexico City's public festivals, despite the suspicion with which colonial officials regarded them. We will see how this performance evolved, reflecting the development of an Afro-Mexican creole culture away from its African roots and more and more toward its new American soil.

2

"Rebel Black Kings (and Queens)"?

Race, Colonial Psychosis, and Afro-Mexican Kings and Queens

And all the different groups of ecclesiastics who live in Mexico [City] were just laughing; they were not frightened by what they were hearing about all the different kinds of news of war concerning the blacks, what they supposedly wanted to do. And we Mexica commoners were not at all frightened by it but were just looking and listening, just marveling at *how the Spaniards were being destroyed by their fear* and didn't appear as such great warriors.

Domingo Chimalpahin[1]

As noted in the previous chapter, the Blacks' inclusion in the 1539 festival was surprising because on December 10, 1537, less than two years before the festival, Viceroy Mendoza had written in his annual report that he had been informed by "un negro" (a certain Black man) that "los negros tenian helegido un rrey y concertado entrellos de matar a todos los españoles y aserse con la tierra" (the Blacks had elected a king and plotted to kill all the Spaniards and take over the land).[2] Mendoza also wrote that, because the informant was Black, he did not give it much weight at first, but that after doing the "proper" investigations, he was convinced of the plot and had "al que tenian helegido por rrey y a los mas principales que se pudieron aver" (the one they had elected as king and the leaders that could be apprehended) hanged, as represented in Figure 2.1. Mendoza's report is the first instance of what would become a fairly common trope in the colonial archive: rebel Black king (and sometimes queen).[3] Yet, without

---

[1] *Annals of His Time*, 219; my emphasis.
[2] "Informe del virrey Antonio de Mendoza," sf.
[3] See, for example, Tardieu, *Resistencia de los negros en el virreinato de México*; *Cimarrones de Panamá*; *Resistencia de los negros ne la Venezuela colonial*.

any other source, it is difficult to verify if what Mendoza was informed of was indeed a Black conspiracy seeking to undermine Spanish dominion or the first record of festive Black kings and queens in Mexico and possibly the Americas.

The trope insists that whenever Afrodescendants resisted colonial rule, they began by electing a king (and sometimes a queen) for the *monarquia africana* (African kingdom) they would establish after killing all of the Spaniards, raping the younger women, and enslaving the Indigenous population. As these three nodes of fear (murder, rape, and subjugation by Blacks) suggest, the trope fed on Spaniards' unease of ruling over a vastly larger Black population.[4] Yet, while enslaved Africans in the periphery of Spain and Portugal's American colonies did revolt and were often led by a male figure, urban Afrodescendants were more likely to join confraternities than maroon communities, as Pablo Miguel Sierra Silva has observed.[5] Nonetheless, colonial officials were suspicious of Mexico City's Black population, seeing revolt plots taking shape in Blacks' every gesture.[6]

In this chapter, I turn to several Mexican documents that accuse urban Afro-Mexicans of electing and crowning kings and queens as initial acts of insurrection. One, "Relación del alçamiento" ("Account of the Rebellion"), the report of the supposed 1612 Black plot, has received a great deal of scholarly attention.[7] Yet surprisingly, no one has looked at the report vis-à-vis Afro-Mexican festive kings and queens. The other, a 1609 report, possibly by the author of "Relación del alçamiento," levies a similar accusation against a group of Afro-Mexicans who supposedly elected a royal court during a Christmas Eve party the previous year. By reading them in tandem, and along with other accusatory sources from the early seventeenth century, I demonstrate that actions cast as sedition in both of these reports – but especially the 1612 report – were in fact part of Afro-Mexican confraternal and festive practices. I thus argue that these condemnatory documents reflect colonial officials' obsession with Black rebellion, which arose from what I call "colonial psychosis," or the psychological imbalance caused by the colonial situation of minority rule in what was

---

[4] See Martínez, "The Black Blood of New Spain"; Nemser, "Triangulating Blackness."

[5] Sierra Silva, *Urban Slavery*, 159–64.

[6] According to Irving A. Leonard, this fear reached a "neurotic" level (*Baroque Times*, 213–25).

[7] "Relacion del alçamiento que negros y mulatos libres y cautivos de la Ciudad de Mexico de la Nueva España pretendieron hazer contras los españoles por Quaresma del año de 1612, y del castigo que se hizo de los caveças y culpados," Mexico City, 1612, BNE, MSS 2010, fols. 158–164.

for many officials a foreign territory – a psychosis that is well illustrated by this chapter's epigraph. I show that colonial psychosis did not leave any aspect of colonial life untouched, and accordingly, Afro-Mexicans' festive practices, and even ostensibly their most orthodox tradition, confraternities, came under attack.[8]

When compared with the public festivals studied elsewhere in this book, these sources present a contradiction: on one hand, festive Black kings and queens are welcomed, even sought, for public festivals, and on the other, when the same performances take place outside the sanctioned, public space of the festival, they are seen as conspiratorial acts. To reconcile this contradiction, I propose that while colonial officials considered Black festive practices innocuous when allowed within the officially authorized space of public festivals (or had them performed as acts of subjugation), they feared – as a result of their colonial psychosis – that these same practices fostered rebellion by giving Afrodescendants freedom of movement and action.

These sources make clear that the suspicion with which officials regarded Afro-Mexican festive and confraternal practices was racially motivated. These sources then also illustrate early modern Iberian racial thinking and can help "reperiodize" our discussion on the history of race and racism. Concretely, as Daniel Nemser has shown in *Infrastructures of Race*, they illustrate that the biopolitics – the control over life – of which the French philosopher Michel Foucault theorized in his Collège de France lectures *Security, Territory, Population* (1977–8), can and should be traced to earlier periods than Foucault proposed.[9] This chapter expands Nemser's previous work on the Amerindian population by focusing on early Iberian thought on Blackness. The chapter also expands María Elena Martínez's much-celebrated work on *limpieza de sangre* by further complicating her view on Blackness as the epitome of blood impurity, as she argued in her own analysis of the 1612 report.[10]

Finally, the two documents at the center of this chapter bookend one of New Spain's most turbulent, unstable periods. This instability was caused,

---

[8] See Valerio, "That There Be No Black Brotherhood."

[9] Foucault defined biopower as "the set of mechanisms through which the basic biological features of the human species became the object of a political strategy, of a general strategy of the power, or, in other words, how, starting from the eighteenth century, modern Western societies took on board the fundamental biological fact that human beings are a species" (*Security*, 1–2 [translated by Burchell]). See Nemser, *Infrastructures of Race*.

[10] See Martínez, *Genealogical Fiction*; "The Black Blood of New Spain."

as it often was, by the absence of a viceroy.[11] In 1609, Luis de Velasco the Younger (r. 1590–5 and 1607–11) ruled as viceroy but would soon thereafter be named president of the Council of the Indies, requiring his relocation to Madrid. Velasco's presence, or rather prudence in 1609 may have prevented the execution of the accused Blacks (although they were imprisoned and tortured). But in 1612, no successor had been appointed and the Audiencia (royal tribunal) was in control of the viceroyalty, as it did in *sede vacante*. This change in administration may have been a key factor leading to the execution of thirty-five Afro-Mexicans, who were hanged and quartered for their alleged involvement in the supposed Black plot. If both reports were authored by same judge, Luis López de Azoca, who in 1609 had called for the wholesale slaughter of runaway Blacks, stating that "gente y applicacion de confianza ... los puedan matar libremente" (applied men of trust should be allowed to freely kill them) if they did not turn themselves in, may have been responsible for the 1612 executions, which mirrored those carried out by Mendoza in 1537 (and by the Audiencia in 1566, when *encomenderos* were said to have plotted to overturn Spanish rule led by Cortés' heir, Martín Cortés).[12]

But the 1608–9 and 1611–12 events were very different. In 1608–09, it was clear to many Spanish residents of Mexico City that the Blacks had at worse engaged in what they termed "drunkenness" and "cosas de negros" (things of the Blacks); only López de Azoca and Viceroy Velasco – unsettled by Black flight in Veracruz – insisted on their criminality.[13] In 1611–12, however, the Blacks had protested en masse the death of an enslaved Black woman at the hands of her owner. Consequently, the city's white residents were indeed fearful that a revolt plot was afoot, and that made all the difference; only the Nahua chronicler Domingo Chimalpahin (1579–1660) seems to have questioned the veracity of the accusations in 1611–12.[14]

The chapter is divided into three sections. The first of these discusses New Spain's anti-Black animus. The aim of this section is to demonstrate

---

[11] This was the case when Velasco' father, Luis de Velasco the Elder, New Spain's second viceroy, died in office in 1564. Spanish creoles being the source of anxiety at the time, a supped anti-Spanish conspiracy was blamed on Cortés' heirs and other creole *encomenderos. This too happened during a* sede vacante: (see, for example, Cushing Flint, "Treason or Travesty)".

[12] "Carta de López de Azoca, alcalde del crimen de la Audiencia de México," Mexico City, February 8, 1609, AGI, Mexico 73, R. 1, n. 4, fol. 3r. On Martín Cortés' alleged rebellion, see Cushing Flint, "Treason or Travesty."

[13] Ibid., fols. 2–3; "Carta del virrey Luis de Velasco, el joven," Mexico City, February 13, 1609, AGI, Mexico 27, n. 63, fol. 3r; Torquemada, *Monarchia indiana*, 1:759.

[14] Chimalpahin, *Diario*, 289–93; *Annals of His Time*, 219–23.

that Novohispanic authorities' suspicion of festive Black kings and queens formed part of a larger anti-Black culture. Section two discusses the Jesuit Alonso de Sandoval's text "On the Nature of Africans." I turn to this text in order to investigate the ideology that underpinned Novohispanic anti-Black policies. I contend that this text illustrates how early modern Iberian society conceived of Blackness as destined for servitude and therefore exclusionary of sovereignty, and that festive Black kings and queens (in communal settings) therefore posed a threat to this ideology because it asserted Black sovereignty – an "ontometaphysical" impossibility in Calvin L. Warren's philosophical assessment of anti-Blackness.[15] The last section turns to how this ideology and anti-Black animus played out in Afro-Mexicans' festive and confraternal lives. The aim of this chapter then is to show a counterpoint to the celebratory texts studied in the other chapters of this book. This counterpoint, I suggest, allows us to appreciate the significance of seeing Afro-Mexicans performing "with their king and queen" before and in such an anti-Black world.

FEAR AND LOATHING IN NEW SPAIN

Mendoza and López de Azoca were not alone in perceiving or portraying Afro-Mexicans' festive and confraternal practices as seditious. Indeed, as the sources studied in this chapter show, colonial officials, from the viceroy to royal magistrates, to church and city administrators, were constantly pre-occupied with New Spain's Black population. In 1579, for example, Viceroy Martín Enríquez de Almanza y Ulloa (r. 1568–80), in his outgoing letter to his successor, Lorenzo Suárez (r. 1580–3), warned the incoming viceroy that "los negros es una de las cosas con que a se de tener mas particular cuenta en esta tierra" (Blacks are one of the things with which one must have more particular caution in this land).[16] That same year, moreover, Enríquez had sent soldiers to the Pacific coast to "reduce" (*reducir*) the runaway slaves that had established a free community there. Enríquez ordered that those run-away slaves who were recaptured "sean capados" (be castrated), a common practice in the sixteenth century, though it had been prohibited by the crown.[17] While intended to dissuade others considering leaving to found

---

[15] Warren, *Ontological Terror*.
[16] "Carta del virrey Martín Enríquez," Mexico City, October 18, 1579, AGI, Mexico 20, n. 29, fol. 2r.
[17] "Para que los negros que anduvieren huidos del servicio de sus amos seas capados," Mexico City, November 6, 1579, AGN, Ordenanzas, vol. 1, exp. 34. See Aguirre

maroon communities, this measure also prevented these ungovernable slaves from producing equally unruly children, and illustrates the kind of biopolitical strategies that characterized New Spain's anti-Black ethos.

As stated previously, not even confraternities were spared colonial suspicion. In his 1572 annual report, for example, Viceroy Enríquez complained about the "inconvenientes" (inconveniences) Afro-Mexican *cofradías* (confraternities) presented to colonial rule:

[A]qui a dias que los negros tenian una cofradia y se juntavan y hazian por si su procesion de diciplinantes como los demas y esto como las otras cosas desta calidad a ydo siempre en crecimiento y siempre dando y tomando que parecia que traya incoveniente.[18]

It has been some time since the Blacks of this city have a confraternity and meet among themselves and make processions of penitents of their own accord, like the other confraternities in the city. And this and the other things of this nature have been becoming more frequent and seem to bring inconveniences.

Enríquez is unambiguous in his desire to prevent "juntas de negros" (Black gatherings) – as he put it in the following paragraph of his report – allegedly in part due to the difficulty of disbanding these groups once they have been formed. This in turn seems like a tacit acknowledgment of the difficulty of retracting autonomy once it had been granted, and an oblique admission of the fragility of colonial rule over its enormous Black population.

The inconveniences colonial officials saw Afro-Mexican sodalities posing to colonial rule seems to have arisen from the freedom of movement brotherhoods – and the urban milieu in general – afforded Afro-Mexicans. Indeed, other officials put it in these exact terms. For example, in his 1609 annual report, Viceroy Velasco complained that Afro-Mexicans had "demasiada libertad" (too much freedom).[19] We will see how López de Azoca, the 1612 report, and other colonial officials saw Black freedom as an existential threat to colonial rule – that is, as an anomaly or oxymoron that contradicted the very foundation of colonial domination based on African slavery.

City officials were also wary of Afro-Mexican confraternal practices. On January 26, 1598, for example, Guillén Brondat, a *cabildo regidor* (alderman) and the city's *procurador mayor* (chief solicitor), complained

---

Beltrán, *Cuijila*, 59–60; Carroll, "Mandinga," 493. On the practice of castrating recaptured runaway slaves, see Lucena Salmoral, *Regulación de la esclavitud*, 41, 60–3.

[18] "Carta del virrey Martín Enríquez," Mexico City, April 28, 1572, AGI, Mexico 19, n. 82, fol. 1v.

[19] "Carta del virrey Luis de Velasco, el joven," Mexico City, February 13, 1609, AGI, México R.17, N.63, fol. 3r.

about two sets of "abuses" that the city's Black residents supposedly committed on a regular basis. One was carrying *cuchillos carniceros* (butcher knives) a practice repeatedly prohibited by both local and regal law.[20] Yet it would not be uncharacteristic of New Spain's Black population, which was heavily involved in cattle ranching and beef production.[21]

The other Black abuse Brondat saw was meeting "so color de cofradía" (under the guise of confraternities):

[Los negros] tienen otro abuso que es aver hecho juntas y conciliabulos so color de una cofradía en el convento de Santo Domingo San Agustin Ospital de Nuestra Señora y desamparados y para esto tienen su caxa que llaman del tesoro con tres llaves y su tesorero mayordomo escribano prioste y allí juntan suma y cantidad de pesos de oro rrobando a sus amos y a los vezinos desta dicha ciudad.[22]

The Black residents of this city meet under the guise of confraternities in the convents of Santo Domingo and San Agustin, and hospitals of Our Lady of Conception, and the Helpless. And for this they have a box, which they call the treasury, with three keys, and their treasurer, majordomo, secretary, and prior. In this box they gather great sums of gold pesos stolen from their masters and other residents of this city.

Brondat's complaint exemplifies the anxiety felt by some colonial authorities, who expressed doubt that these Black brotherhoods were earnest expressions of Catholic belief and functioned instead as fronts for more pernicious activities. Brondat's inclusion of the stolen gold pesos also gives testimony to the common association between Blackness and criminality in colonial Latin America and suggests that such groups could only sustain themselves through illicit means (as we saw with Antonil in the Introduction). In his 1609 report, Viceroy Velasco made the same claim; that any money Afro-Mexicans had must have been "de fuerça seria hurtado" (necessarily stolen).[23] In "*So color de una cofradía*," Karen B. Graubart studies a similar case from Lima, from 1549, where the city's *cabildo* accused enslaved Afro-Limeños of "getting together for dances, robbery and drunken fiestas 'so color de una cofradía,'" indicating an anti-Black, anti-confraternal animus that transcended the Mexican context.[24]

Despite its accusatory nature, however, Brondat's accusation is an important record of Afro-Mexican *cofradías* in the sixteenth century. From later sources, we know that the confraternities he names – Holy

---

[20] See Lucena Salmoral, *Regulación de la esclavitud*; Schwaller, "For Honor and Defence."
[21] See Sluyter, *Black Ranching Frontiers*, 19–60.   [22] *Actas del cabildo*, 14:115.
[23] "Carta del virrey Luis de Velasco, el joven," fol. 3r.
[24] *Libros de cabildos de Lima*, libro 4, 55–6; Graubart, "*So color de una cofradía*," 48.

Christ of the Expiration and the Holy Burial (Dominican convent), St. Nicholas of Mount Calvary (Augustinian convent), Our Lady of the Conception (at the same-named hospital), and Desamparados (at the homonymous hospital) – were indeed attached to these institutions.[25] It is partly because he mentions them that we know that they were active at least by the 1590s. Thus, while we do not know the exact dates when these confraternities were founded, Enríquez's report, Brondat's complaint, and other sources discussed here allow us to see that they were active as early as the late 1560s, which is far earlier than has been posited for them.[26] These sources offer a starting point and an invitation for further research about Afro-Mexican brotherhoods in the sixteenth century. Brondat's complaint also alludes to the governing structures of Black confraternities, which were governed by a board of twelve led by a *mayordomo* (steward), had a treasurer to manage their funds, a secretary to record their activities (often a friar due to Black illiteracy), and a spiritual director (Brondat's "prior"), who could be the same friar who was their secretary. In the end, however, these texts signal out Black sodalities for behaving "como los demas" (like the other) (i.e., Spanish) confraternities, underscoring how Iberian racial thinking thought of these privileges as exclusionary of Black subjects. Yet as Graubart and others have argued, Blacks used brotherhoods to form community, help each other in time of need, and express their Catholic faith and identity through devotion and festive practices, as we will see in the next chapter more concretely.

The best articulation of New Spain's anti-Black ethos, however, may be found in outgoing Viceroy Álvaro Manrique de Zuñiga's (r. 1585–90) advice to his successor, Luís de Velasco the Younger. Manrique de Zuñiga warned the younger Velasco that,

En esta tierra hay gran cantidad de negros y mulatos libres, los cuales son tan dañosos y perniciosos como vuestra señoria sabe, porque no entienden sino en jugar y andar vagamundos y hacer robos y daños, y aunque tributan a su Majestad, la mayor parte deja de hacerlo, porque no se registran como esta mandado, para lo cual yo mande que pena de la vida a todos se registrasen,

---

[25] "Memorial de todas las cofradías de españoles, mulatos e indios," Mexico City, 1706, AGN, Bienes Nacionales, vol. 574, exp. 2. See Germeten, *Black Blood Brothers*, 83.

[26] See Germeten, *Black Blood Brothers*, 83; Bristol, *Christians, Blasphemers, and Witches*, 93–112; Masferrer León, "Por las ánimas de negros bozales." The problem is that this scholarship has relied on later sources such as "Memorial de todas las cofradías" and "Censo de todas las cofradías de españoles, mulatos e indios," Mexico City, 1794, AGN, Cofradías, vol. 18, exp. 8.

enviando orden a los alcaldes mayores y corregidores para que en sus distritos se hiciesen los registros de estos negros y mulatos horros que hubiese y les notificasen que so la misma pena no se ausentasen de la jurisdicción donde se hubiesen registrado. Lo cual servia de dos intentos, el uno de que su Majestad cobrase los tributos que estos le deben pagar, y el otro y *mas principal para la seguridad y bien de la tierra*, mandarlos juntar por los registros y repartirlos rata por cantidad en todas las minas para que sirviesen alli a los mineros, que se lo pagasen, y por cuadrillas, estando sujetos al alcalde mayor sin poder salir de aquel lugar y asiento sin licencia suya *inscriptis*, con lo cual la tierra se aseguraba de los daños y robos que esta gente suelta y vagabunda hace en ella, y los mineros reciban notable beneficio en tener gente de servicio con que se relevaba el trabajo de la mayor parte de los indios. Y los propios negros y mulatos eran tambien beneficiados, porque alli ganarian sus jornales ciertos, y estarian quietos, y los hijos que a estos suce-diesen, criandose en aquella vida, se aficionarian a ella y la continuarian. El tiempo no dio lugar a que esto se ejecutase. En los libros de la gobernacion hallara vuestra señoria lo ordenado, sobre que proveera lo que mas convenga.[27]

In this land there are great numbers of dangerous and pernicious free Africans and mulattos, as your Lordship knows. They are only capable of living as vagabonds, robbing and causing violence. Although they owe tribute to his Majesty, the majority avoid it by not registering as I commanded all on pain of death. I sent an order to the *alcaldes mayores* and *corregidores* to register the free Africans and mulattos in their districts. They will also be punished if they absent themselves from the districts where they are registered. This order serves two purposes. First, his Majesty collects the tribute that must be paid to him. The other intent, *more central to the security and well-being of the country*, is to command them to gather together for registration and then to apportion each one among all the mines, so they can serve there with miners, who will pay them. Others will be apportioned into labor gangs subject to an *alcalde mayor* and not permitted to leave their assigned district or contract without a registered license. This will protect the country from these vagabonds at large and their violence and robberies. The miners will benefit greatly from having these servants to relieve most of the Indians from service. The Africans and mulattos themselves also benefit by earning a steady wage, making them more dependable. Their sons will be raised in this life, will enjoy and continue it. I did not have the time to carry out this plan. In the government records, your Lordship will find the order, which you can carry out as you see fit.

Manrique de Zuñiga's plan is replete with the biopolitics that character-ized colonial society. The viceroy begins by stating the problem: Black freedom, real and imagined. This freedom makes Blacks "dangerous and pernicious" because all they do is gamble, steal, and wander the land.

---

[27] "Carta del virrey Álvaro Manrique de Zúñiga, marqués de Villamanrique," Texcuco, February 14, 1590, AGI, Mexico 22, R. 1; English in Germeten, *Black Blood Brothers*, 76; my empahsis.

Moreover, they do not pay their taxes, a serious offense that denoted disregard for royal authority. This problem, Manrique de Zuñiga suggests, is well known. Manrique de Zuñiga makes clear that this freedom made colonial authorities uneasy. Colonial administrators in fact saw Black freedom as an existential threat to colonial rule. As Spanish officials had begun doing – and other imperial regimes would imitate – the solution to the problem was population control, limiting Black mobility, with the penalty of death for violating orders to stay put. Manrique's plan also reveals what guided his reasoning: collecting taxes for the royal coffers, securing the territory, easing the burden of Indigenous laborers, and, more importantly, providing miners and by extension Spaniards a steady labor force for generations. As Rachel Sarah O'Toole has analyzed, the rhetoric about protecting the native population by alleviating their labor by shifting it to Blacks was part of a colonial discourse meant to bolster the empire's economic aims.[28]

The viceroy's detailed plan reveals the apparatuses the colonial state could and often deployed to control its subaltern population: tracking, confinement, policing, labor, and punishment, including the ultimate punishment, death. Indeed, as I note in what follows, no early modern empire had as many apparatuses of population control in place as the Spanish Empire. Thus, as Nemser has argued, the Spanish Empire is an important locus to begin studying the development of biopower in the early modern world. This chapter contributes to that analysis by focusing on biopolitics' impact on Black lives, especially urban Afro-Mexicans' festive and confraternal practices. Manrique de Zuñiga's plan, however, was impractical, if not impossible to implement in Mexico City, where Afro-Mexicans moved with relative freedom, though not without vigilance – monitored by both the colonial state and their white neighbors. Thus fears of Black freedom rang louder in Mexico City.

This anti-Black ethos is illustrative of Novohispanic colonial authorities' racial thinking, and it is against that perspective that I read López de Azoca's 1609 reports and the Audiencia's 1612 reports. As Viceroy Manrique de Zuñiga's words show, colonial authorities understood freedom along racial lines. And as Nemser has argued, this corresponds to the "racialization of freedom" that is the natural consequence of the racialization of slavery.[29] In this chapter, I extend Nemser's idea, as I argue that as colonial authorities conceived of freedom and sovereignty as exclusionary of racialized subjects, they criminalized Black freedom and sovereignty. The Afro-Mexican

[28] O'Toole, *Bound Lives.* [29] Nemser, "The Iberian Slave Trade."

practice of electing festive kings and queens, especially for confraternal gatherings, thus came to be seen as potentially insurgent. López de Azoca's reports, the 1612 Audiencia reports, and the other colonial texts discussed later in this chapter establish how colonial authorities criminalized that freedom in ways that not only affected Afro-Mexicans' festive and confraternal practices but also came to have fatal consequences.

Two propositions from Foucault's seventh lecture of *Society Must Be Defended* (1975–6) can help theorize the documents discussed in this chapter. The first of these is: "In a normalizing society, race or racism is the precondition that makes killing acceptable."[30] As scholars have argued and indeed as I show in this chapter, the early modern Iberian world possessed a clearly articulated racial system.[31] The question now is whether colonial society was a normalizing society. Foucault defines normalization as follows:

The discourse of discipline is alien to that of the law; it is alien to the discourse that makes rules a product of the will of the sovereign. The discourse of disciplines is about a rule: not a juridical rule derived from sovereignty, but a discourse about a natural rule, or in other words a norm. Disciplines will define not a code of law, but a code of normalization, and they will necessarily refer to a theoretical horizon that is not the edifice of law, but the field of the human sciences.[32]

In the Iberian world, laws were not derived from the sovereign, but from natural and divine laws. It was from these laws that the sovereign derived *his* powers.[33] The sovereign was merely an enforcer of laws that emanated from a sacred order. This is why Spanish monarchs commissioned their viceroys "en descargo de [su] conciencia" (to discharge [their] conscience) – that is, to fulfill their duty to preserve this divine order. It is from this duty that discipline was derived in the Spanish Empire. Discipline's purpose is to ensure normality, the observance of nature's laws and God's laws. In order to ensure discipline, no early modern empire had as many state apparatuses of population control in place as the Spanish Empire, such as the viceroy, the *audiencia* with its *alcaldes*, the Inquisition, *visitadores* (inspectors) with oversight powers, a whole host of *alguaciles* (sheriffs) to monitor daily life, and – among others – sites of population control such as *congregaciónes* (centralized towns),

---

[30] Foucault, *Society Must Be Defended*, 256.
[31] See J. H. Sweet, "The Iberian Roots of American Racist Thought."   [32] Ibid., 38.
[33] On the theory of the divine rights of kings in general, see, for example, Figgis, *Divine Rights of Kings*; Graeber and Sahlins, *On Kings*; Nyquist, *Arbitrary Rule*, 201–6. For early modern Spain, see Cantor and Werthman, *Renaissance*.

recogimientos (disciplinary institutions), *separaciones* (segregated districts), and *colecciónes* (general collections). These sites of population control, into which Indigenous and African-descent populations were funneled, according to Nemser, constituted the "condition of possibility" for modern concentration camps.[34] These institutions were intended to enforce "a code of normalization" based on "natural order." At the local level, this desired order manifested itself in city, church, viceregal, and royal decrees governing behavior, from restrictions on bearing arms, gatherings, and clothing.[35] Crucial to this order was the separation and stratification of the "races."[36]

Normalization ensured colonial hierarchy remained in place. To that end, death, the killing of those who defied the natural order, became not only acceptable but also necessary to maintain it. Thus, after the alleged Black insurrection plots of 1537 and 1612, their purported leaders were summarily executed in order to maintain the status quo and as a grisly display of state biopower (see Figure 2.1).[37] The public hanging of these Black bodies speaks to another Foucauldian idea, namely that "the exercise of discipline presupposed a mechanism that coerces by means of observation."[38] These public hangings made visible to Afro-Mexicans the mechanisms used to coerce them into conforming to colonial rule, as well as made Black bodies visible to all as the sites of both the transgression of colonial rule and the recipient of colonial discipline.

Foucault's other useful proposition – "if the power of normalization wants to exert the old sovereign power to kill, it must go through racism" – brings us to López de Azoca's main desire in sending his report to the Council of the Indies, which he did against the advice of his peers in the Audiencia, who disagreed with his assessment of the situation. When explaining this to the monarch, his addressee, the magistrate states that he disregarded their counsel because he wished that the sovereign be informed of New Spain's Black (male) "threat" and order that "threat" contained. Specifically, the judge recommended the king decree the

---

[34] Nemser, *Infrastructures of Race*, 2. Both *alcalde* and *alguacil* are derived from the Arabic and reflect the policing world the Moors brought to medieval Spain.

[35] See, for example, Lucena Salmoral, *Regulación de la esclavitud*; Schwaller, "For Honor and Defence"; Walker, *Exquisite Slaves*; Salazar Rey, *Mastering the Law*; Villa-Flores, *Dangerous Speech*.

[36] See Lucena Salmoral, *Regulación de la esclavitud*.

[37] "Informe del virrey Antonio de Mendoza"; "Relacion del alçamiento." See Querol y Roso, "Negros y mulatos"; Martínez, "The Black Blood of New Spain"; Nemser, "Triangulating Blackness." I return to this image at the end of the chapter.

[38] Foucault, *Discipline and Punish*, 170–1.

FIGURE 2.1 Anonymous, Execution of the alleged king of the supposed 1537 rebellion plot in the Codex Telleriano-Remensis, fol. 45r detail. Mexico, sixteenth century. Bibliothèque nationale de France, MS Mexicain 385. Courtesy of the Bibliothèque nationale de France

suppression of all Black "maroon" communities by any means, including wholesale slaughter:

[S]era nessesario si v. mag. dello fuere servido que con gente y applicacion de confianza se procuren reduzir y traher al servicio de sus amos estos negros conforme a la cantidad que cada uno tubiere y si no se quisiere rendar [*sic*] *que los puedan matar libremente* porque muy peor sera y de mayor dano si ellos se alzan.[39]

[39] Fols. 2v–3r; my emphasis.

It will be necessary that Your Majesty be served to order that with applied men of trust, these Blacks be captured and brought back to their masters' service, according to the number each master lost. And that if the Blacks do not surrender voluntarily, *the captors may freely kill them*, for it would be worse and of greater harm if they were to revolt.

In a normalizing colonial society, effectively controlling New Spain's Black (rural and urban) population for López de Azoca requires the state be endowed with the power to kill – a license that, as stated earlier in this chapter, Novohispanic colonial authorities availed themselves of on a regular basis. In order to protect and preserve the colonizers' powers and interests, the colonized population must be controlled at all times, even during festivities. This need is clearly articulated in Viceroy Manrique de Zuñiga's advice to his successor about the implementation of a mechanism of registration. Both texts – López de Azoca's and Manrique de Zuñiga's – underscore how colonial authorities deployed biopolitics to maintain colonial order. As Foucault asserts, for the colonizers' survival, "massacres [became] vital."[40] This is how we can characterize the consequences of the alleged slave revolt conspiracies of 1537 and 1612 as violent disciplinary efforts to uphold the colonial regime.[41]

SPAIN AND THE CONSTRUCTION OF BLACKNESS IN THE EARLY MODERN ATLANTIC

Very few works in the field of colonial Latin American literary studies have taken up the question of race and racism, and those that have, have mainly engaged in a one-sided debate on the question of the applicability or inapplicability of these terms (*race* and *racism*) to the colonial context.[42] Ruth Hill, a major proponent of the inapplicability position, for example, has long held that we should only use the categories of *casta* (caste), *limpieza de sangre* (blood purity), and *calidad* (legal status) – the three major systems of classifying peoples in the early modern Iberian world – and argues that these are incompatible with what is meant by race.[43]

---

[40] Foucault, "Nietzsche, Genealogy, and History," 154; my brackets; see also Foucault, *Society Must Be Defended*, 240–1; Nemser, *Infrastructures of Race*, 12–16.

[41] See Foucault, *Security*, 55–86.

[42] See Nemser "Triangulating Blackness." Mariselle Meléndez's *Raza, género e hibridez* (1999) and Daniel Nemser's *Infrastructures of Race* (2017) constitute two notable exceptions.

[43] See Hill, *Hierarchy*, 197–238; Burns, "Unfixing Race"; Thomson, "Was There Race in Colonial Latin America?" For other examples of the Hill camp, see Carrera, *Imagining Identity*, esp. 1–21, and Schwaller, *"Géneros de Gente" in Early Colonial Mexico*, esp. 3–10

Historians of colonial Latin America, on the other hand, while not all in agreement, have held a more fruitful and multivocal debate. Among these historians, María Elena Martínez, Jorge Cañizares-Esguerra, Joan Cameron Bristol, and Rachel Sarah O'Toole have proposed – in O'Toole's words – that *limpieza, casta,* and *calidad* "did the work of race" in colonial Latin America.[44]

In this section, I discuss the construction of Blackness in the early modern Atlantic, positioning myself within the camp that holds that race and racism have been at work in the Atlantic at least since the sixteenth century.[45] I do so principally through the analysis of Chapter 2 of Book 1 of the Jesuit missionary Alonso de Sandoval's (Seville, 1576 – Cartagena de Indias, 1652) manual for ministering to Blacks, *Naturaleza, policia sagrada y profana, costumbres y ritos, disciplina y catecismo evangélico de todos etíopes* (*Nature, Sacred and Profane Laws, Customs and Rites of all Africa, and Discipline and Catechism for Africans*) (Seville, 1627), which Sandoval later expanded and published as *De instauranda Aethiopum salute* (*On Restoring Salvation to Africans*) (Madrid, 1647), the title by which it is better known.[46] That chapter, titled "De la naturaleza de los etiopes, que comunmente llamamos negros" ("On the Nature of Africans, Whom We Commonly Call Blacks"), is

---

and 27–49. Similar to Hill, Carrera argues that "to use the general labels of 'race' and 'racism' [for colonial cases] is to put twenty-first-century constructs of race into play in [colonial] contexts" (1–2). For his part, Schwaller, a cultural historian, contends that not only is it wrong to use the category of race for the sixteenth century, but it is also wrong to use those of *casta* and *calidad* (5). (Schwaller makes no mention of *limpieza*.) Instead, Schwaller argues that "the phrase *género de gente* (types of people) came to encapsulate the belief that colonial society was made up of different kinds of people" (6). While refusing to use the labels of race and racism and advocating against their use, these scholars do recognize hierarchical systems that assigned and confined individuals to certain sectors of society based on their geo-cultural ancestry.

[44] O'Toole, *Bound Lives*, 161; Martínez, *Genealogical Fictions*; Hering Torres, Martínez, and Nirenberg, *Race and Blood*; Bristol, *Christians, Blasphemers, and Witches*, esp. 23–62; Cañizares-Esguerra, "New World, New Stars." Meléndez pioneered this thinking in *Raza, género e hibridez* (1999).

[45] Representatives of this camp include Bristol, O'Toole, Martínez, Nemser, Brewer-García, and Nick Jones, to name a few. In Mexican scholarship itself, there is a strong opposition to using the terms *race* and *racism* for the colonial period: e.g., Gonzalbo Aizpuru, *Vivir en Nueva España*; Gonzalbo Aizpuru and Alberro, *La sociedad novohispana*.

[46] All modern editions (1956, 1987, 2008), including the one I cite from (1987), are based on *Naturaleza*. The Latin title of the revised edition is based on a fellow Jesuit, José de Acosta's (Medina del Campo, 1540 – Salamnaca, 1600) *De procuranda Indiorum salute* (*On Seeking the Salvation of Indians*, Salamanca) (1588), on which Sandoval's own work is modeled, though it was never published in Latin: see More, "From Lines to Networks." For a detailed study of Sandoval's treatise, see Olsen, *Slavery and Salvation.*

an early articulation of the logic that would become the justification for African slavery across the early modern world. Thus, while Sandoval has been rightly recognized as a strong advocate for enslaved Africans in the seventeenth century, he also articulated and discursively reproduced that world's racialization of African slavery.[47] But Sandoval is not an isolated intellectual in this regard. In "De la naturaleza de los etiopes," he espouses a theory of Blackness that was becoming commonplace in the Atlantic at that time, thanks in no small part to African slavery. Yet, while illustrative of a major trend in the early modern Atlantic, Sandoval's text remains unique for the way it weds this theory of Blackness and a theological basis for African slavery.

Besides the historians cited in this chapter, my analysis builds on the pioneering work on race and racism in colonial Latin America by literary scholars Mariselle Meléndez and, more recently, Daniel Nemser and Larissa Brewer-García.[48] Meléndez established how eighteenth-century white *criollos* stereotyped Blackness as an immutable defect. Nemser's work, on the other hand, examines the formation of biopolitics, starting in the sixteenth century, by analyzing Spanish mechanisms of population control as racial regimes.[49] This section contributes to this scholarship by "reperiodizing" our conversation on race vis-à-vis Blackness. Concretely, the section shows how Africans were conceived as theologically and biologically destined for servitude in the early modern Iberian world, and the Atlantic more generally, to justify African slavery, and that this view on Blackness had profound consequences for Afro-Mexicans' festive customs.

As James H. Sweet, Martínez, and others have observed, medieval Europeans used the concept of race differently than subsequent generations would.[50] To them, race – *raza* in Spanish, from the Italian *razza*

---

[47] See Olsen, *Slavery and Salvation*.

[48] Meléndez, *Raza, género e hibridez* and *Deviant and Useful Citizens*; Nemser, *Infrastructures of Race*, "Triangulating Blackness," and "The Iberian Slave Trade"; Brewer-García, *Beyond Babel*, 34–73.

[49] Nemser's book focuses concretely on the concentration of indigenous and mixed-race populations in determined spaces, such as *congregaciones*, centralized towns, *recogimientos*, disciplinary institutions, *separaciones*, segregated districts, and *colecciones* (general collections), in order to police and contain their behavior. Nemser illustrates how ideas of spatial difference were projected onto the physical landscape and laid the foundation for concentration camps, the apogee of spatial difference.

[50] J. H. Sweet, "The Iberian Roots of American Racist Thought"; Martínez, *Genealogical Fictions*, 54–9; Tawil, *The Making of Racial Sentiment*, 33–58; Taylor, "Race and Racism."

– "simply referred to a group of plants, animals, or humans that shared traits through shared genealogy."[51] This idea is akin to the Latin concept of *nationes* (nations), simply meaning birthplace, which shaped the Mediterranean conception of ethnic identity from antiquity.[52] For the ancients as well as medieval Europeans, nation was understood as "a people with its language, habits, and religion."[53] For example, Afro-Iberians were collectively referred to as national groups in early modern Iberia: *nación* in Spanish and *nação* in Portuguese.[54]

This idea would undergo a profound transformation in the late Middle Ages (1250–1500). As scholars have noted, as Europeans increasingly entered into contact with non-Europeans during this period, nation became conceived along color lines.[55] Thus, in the late medieval period, there was a move from a national to a phenotypic conception of human difference. The historian Madeline Caviness, for example, argues that encounters between medieval Europeans and non-Europeans resulted in Europeans' self-perception as white in the second half of the thirteenth century. "One reason that European Christians had come to regard themselves as white by 1250," writes Caviness, "may be that they had been coming in contact in large numbers with brown infidels, and with the sub-Saharan Africans who had been enslaved by Moslems."[56] The category white, then, emerged as a self-referent that helped Europeans distinguish themselves from non-Europeans/Christians. Blackness thus developed as whiteness' foil.

In *Society Must Be Defended*, Foucault proposed that "racism first develops with colonization, or in other words, with colonizing genocide."[57] Foucault's proposition speaks directly to the question of applicability that has dominated the debate about the formation of the modern understanding of race in early modernity in colonial Latin American literary studies. I contend, on the other hand, that it is racism that creates or constitutes the condition for colonization. (Some scholars trace this trend to antiquity.)[58] In other words, it is racism that makes

---

[51] Sweet, "The Iberian Roots of American Racist Thought," 144.
[52] On race and ethnicity in classical antiquity, see Isaac, *The Invention of Racism*; Sechrest, *A Former Jew*; McCoskey, *Race*; Kennedy, Roy, and Goldman, *Race and Ethnicity*.
[53] Taylor, "Race and Racism," 750.   [54] See Kiddy, *Blacks of the Rosary*, 41–62.
[55] Hahn, *Race and Ethnicity*; Heng, *The Invention of Race*; Ramey, *Black Legacies*; Eliav-Feldon, Isaac, and Ziegler, *The Origins of Racism*.
[56] Caviness, "From the Self-Invention," 22.
[57] Foucault, *Society Must Be Defended*, 257 (translated by Macey).
[58] See Isaac, *The Invention of Racism*; McCoskey, *Race*.

colonization a genocidal enterprise. To sustain that race and racism are not applicable to colonial Latin America is therefore to ignore the driving force behind its genocidal biopolitics.

The colonization of the Americas sparked by Christopher Columbus' first voyage in 1492 – often seen as the beginning of modern colonialization – took the form of genocides inflicted on two populations: the Indigenous groups of the Americas and the more than fourteen million Africans enslaved through the Atlantic trade.[59] Yet 1492 was not the beginning of racism, nor of colonization for that matter. Castile, for example, had colonized the Canary Islands in the fifteenth century, enslaving its inhabitants.[60] As Sweet has shown and as is discussed in what follows, by the time Castilians colonized the Canary Islands in the fifteenth century, Iberian and indeed many Mediterranean societies had developed racial systems that shared a common genesis. Columbus would apply this system to the Americas upon arrival, describing the native people of the Americas as "de la color de los canarios ni negros ni blancos" (the color of Canarians, neither Black nor white).[61] When Castilians encountered Canarians in the fifteenth century, they considered them dark-skinned and therefore enslavable.[62]

The Mediterranean racial system Columbus expressed upon landing in the Americas would be used to rationalize both the colonizing genocides of the Conquest and African slavery. This becomes clear if one recalls Juan Ginés de Sepúlveda's iconic position in the Valladolid debate (1550–1). Ginés de Sepúlveda maintained that the Indigenous people of the Americas were so radically different from and inferior to Europeans that there was only one available option to rule them: force.[63] But even Ginés

---

[59] For estimates on the volume of the Atlantic slave trade, see slavevoyages.org.

[60] Canarian slaves were sold in peninsular markets. See Fernández-Armesto, *The Canary Islands After the Conquest*.

[61] Columbus, *Diario de a bordo*, October 11, 1492. For Columbus, the natives' skin color accorded with what he expected: "ni se debe esperar otra cosa, pues [Guanahani] esta este oeste con la isla de Hierro, en Canaria, bajo una linea" (we should not expect otherwise, for Guanahani is east/west of the island of El Hierro, in the Canary Islands, one latitude south) (ibid., October 13, 1492). As J. H. Sweet has noted, "Columbian discourse was explicit. There were three racial possibilities – white, black, and the color of Canarians" ("The Iberian Roots of American Racist Thought," 166).

[62] See Fredrickson, *Racism*, 35–6.

[63] Ginés de Sepúlveda bases his categorization of the indigenous peoples of the Americas on Saint Thomas Aquinas' definition of "barbarian," calling them "quasi-beasts": "Son llamados, pues, simplemente bárbaros los que están faltos de razón [*proprie barbari dicuntur qui ratione non reguntur* (Aquinas, *Super ad Romanus* 1.5)] o por causa del clima, por el cual se ecuentran muchos atrofiados, o por alguna mala costumbre por la que los hombres se convierten casi en bestias" (Barbarians are those lacking reason or those

de Sepúlveda's interlocutor in that debate, Fray Bartolomé de las Casas, whose position nominally prevailed, saw the Indigenous people of the Americas as intrinsically different from Europeans. To las Casas, the Indigenous peoples of the Americas were a "fourth kind of barbarian," who possessed a political society but "no conocen a Cristo" (do not know Christ).[64] Their difference, then, lies in the fact that they lack the sanctifying attribute of "knowing Christ," of being Christians, which in the Mediterranean was tantamount to personhood; not knowing Christ had been used in the Mediterranean to justify the killing of Muslims and reduction of Jews into ghettos and usury. Likewise, Sandoval, an advocate for Afro-Latin Americans as las Casas had been for Indigenous Americans, saw the Blacks to whom he ministered as "innately and intrinsically" different.

If Canarians provided Castilians a new racial referent in the fifteenth century, sub-Saharan Africans, like Jews and Moors, had done so for far longer. While sub-Saharan Africans had been present in the Iberian Peninsula since antiquity, their numbers increased exponentially through the trans-Saharan slave trade dominated by Muslim traders (700–1500 CE).[65] Thus, since late medieval Iberians mostly entered into contact with sub-Saharan Africans through slavery, they came to associate Blackness with subjection. Yet this association did not merely reflect a causality, but rather a worldview. As James H. Sweet has shown, this worldview entered Iberian culture through the influence of the peninsula's Muslim population (711–1492 CE).

At the time Sandoval wrote, the enslavement of sub-Saharan Africans had been rationalized by several Mediterranean societies as a curse from the Abrahamic God for at least a millennium.[66] One theory emerged from a long-standing exegesis of Genesis 9:20–27. This section of Genesis tells the story of the curse Noah placed on his son Ham's descendants. According to the biblical story, one day Noah became inebriated and fell asleep in the nude in his tent. When Ham entered the tent and saw his father naked, he went out and informed his two brothers. The next day, when he awoke from his drunken stupor and heard about what Ham had done, Noah interpreted it as a ridicule and cursed Ham's

---

whose reason is atrophied due to the climate where they live or those who for some bad costume are turned into quasi-beasts) (Ginés de Sepúlveda and las Casa, *Apologia* 61; my brackets).

[64] Ibid., 140.   [65] On slavery in medieval Iberia, see Phillips, *Slavery*.

[66] J. H. Sweet, "The Iberian Roots of American Racist Thought," 148–50.

son thus: "Cursed be Canaan! The lowest of slaves shall he be to his brothers."[67]

While the biblical text does not say anything about Ham or Canaan's skin tone, the connection between slavery and Blackness first developed in the Talmud (fifth century CE).[68] In his study of the curse of Ham, as it has become known in scholarship, David M. Goldenberg points out that ancient Israelites came to see the inhabitants of ancient Nubia (parts of present-day Sudan, Eritrea, and Ethiopia), the Kushites, as Ham's descendants.[69] As Goldenberg notes, Nubia represented the southern end of the known world for ancient Israelites. Thus the Kushites – depicted as Blacks in ancient Egyptian art – represented the remotest people for ancient Israelites.[70] This association of the Kushites and by extension of sub-Saharan Africans with Ham's curse became commonplace in the ancient region around the Red Sea, entering Islam from its founding in the seventh century.

As Sweet notes, in the Muslim world, this connection first appeared in Abū Ja'far Muḥammad ibn Jarīr al-Ṭabarī's (839–923 CE) *Tārīkh al-Rusul wa al-Mulūk* (*History of the Prophets and Kings*), which although written by a Persian author, is considered by scholars the major Arabic historical work from the period.[71] According to al-Ṭabarī,

Ham begot all Blacks and people with crinkly hair ... Noah put a curse on Ham, according to which the hair of his descendants would not extend over their ears and they would be enslaved wherever they were encountered.[72]

As Iberians entered the Mediterranean slave trade partnering with Muslim traders in the late Middle Ages, they adopted this racialized rationalization of slavery, which was well established in Iberian culture by the time the Atlantic slave trade began in the first decade of the sixteenth century. By the time the Atlantic trade began in earnest (ca. 1510), *negro* and *preto* already meant slave in Spanish and Portuguese, respectively.

---

[67] New American Bible (NAB), Gen. 9:25. The biblical story of the curse is an a posteriori justification for the enslavement of the Canaanites by the Hebrews (see Goldenberg, *The Curse of Ham*, 131–40).

[68] J. H. Sweet, "The Iberian Roots of American Racist Thought," 148.

[69] Goldenberg, *The Curse of Ham*, 17–40.

[70] See Bindman, Gates, and Dalton, *The Image of the Black*, vol. 1. Goldenberg argues that ancient Israelites saw Kushites as strong, wealthy in gold, and beautiful (*The Curse of Ham*, 17–40).

[71] See Evans, "From the Land of Canaan," 33.

[72] Quoted in J. H. Sweet, "The Iberian Roots of American Racist Thought," 148.

In "De la naturaleza de los etiopes," Sandoval couples the curse of Ham with the then-emerging theory of Blackness. While both the ancients (Hippocrates, Herodotus, Aristotle, Strabo, Pliny the Elder, etc.) and medieval Christian thinkers (Augustine, Isidore of Seville, Bernard of Clairvaux, Aquinas, etc.) had used the environmental theory – that geography determines personhood – to explain human difference, Sandoval's contemporaries were moving away from it.[73] As Sandoval summarized it:

> Dizen [los Filosofos] que la causa de ser los Etiopes negros, proviene del calor que está en la superficie del cuerpo que abrasa y quema la cute, por ser las tierras en que habitan con extraordinaria violencia heridas del sol, y por consiguientes muy calurosas … Muevense a esto por la experiencia, viendo en los hombres (discurriendo por todo el mundo) tanta diferencia de colores, cuanta la que tiene el temperamento de la tierra que habitan.[74]

> The Philosophers say that the reason why Africans are Black is because of the heat on the surface of the body, which burns and blackens their skin, because the lands where they live are violently hit by the sun, and therefore, very hot. They arrive at this conclusion from experience, seeing among all men around the world as many skin tones as the climates where they live.

Like his contemporaries, Sandoval was not convinced by this theory. In this shift, we can see how imperial expansion had unsettled Europeans' previous understanding of human variety – although belief in geographical determinism reemerged in the eighteenth and nineteenth centuries.[75] What led Sandoval and his contemporaries to doubt the environmental theory was the fact that "Blacks" in Europe had Black children and "whites" in Africa had white children. Sandoval was also intrigued by the fact that African women had "white" children. These children were in fact albinos, but albinism was a mystery to Sandoval's generation.[76] Yet Sandoval does not accept the French barber-surgeon Ambroise Paré's (1510–90) explanation for albinism, namely that, in Sandoval's words, "de lo cual todo es causa una vehemente imaginación que imprime en la materia una

---

[73] Hippocrates, *Airs Waters Places*; Herodotus, *Histories*; Strabo, *Geography*; Pliny the Elder, *Natural History*. On the environmental theory in classical literature, see Isaac, *The Invention of Racism*, 55–168. On race in the Middle Ages, see Hahn, *Race and Ethnicity*; Heng, *The Invention of Race*; Ramey, *Black Legacies*; Eliav-Feldon, Isaac, and Ziegler, *The Origins of Racism*.
[74] Sandoval, *Un tratado*, 73.   [75] See Bernasconi and Lott, *The Idea of Race*; Eze, *Race*.
[76] On albinism in the early modern Iberian world, see Katzew, "White or Black?"

idea de la cosa imaginada" (all is caused by a strong imagination, which imprints in matter an idea of the thing imagined).[77] To which Sandoval responds,

Por donde, aunque yo juzgo que todos pareceres tienen algun fundamento, con todo presumo que otra deve ser la causa desta maravilla [i.e., tener los negros hijos blancos]: porque si el tiemple lo hiziera o el clima los causara, los Españoles que viven en tierra de negros, casados con Españolas, engrendarán negros: y al contrario, en nuestra Europa los morenos engrendarán blancos; de lo cual nos desengaña la experiencia. Assi esto proviene o de la voluntad de Dios o de las particulares calidades que esta gente en si misma tienen intrinsecas.[78]

Whence, although I judge all these opinions to have some foundation, I presume that the cause for this wonder [i.e., albinism among Africans] is another, for if it were caused by the imagination or the clime, Spaniards living in Africa, married with Spanish women, would have Black children, and likewise, Blacks living in Spain would have white children, which is not the case. Therefore, this must either proceed from God's will or some intrinsic quality in this people.

Where geography had been understood as the efficient cause of African Blackness, now parentage became that cause. Sandoval would develop a theory of Blackness where both epidermis and slavery (Ham's curse) are hereditary. Thus Sandoval's answer to his own hypothesis – whether Blackness was the result of God's will or of an intrinsic quality in Africans – is that it is both:

La tez negra en los Etiopes no provino tan solamente de la maldición que Noe echo a su hijo Cham . . . sino tambien de *una calidad innata e intrinseca*, con que le crio Dios, que fue sumo calor, para que los hijos que engendrase, saliesen con ese tizne, y como marca de que descendian de un hombre que se avia burlado de su padre, en

---

[77] Sandoval, *Un tratado*, 73. "L'imagination a tant de puissance sus la semense & geniture, que le rayon, & charactere en demeure sus la chose enfantee" (the imagination has such power over the fetus and the parent, that like a ray of sun light, the thing imagined is imprinted on the fetus), in Paré's words, loosely translated: (*Les oeuvres*, 1020). Paré's idea is found in Genesis 30:25–43, which tells the story of how Jacob outsmarted his father-in-law, Laban, for whom he worked only for the multi-color sheep as wages. According to the biblical story, Jacob outwitted Laban by having the ewes produce more multicolor lambs by waving a multicolor stick before the ewe when the ram was on it. Thus, from Genesis it was believed that offspring would resemble whatever the mother saw. But Paré moves this idea beyond physical sight to the realm of the imagination, though sight is his point of departure. On the maternal imagination, see, for example, Moore, "Monsters and the Maternal Imagination."

[78] Sandoval, *Un tratado*, 74.

pena de su atrevimiento. El cual pensamieno apoya S. Ambrosio; porque este nombre Cam, dize que [quiere decir] *calidus* o *calor*, caliente, o el mismo calor.[79]

The black skin of Africans not only came from the curse Noah put on his son Ham but also is an *innate and intrinsic attribute* of how God created them, which was extreme heat, so that the sons engendered were left this color as a sign that they descend from a man who mocked his father, to punish his daring. This is supported by Saint Ambrose, who says that Ham means *calidus* or *calor*, hot or heat itself.

Sandoval, however, was not the first Iberian intellectual to put Blackness in such terms. In his 1603 *Historia general de la Yndia Oriental* (*General History of the East Indies*), Antonio San Román, a fellow Jesuit, expressed the same idea. Africans, contended San Román, were Black *ad intrinseco*.[80] Sandoval most likely had access to San Román's *Historia*, either at the Jesuit school in Cartagena or in Seville, while he prepared *Naturaleza*.[81] Perhaps Sandoval was expanding on San Román's conception of Blackness.

Moreover, the English chronicler George Best (d. 1584) had arrived at a similar conclusion in 1578, through observations similar to those of Sandoval:

I my selfe have seene an Ethiopian as blacke as a cole brought into England, who taking a faire English woman to wife, begat a sonne in al respects as blacke as the father was, although England were his native countrey, and an English woman his mother: whereby it seemeth this blacknes proceedeth rather of some infection of hat man, which was so strong, that neither the nature of the Clime, neither the good complexion of the mother concurring, coulde any thing alter, and therefore, we cannot impute it to the nature of Clime.[82]

Best's text illustrates how this understanding of Blackness was becoming commonplace in the Atlantic. It is interesting, however, how he conceives

---

[79] Ibid., my emphasis; *Treatise*, 20; translation modified. Germeten's translation does not include the sentence about St. Ambrose. In his treatise on Noah, *De Noe et arca*, St. Ambrose does indeed say "Cham enim *calor* est" (for Ham means heat) (chap. 28, not chap. 23 as Sandoval indicates in the margins of the 1627 edition [fol. 14]; emphasis in the original; see Goldenberg, *The Curse of Ham*, 141–56). Translation modified according to the original. According to Sandoval, another theory, which he rejects, held that "Adam cursed his son Cain for the shamelessness he showed in treating Adam with so little reverence, that Cain lost his nobility and even his personal freedom and became a slave, along with all his children" (Sandoval, *Treatise*, 20). See Goldenberg, *The Curse of Ham*, 178–82.

[80] See Feros, *Speaking of Spain*, 135.

[81] See Haynes, *Noah's Curse*; Whitford, *The Curse of Ham*; Kidd, *The Forging of Races*.

[82] Quoted in Hall, *Things of Darkness*, 11.

its immutability and heredity as an infectious disease, foreshadowing later conceptions of Blackness.

What is unique about Sandoval's theory, however, is the role theology plays in it. While the other articulations of the early modern theory of Blackness cited here do not employ Ham's curse, Sandoval conjoins this emerging notion of Blackness with theology so slavery remains part of the equation. This is noteworthy because in Chapter 18 of this same book (1) of *Naturaleza*, Sandoval affirms that "al principio del mundo no pobló Dios nuestro Señor la tierra de señores y esclavos ... hasta que andando el tiempo, y creciendo la malicia, comezaron unos a tiranizar la libertad de los otros (at the beginning the Lord our God did not people the Earth with masters and slaves ... until, as time went on and men grew in malice, they began to tyrannize others' liberty).[83] This in turn is intriguing because, while Sandoval does not mention slavery in his theory of Blackness, when he takes up the question of whether African slavery is just or unjust in Chapter 17 of this same book (1) of *Naturaleza*, Sandoval evades answering the question himself by reproducing a letter from a fellow Jesuit in Angola. Sandoval had written to the letter's author, Father Luis Brandon, asking whether African slaves were or not "bien avidos" (justly procured). Father Brandon answers Sandoval that he should have no "scruples" about African slavery, not only because Church authorities have not condemned it, but principally because it is Africans who enslaved Africans.[84] Therefore, African slaves are "bien avidos." Sandoval devotes the rest of the chapter to his own examples that underscore Father Brandon's argument. Thus, African slavery is blamed on Africans rather than Europeans. Recalling Sandoval's theory of Blackness, then, slavery is seen as part of Africans' "marca" (mark) and "pena" (punishment) for their biblical forebear's transgression. From the perspective of Father Brandon's argument, they have been condemned by God to enslave each other.

Crucially for Sandoval, bringing salvation to Africans justified slavery: "Y perderse tantas almas que de aquí salen, de las cuales muchos se salvan, por no ir algunos mal cautivos, sin saber cuáles son, parece no ser tanto

---

[83] Sandoval, *Un tratado*, 149.

[84] Ibid., 143–4. It is interesting how this resonates with the trans-Saharan slave trade, both being conceived as enterprises undertaken by non-Christians. More important, this is the same reason Tomás de Mercado had given for declaring African slavery acceptable (Mercado, *Summa de tratos*, book 2, chap. 21).

servicio de Dios por ser pocas, y las que se salvan ser muchas y bien cautivas" (And to lose so many souls that are taken from Africa, for some are not ill gotten, without knowing which, does not seem a great service to God for so few are the ill-gotten ones, and those that are saved many and properly enslaved).[85] Sandoval's position underscores, as Thomas Holt has argued, that in early modernity race worked through religion; the reward of "knowing Christ" justified African slavery even if African slaves were not "bien avidos" (justly procured).[86]

After Sandoval, this understanding of Blackness and slavery would become commonplace, not only in the Iberian world but also in the Atlantic world in general.[87] In his 1649 *Mission evangelica al reyno de Congo* (*Evangelizing Mission to the Congo*), for example, the Catalan Dominican José Pellicer i Tovar echoed Best, San Román, and Sandoval's words:

El ser Negra aquella Nacion, no procede del Calor excesivo del Sol; como algunos han pensado: porque como se ha dicho arriba, el Clima es templadissimo, i los Calores muy moderados. ... El ser Negros propiamente procede de Naturaleza, i Calidad intrinseca; i se reconoce mas, co[n] ver los Hijos que nacen de Negros en España, tiene[n] la Negrura misma de sus Progenitores.[88]

That nation is not Black because of the sun's extreme heat as some have thought for, as we said above, the climate is temperate and the heat very moderate. Their Blackness proceeds properly from nature and an intrinsic quality; this can be seen by the fact that the children of Black parents born in Spain are Black.

What resonates in this conception of Blackness is the role of heredity, which also has its foundation in ancient thought.[89] This theorization of Blackness as intrinsic to the person solved the challenges posed to the environmental theory by the increased (forced and voluntary) circulation of humans in early modernity. This conception of Blackness brings European racial thinking into the biological realm and, as Nemser argues in *Infrastructures of Race*, delineates the foundation for the early modern Iberian world's biopolitics. In the next section, I show how the association of Blackness with slavery in early modernity also meant that freedom and sovereignty were conceived as exclusionary of Black subjects. As I show in that section, this had profound implications for Afro-Mexicans' festive practices.

But Iberian racial thinking is not the only side of the story of Blackness. Afrodescendants naturally conceived of and presented themselves as

[85] Sandoval, *Un tratado*, 144. See Harpster, "The Color of Salvation."
[86] Holt, *The Problem of Race*, 1–24.   [87] See Kidd, *The Forging of Races*.
[88] Fols. 57v–58r.   [89] See Isaac, *The Invention of Racism*, 55–168.

racially different. In a recent article, Chloe Ireton has shown how Blacks in the Iberian world were able to claim Old Christian blood.[90] Confraternities would have certainly allowed or helped Blacks to make such claims, which relied as much on piety as they did on ancestry. Moreover, scholars such as Bennett, R. Douglas Cope, O'Toole, and Jouve Martín have demonstrated how Afrodescendants sought to present themselves as creoles before colonial authorities.[91] So while Iberian thinkers saw Blacks as "the quintessential foreign element that, like 'Jewishness,' could not be fully assimilated into Spanish colonial society," as María Elena Martínez observed, Blacks defined themselves racially as Spaniards themselves did.[92] This was central to Black creoles' identity, as they claimed to have been raised in the true faith amidst their Spanish and white creole counterparts, to whose commonwealth they also belonged. Thus, as these scholars have shown, Afro-Mexicans too played with colonial racial categories, using them to their advantage when possible.

SLAVE REVOLT CONSPIRACIES OR AFRO-MEXICAN FESTIVE PRACTICES?

On February 8, 1609, López de Azoca submitted his report to Philip III (r. 1598–1621) through the Council of the Indies. In his report, the magistrate wished to inform the Spanish monarch about his efforts to save the realm by prosecuting a gathering (*junta*) that "muy gran cantidad" (a very great number) of the city's Black population had held "en casa de una negra libre" (in the house of a certain free Black woman), Melchiora de Monterrey, on Christmas Eve 1608.[93] The gathering itself, albeit problematic for colonial authorities, was not what motivated the judge to write

---

[90] Ireton, "They Are Blacks."

[91] Bennett, *Africans*; O'Toole, *Bound Lives*; Jouve Martín, *Esclavos*; Cope, *The Limits of Racial Domination*.

[92] Martínez, "The Black Blood of New Spain," 515.

[93] "Carta de López de Azoca," fols. 1r, 3r, 6r. In his annual report for 1608, dispatched five days after López de Azoca's, Viceroy Luis de Velasco the Younger states that López de Azoca had told him that the meeting had taken place "en cassa de unas negras, o mulatas tambien libres" (in the house of some free Black or mulatta women), clearly suggesting that the event took place at a commercial establishment "donde otra vezes se juntavan [los negros] gastando alli cantidad de dinero en comer, bever y jugar con mucho excesso que de fuerça seria hurtado a sus dueños" (where [the Blacks] had gathered on previous occasions, spending a great amount of money on food, alcohol, and gambling, with such excess that it must have been stolen from their masters) ("Carta del virrey Luis de Velasco, el joven," Mexico City, February 13, 1609, AGI, Mexico 27, n. 63, fol. 3r). Velasco also wrote in his report that after López de Azoca had informed him of the Blacks' gathering,

TABLE 2.1 *Black confraternities in Mexico City in 1608*

CONFRATERNITY	LOCATION
Exaltation of the Cross and Tears of St. Peter	Parish of Santa Veracruz
Holy Christ of the Expiration and the Holy Burial	Dominican convent
Our Lady of the Conception	Hospital of the Our Lady of the Conception
St. Benedict and Coronation of Christ	Franciscan convent
St. Iphigenia	Mercedarian convent
St. Joseph	Mercedarian convent
St. Nicholas of Mount Calvary	Augustinian convent

SOURCE: Germeten, *Black Blood Brothers*, 83

to the king. It was what the Blacks did there: elected and crowned a Black king, queen, "y otros muchos oficios [que hay] en la casa real" (and many other titles of a royal court).[94] What transpired at the gathering was that celebrants held a festive coronation, but the judge interpreted it as an act of sedition, specifically, as the initial act of a slave revolt. López de Azoca's reaction is particularly remarkable when we consider that this gathering was most likely held by one or more of Mexico City's seven Black *cofradías* at the time, since confraternities normally hosted these coronations in the early modern Atlantic (see Table 2.1).

As the table shows, there were at least seven Afro-Mexican confraternities in the city in 1608. Any or several of these Black corporate groups

"me parecio y a [López de Azoca] lo mismo que bastaria hazer ynformacion del casso por ser contra ordenança que prohibe essas juntas para escussar ruido y platicas del vulgo que de menores principios suelen ynventar grandes chimeras, y los mismos negros tomarian avilantes en lo publico" (it seemed to me, and to [López de Azoca], that it would be sufficient to investigate the matter, since it is against my ordinances, which prohibit these gatherings, to prevent noise and speculations among the people, who make great chimeras of lesser things, and that the Blacks would not be too bold in public matters) ("Carta del virrey Luis de Velasco, el joven," fol. 3r).

[94] "Carta de López de Azoca," fol. 1r, 2r: "abian nonbrado a un negro llamado martin esclavo de baltasar reyes que es el honbre mas rico desta ciudad por rey y a la negra libre donde se juntaron por reyna y les abian Coronado y puesto corona al rey y a la reyna ... Nonbraron duques, condes, condes, marqueses, capitan de la guardia, secretario del rey y otros muchos oficios [que ha]y en la casa real" (they had named a certain Black man named Martín, who is a slave of Baltasar de los Reyes, who is the richest man in this city, for king and the free Black women in whose house they met, for queen, and they crowned them and put crowns on the king and queen. They named dukes, counts, marquises, the captain of the guard, the king's secretary, and many other titles of a royal court).

could have coordinated the Christmas Eve festivities. Melchiora, whose house was used for these gatherings on a recurring basis according to Viceroy Velasco, may have been a member and leader in one of these Black sodalities.[95] While López de Azoca does not mention confraternities in his report, confraternities were the principal form of social organization for Afro-Mexicans. Only one Mexican source, studied in the next chapter, connects Black festive kings and queens to confraternities. But the evidence from the wider Atlantic allows us to reconsider Afro-Mexican confraternities' cultural practices and to read these accusatory documents more critically. Everywhere else in the Atlantic, festive Black kings and queens have been associated with Catholic brotherhoods. It is thus likely that that was the case in Mexico, rather than the exception to the Atlantic tradition.

López de Azoca was informed of the events by an *aguaçil de vagabundos* (sheriff of vagrants), which speaks to the Spanish Empire's policing of racialized bodies.[96] While the Blacks' gathering was ostensibly sanctioned by the state, which normally allowed Blacks to engage in merriments on major holidays, it became problematic for colonial authorities when it was reported by the sheriff that a coronation had taken place.

Only three years later in 1612, in what scholars still consider New Spain's largest Black rebellion plot, Afro-Mexican *cofradías* were accused of repeatedly electing kings and queens as they supposedly endeavored to overthrow Spanish rule. In this section, I discuss López de Azoca's report, as well as two documents relating to the alleged 1612 rebellion plot: the 1612 *audiencia* report and Chimalpahin's account of those events. I analyze these texts to interpret how early modern Iberian racial ideology affected the way some colonial officials perceived and therefore represented Afro-Mexicans' practice of electing and crowning festive kings and queens, especially for their confraternities. I demonstrate two things: first, I show how colonial authorities saw freedom and sovereignty along racial lines and therefore exclusionary of racialized subjects. Second, I demonstrate how this conception of freedom and sovereignty affected Afro-Mexican festive and confraternal practices. These conceptions of Blackness, freedom, and sovereignty provide the reason Novohispanic authorities sought to curtail Black cultural agency in colonial Mexico City. Finally, I distinguish between colonial authorities' construction of

---

[95] "Carta del virrey Luis de Velasco, el joven," fol. 3r.   [96] Ibid., fol. 1v.

the trope of "rebel Black king" and Afro-Mexican confraternal festive kings and queens.

In his report, López de Azoca equates the performance of festive Black kings and queens with "rebel Black king," as Mendoza may have done in 1537. In particular, the judge associates the confraternal festivities that took place in Mexico City on Christmas Eve 1608 with the free Black community of San Lorenzo de los Negros near Veracruz, New Spain's main port of entry.[97] In 1570, an enslaved Bran warrior baptized Gaspar Yanga, and other enslaved Africans fled bondage and sought refuge in the rough terrain beyond Veracruz's Spanish population.[98] Although there is no evidence that Yanga had himself crowned "king," as Mendoza's report shows, enslaved acts of resistance were thought to start with the coronation of a "king." Consequently, Yanga was thought to have been crowned "king" on the feast of the Epiphany, January 6, 1570. This is also how colonial officials interpreted the events of 1608 and 1612, not as demonstrations of Black festive and confraternal culture, but as willful intents to break the social contract that underpinned Novohispanic society. These repeated instances of equating Afro-Mexican cultural life with sedition demonstrate that colonial officials necessarily connected any Black agency with a desire to – or at least a threat to – upend colonial hierarchies.

Colonial authorities tried unsuccessfully in 1609 to disband Yanga's community, and we can see in López de Azoca's and the Audiencia's 1612 reports that this loomed large in the authors' minds. Reading the anonymous 1612 *audiencia* report in conjunction with López de Azoca's report and Chimalpahin's account of the 1612 events thus allows us to interpret the anonymous report differently. Moreover, striking similarities between the magistrate's report and the Audiencia's 1612 document have led scholars to suspect a common authorship.[99] The 1612 report has only survived in transcribed form, in a collection of documents called *Papeles varios de Perú y México* [*Various Papers from Peru and Mexico*] (MS 2010) at the Biblioteca Nacional de España in Madrid. Despite the fact that unsigned *audiencia* reports were uncommon, that transcription omitted the signature

---

[97] Ibid., fol. 2v; Martínez, "The Black Blood of New Spain," 499.

[98] Pérez de Rivas, *Corónica y historia religiosa*, 1:282–94; Alegre, *Historia*, 1:175–83, Naveda Chávez-Hita, *Esclavos negros*, 125–9, Ngou-Mve, "El cimarronaje como forma de expresión"; Tardieu, *Resistencia de los negros en el virreinato de México*, 143–75.

[99] Martínez, "The Black Blood of New Spain"; Querol y Roso, "Negros y mulatos."

of the report's author, which raises the possibility that López de Azoca may have authored both reports.

At the heart of López de Azoca's 1609 report is the Christmas Eve performance of festive Black kings and queens, wherein he conflates the festive monarchs with the idea of the "rebel Black king" in independent maroon communities. In this section, I want to distinguish between the two, and in so doing, challenge the colonial construction of the trope of the "rebel Black king." I use only king because, although López de Azoca and the anonymous 1612 report also mention queen (and indeed some maroon communities were led by women), colonial conceptions of slave revolts were skewed along gender lines wherein male Black bodies presented a threat to female white bodies.[100]

In fact, what the judge presented as "negosio gravissimo y en que rrequiere exenplar y gran castigo en todos" (most grave matter requiring a great and exemplary punishment of all) was a festive Christmas Eve gathering. The judge himself saw this. In his own words, that night there was a "gran bayle y regusijo [sic]" (great dance and rejoicing) and a "famosa cena" (great banquet).[101] The magistrate and his contemporaries could not claim to be unaware of Afro-Mexican festive practices, for not only were these practices well known in the city but Afro-Mexican performers were hired annually by the *cabildo* (city council) for Corpus Christi and other religious and secular festivities. López de Azoca himself cites an incident that illustrates the gathering's ludic nature. According to Lopez de Azoca, the mock queen issued a "warrant" for the arrest of "Isabella of Castile":

La reyna manda que sea presa dona Ysabel de Castilla por yrrespetable que hizo gestos a un grande delante de su magestad. Fecho en mi corte a veynte y seis de diziembre de mil y seiscientos y ocho años. Yo, escribano, don Diego de Alcazar, secretario del Marques del Puño en Rostro.[102]

The Queen orders that doña Ysabel of Castile be apprehended for being disrespectful by making obscene gestures in the presence of Her Majesty. Issued at Court this twenty-sixth of December of the year one thousand six hundred and eight. I, scribe, don Diego de Alcazar, secretary to the Marquis of the Fist in Face.

It was perhaps this part of the performance that led María Elena Martínez to interpret it as a mock coronation.[103] This element of the performance is

---

[100] On maroon communities ruled by women, see Lander, "Founding Mothers."
[101] "Carta de López de Azoca," fol. 2r.　　[102] Ibid.
[103] Martínez, "The Black Blood of New Spain," 502.

indeed striking and – if we can take the judge at his word – could demonstrate that sometimes Black festival king and queen performances could
play with European carnivalesque traditions. Yet neither the long-
standing tradition of Black royal courts nor the fact that Isabel of
Castile had been dead for more than a century was enough to convince
López de Azoca of the innocuous nature of the event, leading him to order
the arrest of forty-nine persons, among them two Spaniards (see
Appendix). One such Spaniard was the so-called Marquis of the Fist in
Face, a certain Juan de Paredes.[104] Even a slave, Lázaro de Mendiola, who
shouted "Long live King Philip III, Our Lord!" and was reportedly
attacked by other participants for the utterance, was arrested and likely
tortured.

If the judge can be taken at his word, his report could contain one of the
few known descriptions of the actual coronation of Black festival kings
and queens:

[Q]ue es verdad que la dicha noche vispera de navidad en casa desta dicha negra
libre ubo muy gran junta de negros y mulatos negras y mulatas, y que allí al dicho
negro Martin, sentado en una silla puesta sobre una tarima, y al honbro debajo de
un dorzel, y un sitial de canto, y los pies puestos en un cojín de terciopelo el dicho
Francisco de Loya, repostero del virrey, le puso una corona harmada sobre un arco
gurnecida de oropel, e hincado de rodillas y descubierto, y abiéndosela puesto dixo
el dicho mulato, "Biba el rey," en alta voz, y los demás negros y mulatos que allí
estavan rrespondieron todos "Biba y rey," y porque un negro dixo "Biba el rey don
Felipe tercero, nuestro señor," le quisieron maltratar y tubieron con el pendensia
y le dieron un piquete con una daga en el rostro, y luego el dicho repostero del
virrey, descubierto y de rodillas como estava, dixo al rey "Gose vuestra magestad
muchos años el reynado," y lo mismo hizieron los demás negros y mulatos que alli
estaban.[105]

It is true that on Christmas Eve there was a great gathering of Black and mulatto
men and women in the house of the said free Black woman. The said Martin,
seated in a chair set on a dais, under a canopy, and a throne, his feet on a velvet
cushion, the said Francisco de Loya, the viceroy's pastry chef, his head uncovered
and on his knees, put a silk crown set in a gold base on his head. After setting the
crown on his head, the said mulatto said, "Long live the king!" in a loud voice, and
the Blacks who were there answered, "Long live the king!" Because one Black man
said, "Long live King Philip III, Our Lord!" they attacked him and cut his face with
a dagger. Then the viceroy's pastry chef, his head uncovered and on his knees, said,

---

[104] "Carta de López de Azoca," fols. 5v–6v. See Appendix for a list of those charged by
López de Azoca.
[105] "Carta de López de Azoca," fols. 1v–2r. For some reason, these documents do not pay
much attention to the queen.

"May Your Majesty's reign last many years!" which all the Blacks and mulattos who were there repeated.

Following the coronation, the Black monarchs then named "duques, condes, marqueses, capitán de la guardia, secretario del rey y otros muchos oficios y cargos [que hay] en la casa real" (dukes, counts, marquises, captain of the guard, the king's secretary, and many other offices and titles of a royal court) (see Appendix).[106] If this is indeed what took place, López de Azoca's report would be a good example of how we can use these types of accusatory sources to reconstruct – however partially – colonial Afro-Latin American cultural practices. This royal court, for example, accords with confraternity charters' stipulation for the election of "principe, reys, duque, condes, marquezes, cardeal & quaes quer outras dignidades" (kings and queens, princes and princesses, dukes and duchesses, counts and countesses, marquises and marchionesses, cardinals, and other royal titles).[107]

López de Azoca's report goes on to explain that when the monarchs descended to the banquet, they were escorted by the captain of the guard. Like the monarchs, the captain was lavishly attired: "yba con un bastón de oro y azul en cuerpo, su espada en la cinta, y bestido de seda" (with a blue staff with a golden tip, his sword on his waist, and dressed in silk).[108] This is not incongruent with what we saw in Chapter 1 with Cavazzi da Montecuccolo's *Istorica descrizione*:

[F]inalmente comparisce il Rè, servito da due Scudieri giovanetti, di sangue illustre, uno de' quali porta una Targa coperta di pelle di Tigre, & una Scimmitarra gioiellata, l'altro tiene in mano un bastone coperto di velluro rosso, guernito d'oro con un Pomo di argento massicio: a' fianchi l'assistono due, che sventollano code di Cavalli, quasi in atto di cacciare le Mosche; e queata trà le Cariche familiari, stimasi la più riguardevole. Un Caviliere de' più favoriti porta il Parasole di damasco cremesino trinato d'oro sempre aperto sopra del suo Signore.[109]

The king comes in last, attended by two young squires of noble blood. One carries a shield covered in tiger hide and a bejeweled cutlass. The other carries a staff covered with red velvet, adorned with gold and solid silver. Two pages accompany the king, swinging horse's tails to keep away flies. This task is the most esteemed of all. Then one of the king's favorites carries a parasol, which is always open on the king.

[106] Ibid., fol. 2r.   [107] "Compromisso," fols. 9v–10r.   [108] Ibid.
[109] Cavazzi da Montecuccolo, *Istorica descrizione*, fol. 257.

At the banquet, the monarchs along with "dos mulatas que abían non-brado a la una por princesa, y a otra hija suya que llamavan la reyna mora" (two other mulattas, whom they named, one, princess, and the other, their daughter, the Moorish queen) sat at the head table, where they were served by "los que abían nonbrado por grandes y titulados, descu-biertos" (those whom they had named grandees and given titles to, served the table, their heads uncovered).[110] Francisco de Loya, who orchestrated the whole event, imitating his role as server in the viceroy's household, "daba la bebida al rey de rodillas y probandola primero" (served the king's drink on his knees, tasting it first).[111] After the monarchs had been served, "senaron [*sic*] los que nonbraron por grandes en otras mesas y en otro aposento de por sí" (those whom they had named grandees dined at another table in another room by themselves).[112] After dinner, "tornaron a baylar" (they went back to dancing).[113] At the end of the evening, "acordaron entre todos que se colgasen [*sic*] aquella persona en la dicha casa, y que la vispera de los reyes acudiesen todos a ella que abía de aver una muy gran junta" (they agreed among themselves that the monarchs should remain in the house, and that the others would return on the eve of the Epiphany for another great gathering), thus linking the festivities with the feast of the three magi kings.

These elements of the gathering illustrate many aspects of Afro-Mexican colonial culture. Three aspects stand out in particular: clothing, food, and dance. The participants' regalia underscores how Afro-Mexicans used sartorial agency to express themselves and challenge colo-nial norms. The evening's events also underpin the centrality of food and dance to Afro-Mexican festive life. Indeed, in his 1608 annual report, Viceroy Velasco described the house where the Blacks had gathered on Christmas Eve as a place "donde otra vezes se juntavan gastando alli cantidad de dinero en comer, bever y jugar" (where they had gathered on previous occasions, spending a great amount of money on food, alco-hol, and gambling).[114] Finally, the participants' reenactment or imitation of their real life occupations – as servants of some of Mexico City's wealthiest residents – points to the possibility that the coronation

---

[110] Ibid.

[111] The report describes Loya as "repostero del virey" (the viceroy's pastry chef). According to *Autoridades*, a "respostero," besides his duty as pastry chef, was also in charge of setting and serving the table as well as taking care of the dinnerware.

[112] "Carta de López de Azoca," fol. 2r.   [113] Ibid.

[114] "Carta del virrey Luis de Velasco, el joven," fol. 3r.

sometimes took a Rabelaisian nature, satirizing colonial society, symbolically inverting colonial order.

The magistrate's report also provides us a glimpse into the social makeup of the celebrants:

Treynta de dizienbre que agora passó fin del año de seiscientos y ocho, un alguasil de bagabundos me dio noticia que la bispera de navidad veynte y quarto del dicho mes se abían juntado y congregado muy gran cantidad de negros y mulatos y negras y mulatas en casa de una *negra libre*, y que abian nonbrado a un negro llamado *Martin, esclavo de Baltassar Reyes, que es el honbre más rico de desta ciudad*, por rey, y a la negra libre donde se juntaron, por reyna, y les abian coronado, y puesto corona al rey y a la reyna, que se la puso un *mulato libre llamado Francisco de Loya, que sirbe de repostero del virrey don Luis de Velasco.*[115]

On the thirtieth of December of the year just passed of 1608, a sheriff of vagabonds notified me that on Christmas Eve, the twenty-fourth of the same month, a great number of Black and mulatto men and women, gathered in the house of a *free Black woman*, and elected a certain *Martin, a slave of Baltasar Reyes, the city's richest resident*, king, and the said free Black woman, queen, and crowned them and put crowns on the head of the king and queen, and that they were crowned by *a free mulatto named Francisco de Loya, who serves the viceroy don Luis de Velasco as his pastry chef.*

This fragment ties the celebrants – especially the king, Martin, and the one who crowned him, Francisco – to Mexico City's richest and most powerful residents, Baltasar Reyes and Luis de Velasco the Younger. López de Azoca himself adds that the celebrants were "muy favoresidos porque sus amos es la gente mas rica y que mas puede en esta ciudad y es de tal manera que los alguasiles no se an detenido a prenderlas" (much favored because their masters are the richest and most powerful people in the city so that none of the sheriffs have tried to arrest them).[116] While the viceroy ordered López de Azoca to investigate the matter, many of the celebrants' masters – owners and employers – tried to protect them from López de Azoca's punitive zeal. When the celebrants' masters refused to turn in their slaves or servants, López de Azoca threatened them with "perdimiento de los oficios y fuedos reales [que] tubiesen y de todos sus bienes para la camara real (loss of offices and royal titles and all their goods to the royal treasury).[117] The masters appealed this order, which was reduced to "perdimiento del esclavo para [la] camara con mas dos mill pesos" (loss of the slave to the royal household and a fine of two thousand pesos), at

[115] "Carta de López de Azoca," fol. 1v; my emphasis.   [116] Ibid., 2v.   [117] Ibid.

which point they complied by turning over their servants.[118] The report also states that all of the Blacks, except for Martin, "son criollos y ninguno nasido en Guinea salbo el Martín que eligieron por rey que dizen que bino muy chiquito de Guinea y se a criado en esta ciudad" (are creoles and none born in African except Martin, whom they elected king, whom they say came very young from Africa and grew up in this city).[119] Martin, then, is a transitional figure who bridges Afro-Mexicans' origins with their present-day reality. That the other participants were all creoles demonstrates the degree to which king and queen celebrations had become ingrained in Afro-Mexican culture.

The judge's list of those charged and arrested provides further details of the social makeup of the participants (see Appendix). Among those arrested were the pastry chef of the archbishop, a cobbler, a silversmith, and a rope maker. Twenty-seven of the celebrants were free, twenty-six of mixed race (*mulato*), and some were related to one another or to Melchiora, the host. This panorama illustrates very well Afro-Mexicans' social makeup at the onset of the seventeenth century (see Table 2.2 and Appendix).

Although the slave Lázaro supposedly protested the coronation, Martin's coronation falls more within the festive tradition studied in this book, whose genealogy I outlined in the previous chapter, than the initial act of plotting a slave insurrection. As Pablo Miguel Sierra Silva argues in his study of slavery in colonial Puebla, urban practices such as

TABLE 2.2 *Social makeup of the participants in the 1608 coronation*

Men (excluding the two Spaniards)	34
Women	13
Black (*negro*)	21
Mulatto	26
Slave	20
Free(d)	27

SOURCE: "Carta de López de Azoca, alcalde del crimen de la Audiencia de México," Mexico City, February 8, 1609, AGI, Mexico 73, R. 1, N. 4, fols. 5v–6v

---

[118] Ibid.   [119] Ibid.

confraternities anchored New Spain's Black population in the urban milieu in such ways that they were more likely to join confraternities than flee to maroon communities.[120] Therefore, contends Sierra Silva, colonizers had no reason to fear "the domestic communities that were intimately enmeshed in their everyday lives."[121] Nonetheless, colonial officials like López de Azoca saw any gestures toward Black freedom as dangerous, and in his view, these coronation ceremonies bespoke a manifest desire to overturn the colonial hierarchy and proclaim independent Black republics. Thus, in an effort to curtail Afro-Mexicans' cultural agency, he compares or equates the Blacks' Christmas gathering with the initial act of a slave revolt. Nothing else could explain López de Azoca's gross misinterpretation of the Christmas Eve fiesta than his neurotic fear of Black resistance. His report in fine demonstrates the criminalization of Black freedom that followed as a natural consequence of the racialization of slavery as Black.

We also see a clear example of the criminalization of Black freedom and sovereignty in the Audiencia's 1612 report.[122] The report begins by complaining about Afro-Mexicans' excessive "libertad y licençia" (freedom and license):

El numero grande de negros y mulatos, cabtivos y libres que hay en este Reyno . . . y particularmente en la Çiudad de Mexico que se multiplan asi con los que naçen en la tierra como los que se traen de guinea . . . *y la libertad y licencia conque esta gente a proçedido, por el rregalo y buen tratamiento que tienen, vestidos y trajes costosos, bayles, casamientos, confradias, y entierros, y las libres casas en que viben de por si atrevida y viciosamente y que ni libre ni captiuos se ocupan en oficios.*[123]

The great number of enslaved and free Blacks and mulattos in this viceroyalty, and particularly Mexico City, which increases with both those who are born here and those who are brought from Africa . . . *and the freedom and license with which this people has acted, because of the goods and good treatment which they receive, and the expensive clothes, dances, weddings, confraternities, burials, and free houses which they have, where they live in sin, has caused that neither free nor slave does any work.*[124]

---

[120] Sierra Silva, *Urban Slavery*, 144–76.   [121] Ibid., 145.

[122] See Germeten, *Black Blood Brothers*, 71–103; Bristol, *Christians, Blasphemers, and Witches*, 93–112; Masferrer León, "Por las ánimas de negros bozales"; Martínez, "The Black Blood of New Spain"; Nemser, "Triangulating Blackness."

[123] "Relacion del alçamiento," fol. 158; my emphasis.

[124] Some scholars believe that López de Azoca is also the author of this report. See Luis Querol y Rosa, "Negros y mulatos" and Martínez, "The Black Blood of New Spain."

While the dictionary in use at the time (Sebastián de Covarrubias' *Tesoro de la lengua castellana* [*Treasury of the Castilian Language*] [1611]) includes *licençia*, it does not define it, but rather just gives its Latin equivalent, *licentia*, as it often does with common words. *Autoridades*, on the other hand, would define it as "libertád immoderada, y facultád de hacer ú decir todo quanto à uno se le antója" (immoderate liberty, and faculty for doing or saying whatever one desires]).[125] As Nemser has noted, the anonymous author here pairs *libertad* (freedom) with *licençia* (license), condemning both Afro-Mexicans' social mobility and moral lives, despite the theological principle of free will.[126] Black *cofradías* were suspect precisely because, as Germeten argues, these brotherhoods were the principal engine of social mobility for Afro-Mexicans as well as the main site of their cultural life. In this highly racialized passage, the anonymous author of the 1612 report, as other sources glossed earlier in this chapter, portrays all Afrodescendants, whether free or enslaved, as "excessively free," both physically and morally. Like the other authors discussed here, this author advocates for greater control by the state, or, to put in Foucauldian terms, more effectively exercising its biopower as a "normalizing society."[127]

In his report, López de Azoca contended it was precisely the "gran libertad" (great liberty) Afro-Mexicans enjoyed that made their Christmas gathering a "negosio gravissimo" (most grave matter):

Yo lo tengo por negosio gravissimo y en que rrequiere exenplar y gran castigo en todos porque esta nueva espana y ciudad de mexico tiene muy gran suma de negros y mulatos libres y esclavos [que] *viven con gran libertad y tienen gran desatenimiento cada dia y cometen muchos delitos.*[128]

I consider the matter most grave, and requiring an exemplary and great punishment of all, because New Spain and Mexico City has a great number of free and enslaved Blacks and mulattos who *live with great freedom and have many discords every day and commit many crimes.*

The 1612 report echoes López de Azoca and other colonial sources cited previously in its characterization of Black liberty as an existential threat to the colonial order. What follows underscores how the two reports mirror each other in other remarkable ways, and show how what has been seen as

---

[125] *Autoridades*, 1:401.
[126] "Relacion del alçamiento," fol. 159. Covarrubias defines *libertad* (liberty) simply as the opposite of slavery: "opónese a la servidumbre o cautividad."
[127] See Foucault, *Security*, 55–86.
[128] "Carta de López de Azoca," fol. 2v; my emphasis.

New Spain's largest Black conspiracy may have been a gross mischaracterization of Afro-Mexican confraternities' clamor for justice and their festive customs.

The alleged 1612 conspiracy began in 1611, when a slave woman died after being whipped by her master. First, some Blacks complained to colonial authorities and asked that the woman's owner, a certain Luis Moreno de Monroy, who insisted the woman had died of "natural illness," suffer some consequences for his abusive treatment of the murdered slave. When colonial authorities ignored the Blacks' demand for justice for the slave woman, whose name is not given in the report, they marched with her body through the principal streets of Mexico City. According to the Audiencia's report,

[M]as cantidad de 1500 negros y negras pareçiendoles que la negra avia fallecido mas por castigo y mal tratamiento de sus amos que por enfermedad natural sin que desto ubiese certidumbre ni presunçion alguna, los negros con mucha furia y alboroto arrebataron el cuerpo de la difunta y salieron con el por las calles de la ciudad por partes de tarde a la ora que avia de ser el entierro dando vozes y gritos lo llevaron a las casas Reales de Palacio en que el Arçobispo residia, y a la del Sancto Officio, de la inquisiçion, y por otros lugares publicos.[129]

[M]ore than 1,500 Blacks, to whom it seemed that the slave woman had died as a consequence of her master's punishment and other mistreatment, and not of natural illness, there being no certainty of this, with much anger and noise took the woman's body at the hour of her burial, which was in the afternoon, and yelling and wailing, took it to the archbishop's palace, the Holy Office, and other public places.

The report casts doubt on the Blacks' claim that the slave woman had died as a consequence of her master's abuse. As in López de Azoca's and other

---

[129] "Relacion del alçamiento," fol. 160r–v. The report offers the following summary of the 1608 Christmas Eve gathering: "El año de 1608, gobernando segunda vez la Nueva España el Virrey Don Luis de Velasco, gran cantidad de negros y mulatos libres y captivos, se juntaron diversos dias y noches en casa de unos negros libres por la Pascua, hasiendo entre fiesta y representaçion de un reynado, coronando Rey y Reyna debajo de dosel y estrado, poniendole casa de mayordomos, capitan de la guarda, otros oficios, titulando grandes y señores de su corte con diversos nombres y honores, comieron y vanquetearon" (The year 1608, during the second reign in New Spain of the Lord Viceroy Luis de Velasco, a great number of free and slave Blacks and mulattos gathered on various days and nights in the house of some free Blacks around Christmas, performing something between a fiesta and a representation of a kingdom, crowning a King and Queen under canopy and on a platform, appointing chamberlains, captain of the guard, other officers, giving title of grandees and lords to their court with different titles and honors, they ate and feasted) (fols. 159v–160r). The report is reproduced, with some errors, in Querol y Roso, "Negros y mulatos."

reports, the Blacks are characterized as guilty, deceptive, and bellicose. The Audiencia's response to the protest was to order those involved in the demonstrations to be sold out of New Spain, effectively ensuring their exile from their communities and social networks.[130] Among those so ordered was a certain slave named Diego, who was the *mayoral* (leader) of one of the two Black confraternities based at the city's Mercederian convent.[131] As the elder of his confraternity, Diego was its ceremonial king (and if married, his wife might have been the ceremonial queen).[132] According to the 1612 report, the protesters' exile further "irritated" the city's Black population, especially the members of Diego's confraternity. The dissatisfaction caused by Diego's exile was necessarily viewed by colonial authorities in the most anxious light and interpreted as an aggressively subversive act. It is at this point that the report contends that, deprived of a community leader and incensed by the official response to an unjust death, the Blacks began to plot to revolt and elected a royal couple to lead them. The plot was supposed to be carried out on Christmas Eve 1611:

Fue por principal y cabeça en esta sedicion un negro Angola, mayoral de la mesma cofradia, esclavo de Juan Carvajal Clerigo llamado Pablo brioso y demas determinaron que otros, casado con una negra de Chritval Henriquez Mercader que esta habia de ser Rey y reyna.[133]

The leader of this sedition was a certain spirited Angolan named Pablo, Friar Juan Carvajal's slave and elder of the same confraternity, whom others determined that, with his wife, Maria, the merchant Christoval Henriquez's slave, should be king and queen.

When, the report continues, shortly after this Pablo fell ill and died, the revolt had to be postponed for Holy Week 1612.[134] If Pablo and his wife were named king and queen of their confraternity as its elders, a new king and queen had to be elected after Pablo's death. But the report presents this festive coronation as the election of new leaders for the uprising:

Ayudo mucho y esforço con estos negros en el alçamiento Isabel mulata esclava de Luis Maldonado de Corral Regidor de Mexico que se persuadio avia de ser Reyna, y un mulato libre moço del Alcalde de corte Don Francisco de leoz Rey.[135]

---

[130] Ibid., fol. 160v.
[131] Ibid., fol. 161r. The two Black confraternities in the Mercederian convents were St. Iphigenia, a legendary third-century "Ethiopian" saint, and St. Joseph (see Germeten, *Black Blood Brothers*, 83).
[132] See Walker, "The Queen of *Los Congos*."   [133] "Relacion del alçamiento," fol. 161r.
[134] Ibid.   [135] Ibid., fol. 161v.

A certain mulatta named Isabel, slave of Luis Maldonado de Corral, president of the *cabildo*, helped the plotters a great deal and persuaded herself that she should be queen and that a certain free mulatto, who is a servant of Don Francisco de Leoz, judge, king.

As in the 1609 coronation, those involved and elected kings and queens were the slaves or servants of the city's richest and most powerful residents, whose prestige may have elevated their own. After Pablo's death, Afro-Mexicans ascended to the leadership of the confraternity. It would seem, from this perspective, that the author of the Audiencia's report, like López de Azoca did in 1609, conflates ceremonial Black kings and queens with "rebel Black king," and interprets the election in the wake of Pablo's death as a rebellion plot, as López de Azoca did the coronation. Thus, like other accounts of (supposed) Black insurrection schemes, the Audiencia's 1612 report relies on and reinforces the trope of the "rebel Black king," an insurgent figure primed to destabilize the entire colonial enterprise. Even Blacks' demand for justice had raised suspicion as it showed their collective dissatisfaction with the status quo. The Audiencia's report illustrates how colonial authorities used the trope of the "rebel Black king" to justify using the sovereign's right to kill in his name, for on this occasion, thirty-five Afro-Mexicans – twenty-seven men and eight women – were hanged and quartered. And it is even possible that there were no elections and coronations in 1612, but rather that the author of the report used the trope of the "rebel Black king," fully aware of its powers to frighten and its instrumentality in justifying the execution of perceived Black subversives.

According to the report, colonial authorities were informed of the plot by two Portuguese slave traders who spoke "Angolan" and overheard the Blacks conspiring to revolt. This is interesting for many reasons. First, the Portuguese serve as authorities on Afro-Mexicans' language. Yet it is unlikely that Angolan, rather than Spanish, was Afro-Mexicans' common language. This claim has the effect of othering the "insurgents" even more; it has the effect of communicating that it is barbaric Africans who want to destroy the Spanish Empire. Claiming that Blacks plotted in Angolan therefore gives more credence to the plot's sinister end. Second, if Portuguese slavers actually transmitted the plot to colonial authorities, it might explain why they began to view the coronations as part of the conspiracy; or inversely, the inclusion of the information offered by the Portuguese in the report helps paint the coronations in this light. Yet the fact that the report makes references to Angolan (language and people) may point to the fact that many urban Afro-Mexicans had Central African ancestry.

The alleged 1612 plot has been the subject of several studies, particularly María Elena Martínez's "The Black Blood of New Spain" (2004) and Daniel Nemser's "Triangulating Blackness" (2017).[136] While both question the historicity of the purported 1612 insurrection plot, neither explicitly links the events to Afro-Mexican festive culture. Furthermore, only Martínez compares the 1612 events to those of Christmas Eve 1608, but stops short of stating that López de Azoca's report contributed to the racist misrepresentation of the 1612 events, construed so as to suppress the Blacks' demand for justice. It is possible that, still angered by their attempts to get some justice for the murdered slave woman, the Afro-Mexican *cofrades* carried on with their annual festive traditions, crowning a king and queen on Christmas Eve and once again at Easter, when the reigning monarchs were exiled (as in Diego's case) or died (as in Pablo's case), as they must have done on many previous occasions of colonial violence. This would show that while racialized systemic violence shaped Afro-Mexicans' lives, it did not define them.

Chimalpahin's (1579–1660) more humane account of the events seems to suggest precisely that:

Axcan miercoles yn ic 2 mani metztli mayo de 1612 anos, yhcuac piloloque cenpohuallonchicuey tlacatl yn tliltique oquichti, auh in tliltique cihua chi come tlacatl yn ihuan piloloque, in ye mochi yc mocenpohua cenpohualloncaxtolli tlacatl in piloloque; oynpan neltico ynic otlatzontequilliloque ynpan yah yn sentencia yn ipampa yniqu intech tlan, ye omoteneuh tlacpac, qui! Macocuizquia quinmictizquia yn intecuiyohuan espanoles. Yn iuh omoteneuh yuh chihuililoque informacion, quil ypan juebes sancto yn ihcuac tlayahualolo ynnehuitequian yn espanoles quinmictizquia, yn iuh quihtoque testigostin; ypampa ynic cenca tlamauhtique ypan omoteneuh semana sancta ynic amo campa huel tlayahualoloc. Auh quil yntla huel quinchihuani yntecuiyohuan espanoles, yntla huel quinmictiani, qui! yc niman yehuantin tlahtocatizquia; quil ce tliltic rey mochihuazquia yhuan ce mulata morisca quil quimonamictizquia, reyna mochihuazquia ytoca Isabel yn otlahtocatizquia Mexico. Auh quil yn ixquich altepetl ynic nohuiyan ypan Nueva Espana, quil ye moch oquimomamacaca yn tliltique yn on can otlahtocatizquia ynic cequintin duques, cequintin marquestin, cequintin condesme.[137]

[136] Other studies include Germeten, *Black Blood Brothers*, 71–103; Bristol, *Christians, Blasphemers, and Witches*, 93–112; Proctor, "Slave Rebellion"; Tardieu, *Resistencia de los negros en el virreinato de México*, 229–76; Palmer, *Slaves*, 110–44; Masferrer León, "*Por las ánimas de negros bozales*"; Riva Palacio, *Los treinta y tres negros*.

[137] Chimalpahin, *Diario*, 288; my emphasis. For an analysis of some of the Nahuatl, see Nemser, "Triangulating Blackness," 354–66.

Today, Wednesday the second of the month of May of the year 1612, was when twenty-eight Black men were hanged, and seven Black women were hanged with them; it added up to thirty-five people who were hanged. Verification was made about them so that they were sentenced and a judgment was issued against them because they were accused, as was mentioned above, of reportedly intending to rebel and kill their Spanish masters. According to the investigation made of them they were reportedly going to kill the Spaniards on Maundy Thursday when they were going in procession scourging themselves, as the witnesses said, because of which they caused great general fear during the said Holy Week, so that processions were not permitted anywhere. And reportedly if they had been able to do it to their masters, to kill them, reportedly a Black was going to become king and a mulatto woman, a *morisca*, named Isabel, was reportedly going to marry him and become queen, they would have been the rulers in Mexico. And reportedly all the different *altepetl* [kingdoms] everywhere in New Spain had been distributed to the Blacks, and there they would rule, so that *some had reportedly been made dukes, some marquises, some counts.*[138]

Uncovering this allegedly rebellious plot allows the participation of Black Mexicans in civic and religious festivities to be criminalized and suggests an underlying fear that confraternities were, all along, just a front for political action.[139] As Nemser points out, Chimalpahin offers "an account of an account" – that is, he offers his account of Novohispanic colonial authorities' version of the events.[140] By framing his account with the Nahuatl word *quil* (reportedly) (*dizque* in Rafael Tena's Spanish translation), Chimalpahin implicitly casts doubt on the Spanish account of the events.[141] Not only does Chimalpahin problematize the Audiencia's narrative of the events by framing it as "an account of an account," but also by recording the victim's declaration of their innocence:

O yxquichtlamanth yn yn italhuililoque yn tenehuililoque yn tliltzitzin, yhuan occequi miectlamantli yn italhuiloque yn amo huel moch nican motenehuaz tlahtolli, ca cenca miec yn intech tlan; yn avo nelli quichihuazquia yn anovo amo, ca çan iceltzin huel yehuatzin quimomachiltia yn t[o]t[ecuiy]o Dios yntla yuhtica, yehica ypampa ca amo huel mellahuac quimocuititihui yn cequintin. Ynmanel oquitzauhctiaque opiloloque, çan oquihtotiaque: "Ma ycatzinco t[o] t[ecuiy]o Dios ticcelican yn miquiztetlatzontequililiztli topan ye mochihua, ca amo ticmati in tleyn in totech tlami ye tictzauhctihui."[142]

---

[138] Chimalpahin, *Annals of His Time*, 219; my brackets. The constituent provinces of New Spain were called kingdoms, Neuva Galicia, Nueva León, etc. A common translation of *altepetl* is city-state.

[139] See Valerio, "That There Be No Black Brotherhood."

[140] Nemser, "Triangulating Blackness," 263.   [141] Chimalpahin, *Diario*, 289–93.

[142] Ibid., 292.

These then are all the things that were said and told about the Blacks; many other additional things were said about them, not all of which tales can be told here, for they were accused of very much that maybe they truly were going to do or maybe not, for only our lord God himself knows whether it is so, because some [of the Blacks] did not acknowledge the full truth of it; though they were punished and hanged, they said on dying, "Let us in the name of our lord God accept the death sentence that has been passed upon us, for *we do not know what we are accused of that we are being punished for.*"[143]

Chimalpahin's version of events should not surprise us for if the conditional is not suggestive enough, this chapter's epigraph is more indicative of his own view:

Auh yn izquitlamantin teopixque Mexico monoltitoque çan mohuetzqmtiaya, amo quinmomauhtiliaya yn quimocaqmltiaya yn ipampa yxquichtlamantli mihtohuaya yaotlahtolli yntechpa tliltique yn cuix quichihuaznequi. Auh yn mexica timacehualtin atle ytlan quinmauhtiaya, çan tlatlachia yhuan tlatlacaqui, çan quinmahuiçohuaya yn españoles yn iuh mopollohuaya in innemauhtiliztica, yniqu iuhqui macamo huel yaotiacahuan ypan nezque.

And all the different groups of ecclesiastics who live in Mexico [City] were just laughing; they were not frightened by what they were hearing about all the different kinds of news of war concerning the lacks, what they supposedly wanted to do. And we Mexica commoners were not at all frightened by it but were just looking and listening, just marveling at *how the Spaniards were being destroyed by their fear* and didn't appear as such great warriors.[144]

Yet if Spaniards were defined by their fear, it was to the detriment of Afro-Mexicans.

Viewed from this perspective, the 1612 document looks more like López de Azoca's report than the conspiracy the document paints, and what has been understood by scholars as possibly New Spain's largest Black rebellion plot could share much more with the repertoire of Afro-Mexican festive traditions than previously suspected. Just as López de Azoca's claims were ignored by the Council of the Indies, the 1612 report does not seem to have elicited any response from the metropole.[145] So what the *audiencia* report casts as "rebel Black kings and queens" may have been in fact confraternal kings and queens. The framing of these

---

[143] Chimalpahin, *Annals of His Time*, 223. "No sabemos *por qué* se nos acusa ni *por qué* nos castigan" (we do not know *why* we are being accused nor *why* we are being punished) in Rafael Tena's Spanish translation (*Diario*, 293; my emphasis).
[144] Chimalpahin, *Annals of His Time*, 218–19; my emphasis.
[145] See Martínez, "The Black Blood of New Spain."

confraternal events as subversive acts was in line with New Spain's anti-Black animus, which in turn was grounded in Iberian racial ideology.

CONCLUSION

These two reports bookend the period in which colonial authorities fought unsuccessfully against the maroon community of San Lorenzo de los Negros. They reveal how fears of Black resistance were galvanized by Yanga's success. More importantly, however, the 1612 report is an important historical document of the vilification of Afrodescendants' claims to civil rights by colonial authorities, showing how rooted in history these tactics (that persist to this day) are. Here Afro-Mexicans' festive practices are maligned through the trope of the "rebel Black king" in an attempt to undermine their clamor for justice for the dead female slave and by extension for all Afro-Mexicans. As at other times, the desired end of the authors of these documents was to curtail Black agency, especially political agency, and in that sense the 1612 report secured the most important victory for colonial authorities. Immediately after the accused were hanged, various limitations were placed on the mobility of Mexico City's Black population, among them a dusk-to-dawn curfew, prohibition to gather in groups of more than four, and a ban on purchasing or wearing expensive fabric and jewelry.[146] So in order to curtail Afro-Mexicans' political agency, colonial authorities sought to rein in their freedom, especially their cultural agency. These documents illustrate how colonial authorities conceptualized freedom and sovereignty as exclusive of Blackness. Afro-Mexicans' practice of electing festive kings and queens for their confraternal gatherings was thus seen as potentially seditious, and often led to deadly reprisals. Although the *cabildo*'s *actas* show that Afro-Mexicans participated regularly in the city's religious and civic celebrations throughout the sixteenth century, after 1612, Afro-Mexicans would only appear once more in a public festival, in 1640 – the text I turn to in Chapter 4. The effects of these measures then seem to have been lasting.

Nevertheless, as I demonstrate in the following chapters, these same festive practices were welcomed when they were perceived to be performed in the name of empire – that is, Iberian hegemony, even in close proximity to incidents of perceived Black revolts. And, while it may seem at first that Afro-Mexicans may have been catering to Iberian

---

[146] See Lucena Salmoral, *Regulación de la esclavitud*, 156–7.

authorities' dreams of domination, I contend that through these performances Afro-Mexicans constructed community and articulated
a distinct creole identity. This chapter has shown the other side of
that homogenic image: how Iberian racial thinking affected the way
colonial authorities interpreted Afro-Mexicans' religious and festive
practices. The way those practices were perceived in turn affected
Afro-Mexicans' lives in important ways, be it the imposition of limits
on their mobility or the Spanish state exercising its sovereign power to
kill.

It can be challenging, therefore, to reconcile these two contradictory
images of Afro-Mexicans, first as violent rebels and second as loving
subjects. A possible path may be offered by what the historian James
Lockhart called the colonial archive's "double image." In the 1960s,
Lockhart proposed that the colonial archive presents a "double image"
of Afrodescendants.[147] According to Lockhart, "in the official municipal
records," as we have seen here, "they appear as a band of
troublemakers."[148] However, "[i]n notarial records," continued
Lockhart, "they appear as an industrious and useful class."[149] In his
analysis of this double image, the historian Patrick J. Carroll contends
that local and viceregal officials, who "often used public documents as
tools for social engineering," present a negative view of Afrodescendants
in order to "shape popular attitudes and beliefs."[150] In so doing, argues
Carroll, they hoped to sow disharmony among subordinate groups. This
may be borne out by the image of the 1537 execution of the alleged king of
New Spain's supposed first slave rebellion plot in the Codex Telleriano-
Remensis (Figure 2.1). Made in the sixteenth century, the third part of the
codex, like the Azcatitlan Codex cited in Chapter 1, recounts the history
of the Mexicas (Aztecs) from their mythical homeland of Aztlan to
Tenochtitlan to the first years of Spanish colonization. As José Rabasa
points out in his study of the Codex Telleriano-Remensis, for the codex's
production, Indigenous *tlacuilque* (artist-scribes) were asked by Spanish
colonial authorities to summarize their preinvasion culture and recount
the first years of Spanish colonization, effectively asking the conquered to
glorify the conqueror.[151] In the image of the execution of the alleged king
of the 1537 supposed revolt plot, which bears significant similarity with
images of lynching of Blacks in the United States, colonial officials communicated to the Indigenous population what would happen to them if

---

[147] Lockhart, *Spanish Peru*, 196.   [148] Ibid.   [149] Ibid.
[150] Carroll, "Black–Native Relations," 249.   [151] Rabasa, *Tell Me the Story*.

they were suspected of the same thing as their Black counterpart, encouraging them to stay away from the latter.[152] Yet as Carroll argues and as Chimalpahin's account of the 1612 events show, Indigenous men and women not only sympathized with Afrodescendants but also formed community with them, further underscoring how the racialized managed to circumvent colonial officials' racialized desires for a divided subaltern population, as O'Toole argues in *Bound Lives*.[153] Black–native relations in Mexico City reached their epitome in 1692, when Afro-Mexicans joined the Indigenous population's revolutionary attempt to end Spanish domination, though the Blacks' role in the events have been neglected by scholars.[154] In the next chapter, I show how Afro-Mexicans used festive culture to navigate colonial psychosis and Iberian racial ideology to redefine their position in colonial society. With Achille Mbembe, we may see these practices as *Afropolitan*, as working "with what seem to be opposites" and refusing "victim identity."[155]

[152] See Elena FitzPatrick Sifford's analysis of this image in "Mexican Manuscripts," 230–5.
[153] See also Restall, *Beyond Black and Red* and *Black Middle*.
[154] See Sigüenza y Góngora, *Alboroto y motín*; Silva Prada, *La política de una rebelión*.
[155] Mbembe, "Afropolitanism."

3

"Savage Kings" and Baroque Festival Culture

Afro-Mexicans in the Celebration of the Beatification of Ignatius of Loyola

On the evening of June 18, 1610, a messenger arrived in Mexico City with the news that Ignatius of Loyola (1491–1556), the founder of the Society of Jesus, had been beatified by Pope Paul V on July 17 of the previous year. The messenger took the news to the Jesuit house, where the sons of Ignatius received it "con la alegría que se puede imaginar" (with the joy one can imagine).[1] This rapturous reaction was recorded in an anonymous account of the festivities that followed, "Relación de las fiestas insignes que en la Ciudad de México se hicieron en la dedicación de la iglesia de la Casa Profesa y beatificación de Nuestro Santo Padre Ignacio" ("Account of the Great Festival Held in Mexico City for the Dedication of the Church of the Jesuit House and the Beatification of Our Holy Father Ignatius"] (ca. 1610; henceforth "Relación") included in the first chronicle of the order in Mexico, Andrés Pérez de Rivas' (1575–1655) *Corónica y historia religiosa de la provincia de la Compañia de Jesús de Mexico en Nueva España* (*Chronicle and Religious History of the Province of the Society of Jesus of Mexico in New Spain*) (completed ca. 1650; first published in 1896). As the Jesuits shared the news with other religious orders that same night, bells, music, bonfires, and fireworks "stirred" (*alborozó*) the sleeping city, transforming it into a "resounding city," as this kind of news often did.[2]

---

[1] "Relación," in Pérez de Rivas, *Corónica y historia religiosa*, 1:242.

[2] Ibid., 1:243. See Baker, "The Resounding City." Aptly enough, Baker points out that: "The resounding city, to a much greater extent than its lettered counterpart, depended on active involvement of the Indigenous (or, in other parts of the Americas, African) population" (12–13). Although, as this book and other studies show, he should have also foregrounded the Black population's involvement, which was central in all parts of the Iberian Atlantic.

Ignatius' beatification brought legitimacy to the young progressive order, founded just fifty years earlier. For one, it put their founder one step closer to sainthood, making him a model for all Catholics. The Jesuits could now use the "spiritual prestige of the would-be saint in order to enhance their ... spiritual [and temporal] status."[3] In fact, the order had already developed strategic relations with both metropolitan and colonial ruling elites throughout the Iberian world, and now had a presence in every corner of the Iberian empire (Portugal was under Spanish rule between 1580 and 1640). Therefore, Ignatius' beatification, like his canonization would be twelve years later, was celebrated in every corner of the Iberian world, from Portugal to Africa to India and Brazil, and from Spain to Mexico, Peru, and the Philippines. In Spain, for example, there were public celebrations of the beatification in Madrid, Murcia, Salamanca, Granada, Segovia, Seville, Valladolid, Girona, Bilbao, and, of course, Loyola, Ignatius' birthplace.[4] And these are only the ones for which documents survive. In the viceroyalty of Peru, Lima and Cuzco hosted festivities.[5] In Mexico, at least the capital and Puebla held celebrations. While there is no record of the festivities staged in other latitudes of the Iberian empire, it is very likely that no city, village, hamlet, mission, or port in the Iberian world neglected to mark the occasion in some fashion.

---

[3] Morgan, *Spanish American Saints*, 3.

[4] Alenda y Mira, *Relaciones*, 149–52; Arellano, "América."

[5] Curiously enough, in Lima, members of the city's male elite "represented" the Spanish court "con su Rey" (with its king): "Seguiose un Alferez con el Estandarte Real, y otros muchos Cavalleros, y Señores de Titulo que acompañavan a su Rey, que venia sentado en un carro triumphal, q[ue] para este hecho se aderço muy bien. Venia el Rey con gran Magestad con su Sceptro en la mano, y Corona en la cabeça, y con el veniam algunos niños en habito de Nimphas, representando a trechos algunas cosas en alabança del Sancto. Significava esto el contenot que los Reynos de España reçibieron con la nueva de la Beatificacion de un gran Sancto Español" (Then came a standard bearer with the Royal Standard and many other Knights and Noblemen who accompanied their King, who was seated in a triumphal car, which was lavishly decorated for this occasion. The king came in great majesty with his scepter and crown. He was accompanied by some children dressed as Nymphs who represented something in praise of the Saint. This performance represented the joy with which Spain received the news of the Beatification of such a Holy Spaniard) (Anonymous, *Relación de las fiestas*, sf.). It is not clear in the text who exactly "represented" the king. Yet while representing the king of Spain, this performance has some resonance with the Black performances I consider here and thus raises some interesting questions. Both performances – this one and Afrodescendants' festive kings and queens – share the same ontology: representing sovereignty. They also do it in the same mode, by making the distant (Spanish and African sovereignty) immanent – that is, "within the limits of possible experience or knowledge" (Merriam-Webster).

As in other parts of the Iberian world, the Jesuits had made strategic alliances with the ruling elite in Mexico City after their arrival in 1572. Thus, when members of the order planned a grand festival to celebrate their founder's beatification, it became a citywide affair. The festivities were scheduled for July 31, the date of Ignatius' death and his new feast day. The preparations included the viceroy, Luis de Velasco the Younger (r. 1590–5, 1607–11), sending two hundred men to expedite the completion of La Profesa, the new Jesuit church, which was still under construction (Figure 3.1).[6] La Profesa readied, the festivities would include a staggering ten Black performances: one with the Eucharistic float (*carro sacramental*) used in the transfer of the Blessed Sacrament from the cathedral to the new Jesuit church – which would be consecrated on that day – another with a float in the shape of an elephant, and eight dances sadly not described in the account. The performances with the floats included a king (no queen) each.

In the following pages, I turn to "Relación" and these performances to investigate, on one hand, colonial Afro-Mexicans' engagement with the material culture of baroque festivals, and on the other, colonial Afro-Mexicans' musical practices, especially their dance customs. Recent scholarship has demonstrated that material culture was central to how early modern Afrodescendants conceived of and expressed themselves as well as engaged with and challenged colonial norms and expectations.[7] Moreover, recent studies on subaltern subjects in early modern festivals has sought to highlight Blacks' agency in shaping their participation.[8] The performances studied in this chapter demonstrate how Afro-Mexicans used material culture to express their Afro-creole subjectivities and negotiate their colonial condition. Additionally, the account illustrates confraternities' role in early modern Afrodescendants' festive practices, as it is one of the few texts that directly links Black confraternities to Afrodescendants' festive customs. This chapter constitutes the first analysis of "Relación," which seems to have gone unnoticed since its publication in 1896.

The chapter is divided into four sections. The first two sections look at "Relación" in order to illustrate how Afro-Mexicans engaged with the

---

[6] "Relación" in Pérez de Rivas, *Corónica y historia religiosa*, 1:245.

[7] See Fromont, *Art of Conversion* and "Dancing for the King of Congo"; Fracchia, *"Black but Human"*; Gómez, *"Nuestra Señora"*; Rarey, "Assemblage, Occlusion, and the Art of Survival"; Walker, *Exquisite Slaves*.

[8] See Jouve Martín, "Public Ceremonies"; Kiddy, *Blacks of the Rosary*; Voigt, *Spectacular Wealth*.

FIGURE 3.1 La Profesa in 1910. Unknown photographer. Courtesy of Fototeca Nacional, Pachuca de Soto, Mexico. Reproduction authorized by Instituto Nacional de Antropología e Historia

materiality of baroque festive culture, drawing from a wide repertoire. The third section discusses Black confraternities' festive practices in the Iberian Atlantic from Mexico. The last section seeks to underscore the role music played in Afro-Mexican festive customs. Due to the paucity of Mexican sources, I once more cast a wide diasporic net in search of answers. The aim of the chapter then is to show, on one hand, how Afro-Mexicans employed baroque material culture in their festive practices, and on the other, the centrality of sound to Afro-Mexicans' festive lives.

The performances studied here stand out because they took place during one of Mexico City's most turbulent periods (1609–12), as explored in the previous chapter. Only the previous year, in 1609, Afro-Mexicans had been arrested and likely tortured for electing a royal court at a Christmas Eve celebration. While many eventually recognized the events for what they actually were – a festive event rather than a revolt plot – Black kings would remain associated with subversion. The 1610 performances thus underscore how Afro-Mexicans were able to negotiate with colonial officials and religious authorities, managing to stage these performances so close to the alleged 1609 plot, repeating a pattern we saw in Chapter 1.

Moreover, religious orders certainly had an interest in having Afro-Mexicans perform in their festivities, but Afro-Mexicans also managed to use this interest to their advantage. In other words, Afro-Mexicans too were desirous to participate in these festivities despite their imperialist overtones, which were overweighed by the attending benefits of participating, such as guaranteeing the continued protection of religious orders or the opportunity to demonstrate to colonial officials that these practices were not as subversive as they suspected. Yet despite all this, in 1612, thirty-five Afro-Mexicans would be executed, their confraternal festive practices apparently used against them once again, as also explored in the previous chapter. Possibly because of this Afro-Mexicans would not appear in a public festival again until 1640, at least as far as the extant record shows, as I will discuss in Chapter 4, although, as noted in the previous chapter, the *actas* (minutes) of the city council show that Afro-Mexicans participated regularly in the city's religious and civic celebrations throughout the sixteenth century.

AFRO-MEXICANS AND THE MATERIAL CULTURE OF BAROQUE FESTIVALS

With La Profesa sufficiently completed to be consecrated (if not altogether finished), the most lavish display in Mexico City since the arrival of the Spaniards began in earnest. The festivities began with vespers in the cathedral on the evening of July 30, after which five floats representing "las victorias que, con su divina gracia y ayuda singular [de Dios, Ignaico] había alcanzado en el mundo, por medio del Instituto y Religión que fundó" (the victories which, with God's divine grace and help, Ignatius won in the world through the Order he founded) were paraded through the city.[9] These floats, which had the form of *carros triunfales* (triumphal carts), were allegories of Ignatius' youth, science, faith, conversion, and state reform, the principal ideals of the order. The following day, a procession between the cathedral and La Profesa passed along a route lined with twenty-four triumphal arches. According to the anonymous account of the festivities, the triumphal arches were offered by Indigenous groups and were made up of local flowers, plants, and live animals: "conejos, liebres, palomas, tórtolas, patas y garzas vivas" (live rabbits, jackrabbits, pigeons, turtledoves, ducks, and cranes).[10] As studied in Chapter 1, these arches drew on Nahua traditions of using trees, flowers, live animals, and birds in their festivities and Americanized the European model, joining the two worlds (Figure 3.2).[11]

The account depicts the incredible opulence of the celebration; a life-size statue of Ignatius placed on an altar in front of the cathedral was so bejeweled that "nunca se pensó que tal y tanta [joya] se pudiera juntar" (it was never thought that such and so many jewels could be brought together) and such an abundance of altars were built, riots of candles lit, and a profusion of jewels, gold, and silver used that the city "parecía un retrato del cielo" (looked like a picture of heaven).[12] Significantly, amidst this remarkable splendor, the author informs us, the Black performances were by far the most "inventive" (*ingeniosas*) elements of the festivities.[13] Surprisingly for a presumably white author, whether creole or Spanish, the author of "Relación" pays far more attention to the Blacks' performances, especially their two floats with a Black king each, than to the white and Indigenous elements of the festival. The author it seems was awed by the Blacks' extravagant displays. Indeed, the account gives the idea that never before (or after) had Afro-Mexicans taken over a festival and the streets of Mexico City so boldly.

Speaking of the crowd in attendance, the account states that "no se podia romper por las calles, sino que como olas andaban unas veces atrás

---

[9] "Relación" in Pérez de Rivas, *Corónica y historia religiosa*, 1:246.   [10] Ibid., 1:249.
[11] See Lopes Don, "Carnivals, Triumphs, and Rain Gods."
[12] "Relación," in Pérez de Rivas, *Corónica y historia religiosa*, 1:245, 6.   [13] Ibid., 1:251.

FIGURE 3.2 Anonymous, *Altar del Convento del Remedio*, Iván Bautista de Valda, *Solenes fiestas que celebró Valencia a la Imaculada Concepción* (Valencia, 1663), fol. 427, detail. Courtesy of Biblioteca Nacional de España

y otras adelante" (it was impossible to move through the streets, but rather people moved in waves, going back and forth).[14] As the procession went from the cathedral to La Profesa, the Eucharist was transported on a *carro sacramental*, or Eucharistic float, which in turn was at the center of the first Black performance, as already noted. This first group of performers belonged to the Confraternity of Holy Christ of the Expiration and the Holy Burial attached to the city's Dominican convent. As noted in Chapter 1, this confraternity was particularly dedicated to the burial of the dead. As such, it must have had regular access to wood, nails, and other materials, which it may have used to build the *carro sacramental*. It is nonetheless interesting to see a Dominican confraternity performing in a Jesuit festival, as the mendicant orders resented the Jesuits' innovative missionary approach and often vied for territory with them. The account, likely authored by an anonymous Jesuit, nevertheless paints a harmonious picture of relations among the religious orders from their initial jubilation upon learning the news of Ignatius' beatification to this Black performance, whose protagonists were "urged" by the Dominican fathers to stage it.

Besides a platform for the Eucharist, the *carro sacramental* also featured a "globe" with two children, one dressed as Ignatius and the other dressed as the Virgin. This "globe," called an *esfera celeste* (heavenly sphere), was a common feature of Hispanic baroque sacramental floats.[15] It was normally painted sky blue with white clouds within and without, and was meant to represent heaven, opening during the performance to reveal children attired as heavenly figures in angelic ecstasy. The performers mobilized all the pomp at their disposal, appearing with their king and his entourage:

En saliendo la procesión de la iglesia, la hizo reparar cuarenta y cuatro piezas que se dispararon junto á un hermoso castillo de siete varas en alto, y de cantería bien fingida que los morenos criollos de una cofradía que tienen en el convento del gloriosísimo Padre Santo Domingo, movidos por aquellos Padres (que en esta occasion se esmeraron en hacernos favor), y también de la devoción que los mismos morenos tienen a Nuestro Santo Padre, le ofrecían esta invención. Tiraban este castillo que venía armado sobre cuatro secretas ruedas, veinticuatro salvajes vestidos de cerdas largas de pies á cabeza y máscaras muy al propio: delante de él venía en hombros de otros cuatro salvajes vestidos de cerdas el rey del castillo, en una silla con maza y traje muy al natural; el cual, puesto delante del Santísimo Sacramento, tocando con la maza el castillo disparó grande número de cohetes, y se rasgó un globo ó nube en que remataba pintada de hermosos celajes

---

[14] Ibid.   [15] See Arellano, *Estructuras dramáticas y alegóricas*, 176–8.

descubriendo dos niños, el uno en traje de la Virgen Santísima y el otro de Nuestro
Padre San Ignacio. ... Entonces el rey salvaje en media docena de octavas, dijo:
cómo estando retirado allá en los bosques, oyó recostado desde su cabaña el eco de
las fiestas que al santo se hacían en México. Pero no hallándose, como que era tan
pobre, con más rico caudal, ofrecía aquel castillo: abrióse al punto una puerta de
él, por donde salieron otros doce salvajes muy bien aderezados que hicieron una
danza muy curiosa que fue alegrando la procesión.[16]

As the procession came out of the Cathedral, it was met by forty-four cannons that
were fired next to a beautiful seven-yard-high castle, of well-feigned masonry, that
the Black creoles of a confraternity have in the convent of the most glorious Father
Saint Dominic, urged by those fathers (who, on this occasion, labored to favor us),
as well as by the devotion which the same Blacks have for Our Holy Father
Ignatius, offered this performance. This castle, which was set on four invisible
wheels, was drawn by twenty-four savages dressed in long animal hide from head
to toe, and who were wearing masks, according to their custom: in front of the
castle, on a chair, with a club, and dressed like a savage, on the shoulder of four
other savages dressed in animal hide, came the king, who upon being put in front
of the Blessed Sacrament, touched the castle with his club and released many
rockets; and a beautifully painted globe or cloud which opened up and revealed
two children, one dressed as the Blessed Virgin and the other as our holy Father
Ignatius. ... And then the savage king, in half a dozen octets, said how being away
in the forest, he heard from his hut the echoes of the fiesta that was being made to
the saint in Mexico City, but as he was poor, having no more valuable asset,
offered this castle. Then a door opened, whence exited twelve more savages very
well dressed, and performed a curious dance that delighted the procession.[17]

One wonders if the children representing Ignatius and the Virgin were
Black, which could have significant racial implications. And if so, did they
appear as they were – that is, Black – or had they been painted to appear
white? This too would have implications for how the performers engaged
with or responded to early modern "blackface," not an uncommon feature of early modern festivals. For example, in Henry II's 1550 entry into
Rouen, although it included fifty actual Tupinambás from Brazil, there
were also two hundred and fifty Normans dressed as Tupinambás.[18]

It is interesting that Blacks were given the responsibility of transporting
the Eucharist when Mexico City's *cabildo* (city council) spent great sums

[16] "Relación," in Pérez de Rivas, *Corónica y historia religiosa*, 1:250. I am grateful to
Manuel Olmedo Gobante for helping me parse this passage.

[17] A *vara* was generally three feet in length, though it varied regionally (see *Diccionario de
Autoridades*).

[18] Anonymous, *C'est la deduction; Relation de l'entrée de Henri II, roi de France, à Rouen, le
1er octobre 1550*, Rouen, 1550 RNB, MS Y28. See Davies, *Renaissance Ethnography*,
117.

of money every year hosting the city's annual Corpus Christi procession in May.[19] Notably, neither the *actas* (minutes) of the *cabildo* meetings nor the secondary literature mentions Eucharistic floats in colonial Mexico City's Corpus Christi, which were instead populated with "giants and gypsies." This context suggests that the Blacks built the float for the 1610 festival, and like the second performance discussed later in this chapter, underscores how Afro-Mexicans engaged with the ephemeral material culture so central to Hispanic baroque festival culture.

One may wonder then, if Mexico City did not have a Eucharistic float, on what did the Afro-Mexicans model their float? The most likely candidate would be a festival book to which they would have had access as a confraternity, in the library of the Dominican convent to which the brotherhood was attached. In the 1680s, a group of painters in Cuzco, Peru, did exactly that, copying the floats depicted in a Spanish festival book, Iván Bautista de Valda's *Solenes fiestas que celebró Valencia a la Imaculada Concepción* (*Solemn Festivities Held in Valencia for the Immaculate Conception*) (Valencia, 1663), onto canvases (Figures 3.3–4).[20] Yet it is difficult to say on which festival book the Afro-Mexicans drew. Indeed, the Blacks' float was unique in the repertoire of baroque floats and carts. The float seems to have taken a unique shape, as the best catalogue of Hispanic baroque floats, Valda's *Solenes fiestas*, from which the Cuzco artists copied, does not feature any castle-shaped float.

Alternatively, the float could have been the original creation of a local artist or artisan. The creator may have even been Black. Afro-Mexicans did not lack for artistic talent; many Afro-Mexicans were artists and artisans or worked as artists' and artisans' apprentices and assistants.[21] Their experience as painters, carpenters, sculptors, metalsmiths, tailors, and seamstresses would have easily enabled them to create the spectacular floats and outfit the performers with rich costumes. Afrodescendants practicing these trades may have joined Black confraternities in favor of those based around their professions, leading to a wide range of skills and crafts practiced by their members. Moreover, Afro-Mexican painters, carpenters, sculptors, metalsmiths, and tailors would have been barred from *gremios*, or professional guilds (called *cofradías* at the time), a privilege reserved for Spaniards.

---

[19] See Curcio-Nagy, "Giants and Gypsies."
[20] See Dean, "Copied Carts" and *Inka Bodies*.
[21] Velásquez Gutiérrez, *Mujeres de origen africano*, 369.

FIGURE 3.3 Anonymous, *Parroquia del hospital de los naturales*, Cuzco Corpus Christi Series, 1680s, Parish of Santa Ana, Cuzco, Peru. Courtesy of ARCA: Arte colonial americano

While little research has been conducted on Afro-Mexican artists and artisans, two of colonial Mexico's most famous painters were of African descent. Juan Correa (1646–1716) was a mulatto and his student José de Ibarra (1685–1756) was a *moreno*, a Spanish euphemism for Blacks derived from the word *moro* (Moor, thus literally meaning Moorish).[22] Afrodescendants dominated artistic production elsewhere in the Americas, particularly in Brazil and Cuba.[23] Additionally, Afro-Mexican confraternities could mobilize their financial resources gathered from membership fees, donations, and services they provided, such as funerals, to commission local artists to aid in the construction and adornments of the floats. The creation of these festival floats and costumes was an opportunity for Afro-Mexican tradesmen and craftspeople to flaunt their talent (and financial resources) to the whole city.

[22] See *morena* in Cobarrubias Orozco, *Tesoro de la lengua castellana*; Velázquez Gutiérrez, *Juan Correa*.
[23] See Araújo, *A mão afro-brasileira*; Lugo-Ortiz and Rosenthal, *Slave Portraiture*; De la Fuente, "Afro–Latin American Art"; Sullivan, "The Black Hand."

FIGURE 3.4 Anonymous, *Carro de los tejedores de seda*, Iván Bautista de Valda, *Solenes fiestas que celebró Valencia a la Imaculada Concepción* (Valencia, 1663), fol. 522, detail. Courtesy of Biblioteca Nacional de España

Furthermore, the performance with the Eucharistic float, in particular, underscores the kind of alliances Afrodescendants developed in the early modern Atlantic. Here the Black confraternity helped the Jesuits honor their founder and the Dominicans show their goodwill toward the Jesuits, hoping that both orders would defend – as they must have – their festive traditions, which often came under attack from colonial officials.[24] Finally, both performances also point to the work the Jesuits did with urban Afro-Mexicans, even if they did not host a Black confraternity. While the Jesuits' work with colonial Afrodescendants has been better studied in the South American context, early Jesuit missives from Mexico City attest to their work with the city's Black population, a topic that merits further research.[25]

[24] See Valerio, "That There Be No Black Brotherhood."
[25] See, for example, *Monumenta mexicana*, 1:296, 437, 529; Martínez Ferrer, "Pedro López," 185. On the Jesuits in South America, see Olsen, *Slavery and Salvation*.

SAVAGE KINGS

While in 1539, in Mexico City, the Black king and queen appeared wearing "grandes riquezas ... de oro y piedras ricas y aljófar y argentería" (great riches of gold and precious stones and pearls and silver), giving the impression of European-style or at the very least, lavishly costumed monarchs, here the king appears dressed "de cerdas largas de pies á cabeza" (in long animal hide from head to toe), as seems to be suggested by his "traje muy al natural" (very natural accoutrement).[26] Given the fact that the performers are *negros criollos* (American-born Black creoles), their appearance is revealing. The difference in appearance in 1539 and here could indicate a change in colonial expectations of what constituted an "African" performance. It would then seem that, aware of this expectation, Afro-Mexicans responded accordingly. This does not then mean that Afro-Mexicans lost agency in shaping the performance. Indeed, the mixture of perceived "civilized" (European) and again perceived "savage" (African) traditions can serve as an allegory of the performers' creole identity, understood as a fusion of distinct cultures (see Introduction). This would in turn inscribe the performance within the *exotic genre*. As defined by Peter Mason, the exotic genre represented non-Europeans as colorful people whose appearance and habits differed radically from those of Europeans.[27] This shift in expectations might be better illustrated by the second Black performance discussed in what follows. The section on dances and music will further underscore this in its analysis of how Afrodescendants in the early modern Atlantic combined European, African, and even American dances and musical instruments to create their distinctive Afro-creole music traditions.

As noted, the second performance also featured a Black king atop a float shaped like an elephant. This further demonstrates how Afro-Mexicans engaged with colonial notions of Africa:

Acabada de ver esta [primera] invención al punto encontró la procesión con otra, asimismo de morenos, nuevamente traidos á este Reino de diversas provincias de Etiopia, traían un elefante de maravillosa grandeza y gracia. Espantó ver su figura y forma tan al natural retratada. Toda esta gran máquina estaba armada sobre unas ruedas que con facilidad se movían. En lo alto de este animal estaba sentado un moreno en forma de rey, con su cetro en la mano y corona en la cabeza, representando muy al vivo al de Etiopia. Era cosa maravillosa, cómo esta gran bestia venía á reconocer y hacer reverencia á la Soberana Majestad de Dios Nuestro Señor, puesta debajo de

---

[26] Díaz del Castillo, *Historia verdadera*, 755.   [27] Mason, *Infelicities*.

aquellos accidentes; hizo luego una hermosa retirada hacia fuera para dar lugar á la gente y hacer lo que no causó menos gusto que admiración, porque todo el vientre del elefante que era hueco y muy capaz, á la manera del otro caballo de Troya que estaba lleno de soldados, éste lo estaba lleno de cohetes, morteruelos y bombas, á quienes pegando fuego por un secreta cuerda alqui-tranada, antes que por de fuera se viese dispararon allá dentro dos bombas, y rompiendo el mismo vientre del elefante salieron con un ímpetu y velocidad grande, así por él como por los ojos y trompa, tantos cohetes, que fue cosa que puso admiración y dio mucho gusto.[28]

After seeing [the first] performance, the procession came right away to another, also by Blacks, recently brought to this Kingdom from Africa, who brought an elephant of marvelous size and beauty. It was a wonder to see its figure and form so naturally done. All this machinery was set upon wheels that moved with great ease. Up above this animal there was a Black king, with a scepter in one hand and a crown on his head, convincingly representing the king of Africa. It was a great thing to behold how this beast made reverence to God's sovereign majesty when it approached the Eucharist. It then moved aside to let the people through and do something that caused no less joy or admiration, for its belly was hollow and roomy, like the Trojan horse, and like that of soldiers, this one of rockets, mortars, and bombs, which lit with a secret cord, blew two bombs before those outside saw it, and blowing up the elephant, shot from there and its eyes and trunk, with such speed and force, so many rockets that they caused great admiration and joy.

While the author contends that this group of Blacks was "nuevamente traidos á este Reino de diversas provincias de Etiopia" (recently brought to this Kingdom from Africa), it is unlikely that that was the case. As in 1539, a Black group ingrained in the urban Mexican milieu, such as a confraternity, would have been better poised to stage a performance like this. Indeed, while the author contends that performers were "representando muy al vivo al [rey] de Etiopia" (convincingly representing the king of Africa), this concrete performance had more European roots than African ones.

The image of the king of Africa astride an elephant had become a common trope of Renaissance and Baroque festivals as an allegory of the African continent. For example, in 1626, the French Royal Ballet staged the court ballet *The Grand Ball of the Dowager of Billebahaut*, which featured a procession of "foreign dignitaries" from across the globe. In a drawing of the theatrical costumes by Daniel Rabel (1578–1637), a crowned Black "cacique" (chief) rides

---

[28] "Relación," in Pérez de Rivas, *Corónica y historia religiosa*, 1:250–1.

FIGURE 3.5 Daniel Rabel, *Black Cacique on Elephant*, for *Le Grand Bal de la Douairière de Billebahaut*, Paris, 1626. Courtesy of the Bibliothèque nationale de France

atop an elephant surrounded by drummers and soldiers (Figure 3.5).[29] Likewise, and perhaps as the culmination of this tradition, the Afro-Brazilian painter José Teófilo de Jesus (ca. 1758–1847) depicted a Black king mounted on an elephant to represent Africa in his allegories of the four continents, which in the absence of Mexican examples has been chosen as the cover of this book (Figure 3.6). Like ambassadors in performances of Afro-Brazilian kings and queens, these motifs were inspired by real African embassies to Europe, as Kate Lowe has studied.[30] Though these Mexican examples are different in form, Afro-Brazilians then were not the only ones inspired by actual African embassies to Europe and the Americas.

Such images, however, were not uncommon in European art, as Lowe has analyzed.[31] For example, in the Capitoline museums in Rome, we find a fresco of Hannibal crossing the Alps attributed to Jacopo Ripanda (d. ca. 1516; Figure 3.7). The fresco, which depicts Hannibal, a North African,

---

[29] See Welch, *A Theater of Diplomacy*, 62–8. I am grateful to Noémie Ndiaye for bringing Rabel's image to my attention. See Ndiaye, "The African Ambassador's Travels."
[30] Lowe, "'Representing' Africa."　　[31] Lowe, "Visual Representations of an Elite."

FIGURE 3.6 José Teófilo de Jesus, *Africa*, 1810. Courtesy of the Art Museum of Bahia

FIGURE 3.7 Attributed to Jacopo Ripanda, *Hannibal in Italy*, ca. 1600. Palazzo dei Conservatori, Musei Capitolini, Rome. Courtesy of the Musei Capitolini

astride an elephant, forms part of a series of frescoes painted at the beginning of the seventeenth century in Michelangelo's new Roman tribunal, Palazzo dei Conservatori. In 1563, moreover, the Dutch engraver Jan Mollijns (1532–65) engraved a similar image, featuring a dark-skinned man (a "Blackmoor" according to the British Museum, which owns the image) riding an elephant (Figure 3.8). This particular elephant had been brought to Antwerp from Portugal (where it had been given to the Spanish prince Don Carlos [1545–68] by his grandmother Mary of Austria [1528–1603], queen consort of Portugal, who got it from India) that same year and was to be ultimately destined for the new Emperor Maximilian II's (r. 1564–76) menagerie in Vienna. Yet this was one of a few Renaissance performances to use live elephants, for due to the rarity of real elephants in early modern Europe, ephemeral, wooden or cardboard ones were used instead.

FIGURE 3.8 Jan Mollijns, *September 14th (Strong on My Feet)*, 1563. British Museum, London. Courtesy of the British Museum

As a matter of fact, Mexico City's performance is very similar to another staged for Philip II, then prince of Spain, in Benavente, Zamora, in 1554. That year Philip traveled from Spain to England to marry his cousin Mary I of England.[32] Philip's journey was painstakingly documented by a *lacayo* (servant, literally "lackey") of his ill-fated son, Don Carlos, Andrés Muñoz, in his *Viaje de Felipe Segundo á Inglaterra* (*Journey of Philip II to England*) (Madrid, 1554). In Benavente, the princes were hosted by the Duke of Benavente, a personal friend of Philip's. As was customary, the duke provided copious entertainment for the princes. One evening, the duke had the interior courtyard of his castle richly adorned and a series of floats processed inside for the princes' diversion; the first featured a Black performer riding a wooden elephant:

Fué la primera [ivención] que entró un poderoso elefante, muy al propio y por lindo estilo hecho, que era un cuartago en quien la cabeza d'este lleva armada la del elefante con el cuello y manos, y el otro medio cuerpo en las ancas, tan al natural, que era cosa maravillosa verle. Encima del cual iba un moreno, con una camisa sola vestido, y el brazo derecho arremangado con un venablo en la mano, imitando en la postura y traje á los indios de las partes de África del Occéano.[33]

The first performance to enter was that of a powerful elephant, very natural and beautifully made. The head of this elephant was the size of a horse with its neck and forelegs, and the other half a horse at its rump; so natural, that it was a marvel to behold. On top there was an African, only wearing a shirt, with his right sleeve rolled up, and an arrow in his hand, imitating in his posture and attire, the Indians of West Africa.

In calling the Black performer an *indio africano* (African Indian), Muñoz further inscribes the performance within the exotic genre (as Rabel had done with the Black king by calling him a *cacique*, the Taino word for chief the Spanish adapted for Indigenous leaders beyond Arawak erstwhile territory), which does not distinguish among Africa, America, or Asia, a phenomenon Mason dubbed *ethnographic interchangeability*.[34]

Moreover, in 1609, Black performers appeared with their king for Dresden's celebration of Shrovetide. In one of the performances, recorded by court painter Daniel Bretschneider the Elder (dates unknown), the king, possibly performed by the festivities' patron, Duke Christian II of Saxony (r. 1591–1611), rides atop a platform drawn by two elephants (Figure 3.9). In the other, the king, also possibly Christian II, is carried while he sits on a throne, scepter in hand, under a parasol (Figure 3.10).

---

[32] See Ruiz, *A King Travels*, esp. 1–33.   [33] Muñoz, *Viaje*, 45.
[34] Mason, *Infelicities*, 40.

FIGURE 3.9 Daniel Bretschneider the Elder, "Standard-Bearer and Moorish musicians," 1609. In *Abriß und Verzeichnis aller Inventionen und Aufzüge, welche an Fastnachten, Anno 1609 im kurfürstl. Schlosse zu Dresden aufgeführt wurden*. Saxon State and University Library Dresden, Mscr.Dresd.J 18. Courtesy of Deutsche Fotothek

FIGURE 3.10 Daniel Bretschneider the Elder, "Rider with standard," 1609. In *Abriß und Verzeichnis aller Inventionen und Aufzüge, welche an Fastnachten, Anno 1609 im kurfürstl. Schlosse zu Dresden aufgefuhrt wurden.* Saxon State and University Library Dresden, Mscr.Dresd.J 18. Courtesy of Deutsche Fotothek

However, the Afro-Mexican iteration of this performance bears some significant differences from the European model. For one, the European examples are performances sponsored by royal figures where the Black performers, if they were indeed Black, though physically present, may have had little if any say in shaping them. There is also the possibility that the performers were "white" actors in black paint. By contrast, as far as we know, the performance and materials of the Mexican example were conceived, designed, and executed by Afro-Mexicans themselves. Unlike their European counterparts, then, Afro-Mexicans exercised a great deal of agency in shaping their performance. Rather than being exoticized, Afro-Mexicans exoticized themselves, more so in order to present a legible performance to European eyes than in order to portray themselves as they were. In other words, they staged performances that (cor)responded with/to baroque notions and expectations of what Blackness/Africanness looked like. This may have been easy for *criollos* who may have not seen themselves as Africans but rather as Mexicans; as for Europeans, Africa may have only been a reference for them. In fine, in this second performance we see Afrodescendants embracing an originally European practice, but one that resonated with Afrodiasporic customs.

One may wonder why Afro-Mexicans were interested in participating in these clear celebrations of empire. They did so for a plethora of reasons. One major reason was to present themselves as agreeable colonial subjects loyal to the crown. This was particularly important for the performance of festive Black kings and queens, as colonial authorities had confused the performance with the initial act of rebellion on several occasions, as explored in the previous chapter. By performing "with their king (and queen)," Afro-Mexicans wanted to clarify to colonial authorities that this was not a subversive performance or prelude to insurrection.[35] By showing themselves to be devout, amenable subjects, even "with their king (and queen)," Afro-Mexicans could win concessions and ease colonial suspicions. Thus these performances underscore how Afro-Mexicans used the conventions of early modern festivals to express their Afro-creole subjectivities and "redefine their position in colonial society."[36]

Finally, although the text does not say whether this second float was sponsored by another Black confraternity, it is likely that that was the case, as festive Black kings (and queens) are uncommon outside the confraternal context. At the time of this performance, there were seven Black

---

[35] Díaz del Castillo, *Historia verdadera*, 755.
[36] Jouve Martín, "Public Ceremonies," 194.

TABLE 3.1   *Black confraternities in Mexico City in 1610*

CONFRATERNITY	LOCATION
Exaltation of the Cross and Tears of St. Peter	Parish of Santa Veracruz
Holy Christ of the Expiration and the Holy Burial	Dominican convent
Our Lady of the Conception	Hospital of the Our Lady of the Conception
St. Benedict and Coronation of Christ	Franciscan convent
St. Iphigenia	Mercedarian convent
St. Joseph	Mercedarian convent
St. Nicholas of Mount Calvary	Augustinian convent

SOURCE: Germeten, *Black Blood Brothers*, 83

brotherhoods in Mexico City (Table 3.1). One of the other six, besides Holy Christ of the Expiration and the Holy Burial, could have performed with this float. Moreover, a confraternity, as one of the few social institutions available to Afro-Mexicans, would have allowed the members to pool their material and financial resources and skills and talents to put this float together.

CONFRATERNITIES IN PUBLIC FESTIVALS

Part of what makes the "Relación" so valuable is that it is one of the few texts to directly link confraternities to Afrodescendants' festive practices, illustrating how these groups facilitated their festive customs. Yet confraternities had been involved in public celebrations in the Iberian world from the fifteenth century, as discussed in Chapter 1. It was this Iberian precedent that, in part, made possible the similarities between the performances in Mexico City and Benavente, in no small measure because Afro-Mexicans were familiar with the repertory of baroque festive culture, and crucially, because confraternities were the principal sites of Afro-Mexicans' cultural action.

In the Iberian Peninsula, besides the celebration of the feast of their patron, Black confraternities also participated in public religious and civic festivals. The founding charter of Sanct Jaume (Barcelona's first Black confraternity), for example, encourages the members to continue taking part in the city's annual Corpus Christi celebration, "lo qual ja acostumen de fer" (as they were already accustomed to doing).[37] Corpus Christi was one of the most important feasts of the Catholic calendar, and was celebrated with great pageantry in the early modern Catholic world.[38] This splendor, which was meant to reinforce the Catholic Church's doctrine on the Eucharistic presence – so central to Counterreformation theopolitics – sought to incorporate all sectors of society.[39] In 1497, for example, when Queen Isabella entered Seville on Corpus Christi, the city council ordered "que deuian salir al dicho recibimiento todos los negros que ouiese en esta çibdad" (that all the Blacks in the city should join the rest of the citizenry in welcoming) the Catholic monarch.[40] When this order was issued by the city council, Seville already had several Black confraternities, which must have participated in these festivities.

In another account of Philip II's travels in 1585, this time to Aragon, Catalonia, and Valencia, with his heir apparent, the future Philip III, to open these kingdoms' *cortes* (parliament), the Dutch Henrique Cock's *Anales del año ochenta y cinco* (*Annals of the Year Eighty-Five*) (Madrid, 1585), both king and heir are party to Afro-Iberians, some with confraternities, performing in the streets of Barcelona. On the feast of St. Stephen (December 26), the king and prince witnessed Blacks taking part in a religious celebration. After describing "a battle of some devils," Cock states that the previous performance "le siguió una danza de moriscos y luego los negrillos" (was followed by a Moorish dance and that of the Blacks).[41] The Blacks' performance was followed by a procession of Barcelona's confraternities: "Luego vinieron los pendones de las cofradías, por su orden, cuyas imágenes tomó todas el príncipe" (Then came the confraternities with their standards, according to their rank, whose images were taken in by the prince).[42] Although Cock does not go

---

[37] Quoted in Bofarull y Mascaré, *Colección de documentos inéditos de la Corona de Aragón*, 8:467.

[38] Pope Urban IV instituted the Solemnity of Corpus Christi on the Thursday after Pentecost in 1264 (see Rubin, *Corpus Christi*, 164–287).

[39] This pageantry increased in volume as the Eucharist became a central concern of the Catholic Church during the post-Tridentine Counter-Reformation.

[40] AHS, Cuaderno de Actas Capitulares, June 27, 1497. Quoted in Gestoso y Pérez, *Curiosidades*, 2:101. A similar order had been issued in 1477 (Gestoso y Pérez, *Reyes Católicos*, 8). Queen Isabella was a significant promoter of Corpus Christi celebrations in Spain. The same document states: "bien sabía su merced quel tenía cargo de fazer salir los juegos y danças cuando la Reyna nra. sra. mandase fazer la fiesta del cuerpo de nro Señor" (your lordships [i.e., the city council] well know how [the mayor] has ordered to arrange for the performances and dances when the Queen our lady orders the celebration of the feast of the Body of Our Lord) (quoted in Gestoso y Pérez, *Curiosidades*, 2:101).

[41] In Gestoso y Pérez, *Curiosidades*, 2:537.   [42] Ibid.

into detail, St. Jaume most certainly was among the confraternities that processed before the monarch. City records show that St. Jaume had processed through the streets of Barcelona when Philip II had visited previously in 1564. On that occasion, when the confraternities of the city filed before the monarch, St. Jaume came in fifth place out of thirty confraternities.[43] St. Jaume is the only confraternity identified by a religious name; all of the others are identified by professions (though they all had religious names, as we will see). The confraternities that came before St. Jaume were those of farmers (*parayres*), carpenters (*ffusters*), tanners (*blanquers*), and gardeners (*hortolans*). This list places St. Jaume among the group with the humblest occupations, which would have been the kind of labor available to free Blacks in early modern Iberia. St. Jaume was a national confraternity – that is, determined by race/ethnicity rather than labor. Confraternities, then, lined up according to rank, as Cock writes, but from lowest to highest, which is the form many Catholic processions still take today.

This same order was observed when Philip III visited Barcelona again in 1599. On this occasion, the confraternity that preceded St. Jaume was that of the young gardeners (*jovens ortolans*). The older gardener confraternities of St. Anthony (Sanct Anthoni) and St. Peter (Sanct Pere) that had come before St. Jaume in 1564 came later in the procession, toward the middle.[44] This shows that rank was not fixed for Europeans confraternities, for by 1599, the gardeners of 1564 had ascended in rank and the young gardeners occupied their old place in the lineup. St. Jaume, however, seems to have been fixed in its place, highlighting the limited social mobility available to Blacks. For example, Los Negritos, Seville's oldest Black confraternity, only presided over all the other Sevillian confraternities in the city's Corpus Christi procession when it was no longer a Black confraternity in the

---

[43] AMB, "Ordinatió y forma de la cerimonia y festa feta per la ciutat de Barcelona per rahó de la nova entrada del catholico e molt alt senyor don Phelip, rey y senyor nostre, vuy beneventuradament, fill de la bona memoria de don Charles, emperador y rey nostre, la qual entrada es la primera que ha feta en esta ciutat de Barcelona com a rey," Barcelona, January 10–March 1, 1564, sf. Reproduced in Duran i Sanpere and Sanabre, *Llibre de les solemnitats de Barcelona*, 2:1–13.

[44] AMB, "Ordinatió y forma de la cerimonia y festa feta per la ciutat de Barcelona per rahó de la nova entrada del catholico e molt alt senyor don Phelip, rey y senyor nostre, vuy beneventuradament, fill de la bona memoria de don Felip, rey y senyor nostre, la qual entrada es la primera que ha feta en esta ciutat de Barcelona com a rey," Barcelona, May 14–18, 1599, sf. Also reproduced in Duran i Sanpere and Sanabre, *Libre de les solemnitats* 2:126–36.

eighteenth century.[45] This demonstrates how European authorities only wished to extend partial autonomy to Black subjects. It does not speak, however, of the world of freedom Afrodescendants managed to build from these small concessions. Their festival practices and participation in public festivals, then translated into intra- and intercommunal social capital, give us a window into that world. With this Iberian precedent, confraternities would be instrumental to the development of Afrodescendants' creole culture in the Americas, as the "Relación" studied here demonstrates.

These examples underscore how important confraternities were to early modern Afrodescendants' festive practices, and Afro-Mexicans were no exception. As noted in the Introduction, while this connection has been studied extensively in Brazil and to a lesser extent in Peru and the River Plate region, besides the 1612 Audiencia report studied in the previous chapter, "Relación" is the only other Mexican text that makes this connection explicit. It is therefore critical for expanding our understanding of how confraternities helped Afro-Mexicans develop and express their festive culture and how they used it to negotiate their colonial condition. This in turn would broaden the scope of the literature on colonial Mexico City's Black confraternities, which has up to now associated them with the Black conspiracy of 1612.[46]

AFRO-CREOLE DANCE AND MUSIC IN THE EARLY MODERN
IBERIAN ATLANTIC

As noted at the outset, in Mexico City in 1610, the two performances of Black festive kings were followed by eight Black dances:

Luego entraron ocho danzas de los morenos, cada una tan artificiosa que pedía particular memoria, y se le debía á esta buena gente que con extraña devoción gastó su pobre caudal en sacar vestidos nuevos de Damasco y sedas, todos ellos tan bien aderezados, que así por esto, como por los ingenios de las danzas, curiosidad de los vestidos, y són de las flautas y tamboriles, no poco alegraron la procesión.[47]

---

[45] Moreno, *La antigua hermandad*, 26. In 1604, Los Negritos unsuccessfully petitioned to have their seniority over all other confraternities recognized (Sánchez Herrero and Pérez González, *CXIX reglas de hermandades y cofradías*, 9).

[46] See Germeten, *Black Blood Brothers*, 71–103; Bristol, *Christians, Blasphemers, and Witches*, 93–112; Masferrer León, "*Por las ánimas de negros bozales.*"

[47] "Relación," in Pérez de Rivas, *Córonica y historia religiods*, 1:250–1.

Then entered eight Black dances, each of memorable artifice, which was owed to this poor people who, with extraordinary devotion, spent all they had to procure new dresses of damask and silk, all very well made, and because of this, and of the artifice of their dances, the curiosity of their costumes, and the sound of flutes and tambourines, brought great joy to the procession.

The author notes how the Blacks' presumed poverty made their splendid offerings all the more remarkable and devout. Yet they appear here not as paupers but rather costumed in "vestidos nuevos de Damasco y sedas, todos ellos tan bien aderezados," (new dresses of damask and silk, all very well made). Indeed, the author repeatedly emphasizes that the Blacks financed their performances. The Black performers appear dancing to the tune of "flautas y tamboriles" (flutes and tambourines), and undoubtedly other instruments. They form a gleeful troupe joyously guiding the procession from the cathedral to the new Jesuit church, as in the consecration of Solomon's temple.[48]

While this and other festival accounts do not say exactly what kind of dances Blacks performed on these and other occasions, Black dances ("bayle de negros") were recorded in Spanish literature as early as the fifteenth century, and were a recurring theme of Baroque comic theatre, especially short pieces called *entremeses*, which were normally performed between acts or as stand-alone pieces at palace celebrations.[49] These dances were known by proper names such as *cumbé*, *paracumbé*, *gurumbé*, *guirigay*, *zarambeque*, and *gurujú*, among others.[50] While the African linguistic imports of these names, if any, have been lost in translation (i.e., a la Hall [see Introduction]), scholars have amply demonstrated their sub-Saharan, particular West and Central African, influences, if not origins.[51] What is clear is that these dances were a fixture of baroque theatre and Afro-Iberians' festive customs.[52]

On January 6, 1658, for example, a *zarambeque* was featured in an *entremés* performed for Philip IV's second wife, Mariana of Austria, at the royal palace in Madrid. Composed by the playwright Agustín Moreto y Cavana, the *entremés* was meant to commemorate the birth of Prince

---

[48] See II Chronicles 5.

[49] *Diccionario de Autoridades* 3:519. See Trambaioli, "Apuntes"; Castellano, "El negro"; Becco, *El tema del negro*; Martín Casares and Barranco, "Popular"; Jones, *Staging*; Fra-Molinero, *La imagen*.

[50] Trambaioli, "Apuntes," 1773; Becco, *El tema de negros*, 21–46. On *gurumbé*'s influence in flamenco, see the documentary *Gurumbé* (2016).

[51] See Trambaioli, "Apuntes"; Jones, *Staging*, 48–52; Barranco and Martín Casares, "The Musical Legacy of Black Africans in Spain"; Navarro García, *Historia del baile flamenco*.

[52] See Trambaioli, "Apuntes"; Jones, *Staging*, 48–52; Fra-Molinero, *La imagen*.

Philip Prospero on November 28 of the previous year, which was celebrated with many festivities throughout the Spanish Empire, since the
king's firstborn and heir apparent, Prince Balthasar Charles (b. 1629), had
died in 1646.[53] In the *entremés*, two Madrid city officials are looking for
the best way to honor the prince's birth. Many characters, including
geographic personifications of the four elements – Galicia as earth, India
as water, Italy as air, and curiously Angola as fire – offer to help celebrate
the prince's birth. "Angola Negra" (Black Angola) appears toward the
end of the *entremés* offering to teach the prince ("nucio primo" [our
prince]) the *zarambeque*: "Sale Angola Negra en su traje, con el elemento
del fuego echando fuego" (Enters Black Angola with her costume, with
the element of fire throwing fire) and pronounces:

> Ya como unam plesona
> turu venimo
> a inciñá zalambleuqe
> a nucio primo.[54]

> We all come
> as one people
> to teach our prince
> the *zarambeque*.

Angola's personification of fire corresponds to an ancient and early modern
association of Africa with Vulcan and thus heat (see Chapter 4).[55] Angola
here then functions as a metonym for Africa. Like the other elements, Black
Angola performs a double personification: first as fire, and second as the
people from the land she represents. In the next chapter, I discuss a text that
demonstrates how Mexico City's Black community presented itself before
the viceroy as "toda [una] nación" (a whole nation). This indicates
Afrodescendants' categorization as a "nation" or ethnic group as well as
their awareness of belonging to a global diasporic community. Angola's
distorted Spanish, like the name of the Black dances themselves, as
Trambaioli and others have pointed out, is meant to "imitar, o, mejor
dicho, evocar de forma onomatopéyica las lenguas africanas" (imitate, or
better put, onomatopoeically evoke African languages).[56] This type of speech

[53] Philip Prospero would die in 1661. On Afro-Limeños' participation in that city's celebration of the birth of Balthasar Charles, see Jouve Martín, "Public Ceremonies."
[54] Moreto y Cavana, *Loas*, 190–1.   [55] See Sandoval, *Un tratado*, 69.
[56] Trambaioli, "Apuntes," 1774. The normative Spanish would be something like: "Ya
como una persona/ todos venimos/ a enseñarle el zarambeque/ a nuestro primogénito."
On "habla de negros," see Jones, *Staging*.

became known as *habla de negros* (*fala de negros* in Portuguese) and was the language used for many Black characters, actors, and performers in dramatic works and festival performances in both the Spanish and Portuguese Empires.[57] While the text is silent as to the "nationality" of the actor who played Angola in the *entremés*, we cannot discard the possibility that Angola may have been personified by an Afro-Iberian actor. It was not uncommon to find Afro-Iberian actors in these roles, especially since Spain and Portugal's Black population in this period neared twenty thousand in both nation-states.[58] At the same time, it was in this period that blackface began to emerge as a theatrical device, in both paint/mask and speech form.[59]

Closer to home, both geographically and temporally, around 1609, Gaspar Fernandes (1566–1629), a Portuguese-born *maestro de capilla* (choirmaster) active in Santiago (present-day Antigua) de Guatemala from 1599 to 1609, and Puebla, Mexico, from then until his death (i.e., 1609–29), composed a *villancico* (Christmas carol) titled "A negrito de Cucurumbé" ("The Black Boy from Gurumbe)":

> A negrito de Cucurumbé
> bisicaino lo sá mia fé;
> qui vai buscán a mé,
>
> ¿y si cansarte?
> ma si qui cánsame.
>
> Que peso hártame
> de si pan que dame
> qui tasi pañoli
> de Santo Tomé,

---

[57] Tinhorão, *Os negros em Portugal*, 201–5; Alkmim, "Falas e cores," 247–51. Other examples of Spanish *entremeses* featuring Black dances include Simón Aguado's *Entremeses de los negros* (1602), Vicente Suárez de Deza, *Los borrachos* (1663), Francisco de Avellaneda, *Baile entremesado de negros* (1663), and Bernardo López del Campo, *El zarambeque de Cupido* (after 1670). Black dances appear in plays and poems by major golden age authors such as Luis de Góngora (e.g., *En la fiesta del Santísimo Sacramento*, 1609), Lope de Vega (e.g., *El Capellán de la Virgen*, 1623), and Francisco de Quevedo (e.g., "Bodas de negros," 1626). In 1602, Andrés de Claramonte y Corroy debuted *El valiente negro de Flandes*, a play about a slave who buys his freedom and becomes a soldier. He accompanies the Duke of Alba to the Netherlands, where he fights bravely, is consequently rewarded by King Philip II with noble titles – among them a knighthood in the Order of St. James – upon their return to Spain, and marries his former master's daughter. *El valiente negro de Flandes* remained popular throughout the seventeenth and eighteenth centuries.

[58] See Castellano, "El negro esclavo"; Jones, *Staging*; Fra-Molinero, *La imagen*.

[59] See Lane, *Blackface Cuba*; Jones, *Staging*.

Cucurumbé

Coplas
Si dia piensas
si días bebes,
mientes sangre de Dios es,
que por eso tanto puedes,
que vuelves hombre al revés
cuando comas como bebes.

The Black boy from Gurumbe
Vizcayno knows my faith
He went looking for me

Does it make you tired?
Yes, that tires me.

How that prisoner annoys me
and of the bread they give me
is of the clothes
of Saint Thomas
Gurumbe

Verses
If you think daily
If you drink daily
As long as it is the blood of God,
For that, as much as you can.
So that you should again become a man
When you eat as you should.[60]

In this *villancico*, the disembodied Black voice affirms its faith in the
Eucharist. Fernandes' repertoire included many similar *villancicos*, and as
we know, New Spain's most famous author, Sor Juana Inés de la Cruz
(1648–95), wrote several *villancicos de negros*.[61] Many of Fernandes'
villancicos in fact were adapted from literary texts.[62] As Sor Juana's
villancicos suggest, the Black dances just enumerated were known in
Mexico. While it can be argued that Fernandes probably became familiar
with these dances in the Iberian Peninsula, the same cannot be argued
about Sor Juana, who never left Mexico.

---

[60] As cited in Sturman, *The Course of Mexican Music*, 86. I am grateful to Robert L.
Kendrick for bringing Gaspar Fernandes' corpus to my attention.
[61] See Fernandes, *Cancionero musical*; Chávez Bárcenas, "Villancicos"; Jones, "Sor Juana's
Black Atlantic."
[62] See Sturman, *The Course of Mexican Music*, 84–6. For a discussion of Black *villancicos* in
Nueva Granada (Colombia) and Peru, see Brewer-García, *Beyond Babel*, 41–56.

Baroque representations of Black dances drew from what authors saw in the streets of Iberian cities. These dances were indubitably of African origin. In 1786, for example, an Afro-Brazilian Rosary brotherhood from Salvador da Bahia, Brazil, petitioned the queen of Portugal, Dona Maria I, to allow them to perform "Angolan" dances, which had apparently been banned in Bahia. One of the reasons the Blacks offered for requesting this permission was the fact that these dances "em muitos Paizes da Christandade inda se praticão" (are still practiced in many Catholic nations):

Dizem os Pretos devotos da Glorioza Senhora do Rosario da Cidade da Bahia, q [ue] antigamente lhes era permitido para maior e geral aplauzo da festividade da mesma Senhora, mascaras, dancas no idioma de Angola com os instrumento concernentes Canticos e louvores; e por q[ue] se achão privados; *e em muitos Paizes da Christandade inda se praticão*, e so neste existe a privacião: Rogão a V. Mag. por sua Alta Piedade e Real Grandeza, Servico de Deos, e da mesma Senhora, se digne conceder lecenca aos Supp. para os ditos festegjos [*sic*] em Razão de parecer muito do agrado da sempre Glorioza Mayde Deos.[63]

The Black devotees of the Glorious Lady of the Rosary of the city of Bahia declare that from olden times it was permitted them for the greater and general applause of the festival of the Virgin, masquerades, dances in the language of Angola with instruments concerning spiritual songs and praises and because they are now banned [in this city] but still practiced in many Catholic nations and this is only a loss [for this city and its Black residents]. They implore your majesty for your high piety and royal grandeur, in the service of God and of the same Our Lady [the Virgin], be pleased to concede permission to the petitioners for the said festivals by reason of the very appearance of pleasure of the always glorious Mother of God.[64]

Here the Blacks of the Bahia Rosary brotherhood express or at least appeal to a global knowledge of Afro-Christian practices in the Iberian world; they know that African-inflected dances are performed in other Iberian spaces. This awareness points to the circulation of knowledge through the mobility of persons across Iberian spaces, both through the slave trade and through other, "free" forms of movement. We cannot exclude festival accounts from these circuits of knowledge, which would indicate book-based knowledge of Black festival practices in the Iberian world as an additional avenue for its spread, and the similarities between Benavente and Mexico City's celebrations perhaps underscore these multiple means of circulation.

While the "Relación" is silent on the nature of the dances Afro-Mexicans performed in the streets of Mexico City in 1610, the kind of diasporic

---

[63] "Requerimento dos Pretos devotos da S[enhora] do Rosario da Bahia," Bahia, 1786, AHU, Bahia, cx. 71, doc. 12235 (cota antiga), sf.; my emphasis.

[64] Quoted in and translated by Mulvey, "Slave Confraternities," 47; translation modified.

framework Charles Chasteen proposed in *National Rhythms, African Roots* and upon which I have been expanding in this book, may help us gain some notion of the kinds of dance performances Afro-Mexicans staged for this and other occasions. Closer to Mexico City, for example, two *residencias* (audits) made of the governance of Veracruz, the main slave port of New Spain, are among the few Mexican sources that describe, albeit elliptically, the dances Afro-Mexicans normally performed for Corpus Christi in the cities of the viceroyalty. As stated in Chapter 1, Black dance troupes were normally paid for these dances, though it is unlikely that the dancers in Mexico City's 1610 festival were paid for their performances. In Veracruz in 1664, five groups of Afrodescendants were paid twelve pesos each to perform five different "national" dances for the city's Corpus Christi procession: these were *congos, matambas, lobolos,* and *bendos* or *bandos*.[65] While *congo* (Kongolese), *matamba* (Angolan), *bendo* (Sierra-Leonese) and *bando* (Ghanaian) are relatively familiar ethnonyms, I have not encountered *lobolo* elsewhere. Nonetheless, those ethnonyms we know give a balanced presence of West and Central Africans in New Spain at the time. This balance reflects the change that occurred in the slave trade to Mexico after the dissolution of the Iberian union in 1640.[66]

But Afrodescendants did not only perform African-inflected dances in the diaspora. For example, in Veracruz, in 1671, a group of *negros criollos* (creole Blacks) were paid seventy-seven pesos for a dance.[67] *Negros criollos* performed other important parts of the festivities, including "bringing out the giants," suggesting that by 1671, Afro-Veracruzanos had taken over the roles previously carried out by Blacks born in Africa in the city's Corpus Christi celebration, for which they were paid more than the former.[68] Yet the *residencia* does not describe the *negros criollos'* dance. To find better evidence of colonial Latin Americans' creole music practices, we must cast a wider diasporic net.

Interestingly, Madrid's 1657 Corpus Christi festivities featured a dance with a *tarascona* (female giant) with the appearance of a Black woman (Figure 3.11).[69] Did Mexican *tarascones* share in this racialized aesthetics? If so, by whose design? These are important questions that future research may be able to answer.

---

[65] "Residencia de Alonso Esquivel, corregidor de la ciudad de Veracruz, por Fernando Solis y Mendoza, su sucesor," AGI, Escribanía de Cámara de Justicia, l. 300A, p. 7, fol. 127v. I am grateful to Joseph M. Clark for sharing these sources with me.

[66] See Borucki, Eltis, and Wheat, *From the Galleons.*

[67] "Residencia de Alonso Esquivel," fol. 149.   [68] Ibid.

[69] I am grateful to Nathalie Miraval for bringing this image to my attention.

FIGURE 3.11 Unknown artist, "Tarascona," *Danzas para las fiestas del Corpus de este año 1657*, Archivo de la Villa de Madrid, AVM 2-197-16. Courtesy of the Archivo de la Villa de Madrid

In colonial Peru, we find several examples of Afro-Peruvians' music culture in the monumental nine-volume *Trujillo del Perú* (*Trujillo of Peru*) (1782–5), comprised of 1,411 watercolors and twenty musical scores.[70] Commissioned by Trujillo's bishop at the time, Baltasar Jaime Martínez Compañón (r. 1779–90), and sent to Charles III (r. 1759–88) in Madrid, along with some of the objects depicted (Inca art, specimens of northern Peruvian flora and fauna, etc.), this astonishing document has been called a "paper museum" of late colonial northern Peru.[71] While some of the watercolors show decidedly

---

[70] BPR, MSS P/360-P/368.
[71] See Soule, *The Bishop's Utopia*; Trever and Pillsbury, "Martínez Compañón."

FIGURES 3.12–14 Afro-Peruvian musical traditions, in Baltasar Jaime Martínez Compañón, *Trujillo del Perú*, Biblioteca del Palacio Real, MSS II/344, fols. 159–61, ca. 1789. Courtesy of Patrimonio Nacional, Madrid, Spain

African-inflected dances, others illustrate dances Afrodescendants developed in the Americas (Figures 3.12–14). Additionally, one of the watercolors shows Afro-Peruvians playing both African and European musical instruments (Figure 3.13). One watercolor even depicts an identifiable Afro-Peruvian

FIGURES 3.12–14 (cont.)

dance, the *zamacueca*, the precursor of today's *cueca*, the national dance of Peru, Chile, and Bolivia (Figure 3.14). In the illustration, two Black figures dance the *zamacueca* before a Spanish observer who is shaded by a parasol held by his Black servant. Interestingly, this image has some resonance with Black festive kings and queens, who sometimes appear under a parasol, as in Julião and D'Asti's images referenced in Chapter 1 (see Figures 1.4–7, 1.9). In the foreground of the same watercolor from *Trujillo del Perú*, we can see what

FIGURES 3.12–14 (cont.)

looks like a Black drummer boy playing a military-style drum. Black drummers had been used in the Spanish royal army since the time of Charles V.[72] In
1529, for example, Christoph Weiditz (1498–1559), a German painter who
accompanied Charles V to his imperial coronation, recorded a similar Black
drummer in a red shirt, in Charles' coronation entourage traveling to Bologna
(Figure 3.15). In the accompanying text, Weiditz writes that "allso Reitten die

[72] Lowe, "The Stereotyping of Black Africans," 37. See also Strong, *Art and Power*, 78–81.

FIGURE 3.15 Christoph Weiditz, *Drummer at the Entrance of the Emperor*, ca. 1529. Courtesy of the Germanisches Nationalmuseum

herbaucker In spanig Wen der Kayser In ain statt Reitt" (thus ride the army drummers in Spain when the emperor rides into a city), suggesting, as Kate Lowe contends, that Black drummers were a staple of Spanish Renaissance royal entries.[73] The drummer in *Trujillo del Perú* could represent Black drummers in colonial Black militias, or any colonial militia.[74]

---

[73] Translation by Lowe, "The Stereotyping of Black Africans," 37.
[74] See Vinson, *Bearing Arms*; Bowser, *The African Slave*, 306–10.

The images in *Trujillo del Perú* also show the musical instruments Afrodescendants used, mixing European ones with African ones. In one image, we see Afro-Peruvians playing the *marimba*, an African instrument, in the foreground and a Spanish guitar in the background (Figure 3.13). The *marimba* was a popular instrument among Afro-Mexicans as well, perhaps because these instruments are portable and, like African drums, can be used in street dances.[75] Finally, *Trujillo del Perú*, includes a supposed African song, "El congo," underlining the kind of creole music generated by Afro-Latin Americans (Figure 3.16).

> A la mar me llevan sin razon
> A la mar me llevan sin razon
> Dejando mi madre de mi corazon
> Dejando mi madre de mi corazon
>
> Ay que dice el congo
> Lo manda el congo
> Cusucu van vees
> Tan cususcu vaya
>
> Esta nao y nobedad
> Nao y nobedad
> Nao i nobedad
> Quel palo de la geringa
> Derecho derecho
> Va a su lugar
>
> They're taking me out to sea without reason
> They're taking me out to sea without reason
> Leaving my beloved mother behind
> Leaving my beloved mother behind
>
> Oh what does the congo say
> What does the congo ordain
> Cusucu watch it go
> So cusucu it goes
>
> This ship and a new world
> This ship and a new world
> This ship and a new world
>
> This wood of pain
> Sails straight
> To its port

[75] See Githiora, *Afro-Mexicans*, 61–2.

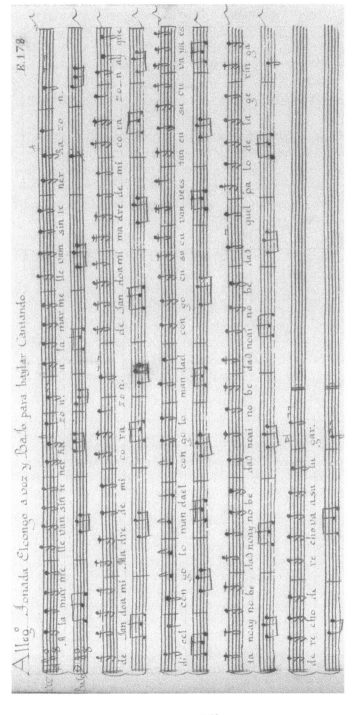

FIGURE 3.16 Anonymous, "El congo." In Baltasar Jaime Martínez Compañón, *Trujillo del Perú*, Biblioteca del Palacio Real, MSS II/344, fol. 197, ca. 1789. Courtesy of Patrimonio Nacional, Madrid, Spain

163

Intended "para baylar cantando" (to dance singing), this song reflects the rhythms common to Black musical creations. The song, moreover, foreshadows the Cuban poet Nicolás Guillén's (1902–89) poem "Vine en un barco negrero" ("I Came in a Slave Ship") and reflects how the act of enslavement endured in Afrodescendants' collective memory – expressed here through a mournful song – that is, assuming the song is of Black authorship.

These examples illustrate the cultural mixing that went into the formation of Afro-creole music and dance, as Chasteen contends in *National Rhythms*. Thus, we must also assume that Afro-Mexicans did not only perform African-inflected dances, but also music, in 1610 and on other occasions. As Moreto y Cavana's *entremés*, the Bahian Rosary confraternity petition, the *criollo* example from Veracruz, and the use of European or Europeanized instruments (flutes and tambourines) in the 1610 festival suggest, Afro-Mexicans danced African, European, and creole choreographies. And as the 1732 Portuguese example glossed in what follows shows, confraternities were central sites for the development and performances of these dances and musical practices.

Another colonial source that bears witness to colonial Afro-Latin Americans' music culture is the satirical travel guide by Alonso Carrió de la Vandera (also known as Concolorcorvo), *El lazarillo de ciegos caminantes* (*Guide for Blind Walkers*) (Lima, 1773).[76]

Las diversiones de los negros bozales son las más bárbaras y groseras que se pueden imaginar. Su canto es un aúllo. De ver sólo los instrumentos de su música se inferirá lo desagradable de su sonido. La quijada de un asno, bien descarnada con su dentadura floja, son las cuerdas de su principal instrumento, que rascan con un hueso de carnero, asta u otro palo duro, con que hacen unos altos y tiples tan fastidiosos y desagradables [sonidos] que provocan a tapar los oídos o a correr a los burros, que son los animales más estólidos y menos espantadizos. En lugar del agradable tamborilillo de los indios, usan los negros un tronco hueco, y a los extremos le ciñen un pellejo tosco.[77]

Bozales' entertainments are the most barbaric and vulgar one can imagine. Their song is a howl. Its unpleasant sound can be deduced by just looking at their instruments. The jaw of an ass, defleshed, with its teeth loose, are the cords of its principal instrument, which they scratch with a ram's bone, antler or another hard stick, with which they make fastidious and unpleasant alto and soprano noises, which causes people to cover their ears and the ass, which are the most stupid and

---

[76] See Meléndez, *Raza, género e hibridez*.
[77] Carrió de la Vandera, *El lazarillo de ciegos caminantes*, 175.

least easily frightened animals, to run. Instead of the pleasant drums of the Indians, Blacks use a hollow trunk, to whose ends they affix a rough hide.

While Carrió de la Vandera's tone is unabashedly satiric, he describes some of the instruments that we can see Blacks playing in *Trujillo del Perú*. We find the expected, ubiquitous drum. But Carrió de la Vandera also describes an instrument not discussed previously: the *quijada* (donkey jaw), a central instrument of *son jarocho*, a Mexican music genre with many African influences that, for obvious reasons, developed in Veracruz.[78] Traditional performances of *La bamba*, the most famous *jarocho*, and other Afro-Mexican pieces include *quijadas*. Carrió de la Vandera's text establishes a connection between Afro-Peruvian and Afro-Mexican musical practices. Carrió de la Vandera also identifies polyphony in the Blacks' music: "altos y tiples" (altos and sopranos). This is important because it denotes sophisticated musical layers in Afrodescendants' vocal music. While in accord with the growing scientific view on race of his age, Carrió de la Vandera presents non-Europeans (Blacks and Indigenous people) as "savages" in *El lazarillo*, when parsed, this example offers a different perspective and underscores how Afrodescendants' festive and other practices can be recovered from negative evidence.[79]

The diasporic connections even reach across the Atlantic. On October 6, 1732, the weekly satirical *Folheto de ambas Lisboas* (*Pamphlet of Both Lisbons*) described Afro-Lisboetas music in terms similar to Carrió de la Vandera's.[80] On Sunday, October 1, a Black Rosary confraternity celebrated their feast day in the churchyard of the parish of Salvador in Alfama. Like Carrió de la Vandera, the *Folheto* describes the music as bizarrely dissonant:

No adro estava hum rancho de instrumentos, com huma bizarra dissonancia; porque estavaõ tres marimbas, quatro pifanos, duas rebecas do peditorio, mais de trezentos berimbaus, pandeiros, congos, e cangáz, instrumentos de que uzaõ.[81]

There were myriad instruments in the churchyard, with a bizarre dissonance; because there were three marimbas, four piccolos, two fiddles, more than three hundred berimbaus, tambourines, African drums, the instruments they use.

---

[78] See García de León, *Fandango*; Miranda Nieto, *Musical Mobilities*; Pérez Fernández, "El son jarocho."

[79] On race in *El lazarillo*, see Meléndez, *Raza, género e hibridiz*, 132–65.

[80] The *Pamphlet*'s title alludes to division of old Lisbon into two major districts, Bairro Alto to the north and Alfama to the south.

[81] Anonymous, *Folheto de ambas Lisboas*, no. 7, fol. 3. See J. H. Sweet, "The Hidden Histories of African Lisbon."

This passage underscores that Afrodescendants were a constant feature of Iberian satire, yet at the same time offers evidence of their musical sophistication, even while characterizing it as barbaric. Here, as in the examples from *Trujillo del Perú*, European instruments are mixed with African ones. The *berimbau*, for example, is the instrument we see today in *capoeira* performances – the originally African martial dance that has become the Afro-Brazilian martial art we know today.[82]

As we saw in Chapter 1 with Cavazzi da Montecuccolo's *Istorica descrizione*, these Afro-European music practices began to take form in Africa itself:

Il Rè hà una Corte, che non uguaglia quelle de' Principi Europei, tuttavia vi è fasto, e nobilità proportinata alle alter cõdizioni del Regno. Quando egli esce in publico, le Guardie, armate di archi, li lancie, e di moschetti, inordinatamente sanno la scorta: dietro ad essi vanno I Sonatori, toccando i loro barbari stromenti, & e anche i Pisseri, havendone da Portughese appreso l'uso, col quale festevole, benche non armonioso concerto, accordano sovente musicali encomij intorno alle prodezze, & alla magnificenza del Rè presente, e de' suoi Aui; & in questa sorte di componimenti, sommamente adulatorij, sono aiutati da certi Araldi, che maneggiando Mazze di ferro con alcuni Campanelli, si fanno senitre ben da lontano.[83]

The king has a court which, although it does not equal those of the princes of Europe, still has pomp and nobility proportionate to the other conditions of the kingdom. When he goes out in public, guards, armed with bows, lances, and muskets make up his escort. Behind them go the musicians playing their barbarous instruments and fifes, which they have learned to play from the Portuguese, disturbing, with their dissonant noise, the king's valor and magnificence, as well as his ancestors. In this kind of composition, they are aided by some heralds who make themselves heard from afar with metal clubs and small bells.

While Cavazzi da Montecuccolo, like Carrió de la Vandera and the *Folheto*, gives a negative valuation of Africans' music practices, when we read them critically and compare them to Afrodescendants' musical legacy in the Americas, we can imagine that, on the contrary, they made beautiful, sophisticated sounds instead of the barbarous cacophony these authors wish to portray.[84]

While these sources are widely dispersed in time and space, they give us some notion of early modern Afrodescendants' musical and dance practices. Though they are fragmentary and laconic, with those discussed in Chapter 1 and the next, they are among the few sources that attest to the

---

[82] On the history of capoeira, see Röhrig Assunção, *Capoeira*.
[83] Cavazzi da Montecuccolo, *Istorica descrizione*, fol. 257.
[84] See Chasteen, *National Rhythms*; Fryer, *Rhythms of Resistance*.

kind of music and dance early modern Afrodescendants practiced. In the absence of sources from Mexico City, they may reflect urban Afro-Mexicans' own music and dances beyond the king and queen performance.

CONCLUSION

"Relación" bears testimony to an important moment in the history of Afro-Mexicans' festive practices. It demonstrates how Black festive kings and, in other instances, queens were further transformed and creolized in Mexico, even if the festival celebrated the Iberian Empire via its new would-be saint, Ignatius of Loyola. If the kings and the dances appear here as two separate set of performances, the text I study in the next chapter combines the two, as a select group of Afro-Mexicanas perform a *danza hablada* (dramatic dance) that reenacts the story of the Queen of Sheba's visit to King Solomon.[85]

While this chapter alone explicitly discussed how Afro-Mexicans engaged with the material culture of early modern festivals, all of the texts studied in this book show this, from the "grandes riquezas ... de oro y piedras ricas y aljófar y argentería" (great riches of gold and precious stones and pearls and silver) of 1539, to the materials used in the 1608, 1611, and 1612 coronations discussed in the previous chapter, to the rich fabric the *morenas criollas* (creole Black women) use in the performance that I take up in the next. Thus all of the performances studied in this book demonstrate how Afro-Mexicans engaged with the material culture of early modern festivals to express their creole subjectivities and negotiate their colonial standing. The performances discussed in this chapter, however, exemplify this more poignantly because of Afro-Mexicans' use of floats and carts, a quintessential element of early modern festivals. While the materials used in the other performances studied in this book can be thought of as small, more personal, though not insignificant items, here Afro-Mexicans outshine their white and Indigenous counterparts with their extravagant displays, which used floats and carts as support. In no other of the known colonial Afro-Mexican festival performances did Afro-Mexicans take over the festival and the streets of Mexico City so boldly.

---

[85] I Kings 10; II Chronicles 9.

4

"Black and Beautiful"

Afro-Mexican Women Performing Creole Identity

> I am a carnival of
> stars a poem of blood
> Sonia Sánchez

Around late October or early November 1640, in the throne room of the viceregal palace of Mexico City (Figure 4.1), a select group of eleven women performed a choreographed dance for the incoming viceroy, don Diego López Pacheco Cabrera y Bobadilla, whose many titles included the seventh Duke of Escalona and the seventh Marquis of Villena (r. 1640–2).[1] The text that describes the performance, *Festín*, identifies the dancers as "morenas criollas" (creole Black women) "produzidas en este Indiano suelo" (born on American soil).[2] (*Moreno/a* –derived from *moro/a*, Moorish man or woman, was a euphemism free Afrodescendants increasingly used to distance themselves from enslaved, presumably darker-skinned Blacks, or *negro/a/s*.[3]) The women's dance came toward the end of a long series of performances staged throughout New Spain for the new viceroy following his landing at Veracruz in June of the same year. In the performance, the women reenacted the biblical story of the Queen of Sheba's visit to King Solomon in the ninth century BCE.[4]

The women's performance is described in what may be the only colonial printed (and otherwise) Latin American text dedicated in its entirety

---

[1] Hernández Reyes, "*Festín*," 339–40n2.   [2] Torres, *Festín*, fols. 1r, 2r.

[3] Cobarrubias defines *morena* as "color, la que no es del todo negra, como la de los moros, de dó[n]de tomò nombre, o de mora."

[4] This story is told in 1 Kings 10:1–13 and 2 Chronicles 9:1–12; see Clapp, *Sheba*; and Philby, *The Queen of Sheba*.

FIGURE 4.1 Old Palace of the Viceroys, Mexico City, built seventeenth century. Currently the Palacio Nacional, office of the president. Wikimedia Commons

to a Black festival performance: *Festín hecho por las morenas criollas de la muy noble, y muy leal Ciudad de México al recibimiento, y entrada del Excellentísimo Señor Marqués de Villena, Duque de Escalona, Virrey de esta Nueva España* (*Dance Performed by the Creole Black Women of the Most Noble and Most Loyal City of Mexico for the Reception and Entry of His Excellency the Marquis of Villena, Duke of Escalona, Viceroy of New Spain*), which was published in Mexico City in 1640. Of all the texts studied in this book, *Festín* is the most literary and best fits the category of festival book, insofar as it was the only one published contemporaneously. *Festín* is exceptional in many other ways. For one, it is the only source studied here that describes a Black performance for the festivities that normally accompanied the arrival of a new viceroy. Furthermore, and more importantly, it is the only text studied here where women are the protagonists. Finally, of all the performances studied in this book, the one described in *Festín* is the only one where all the performers are recognized as creole.

Festín was authored by Nicolás de Torres (dates unknown), a scholar and secular cleric who composed the Latin text for the performance (Figure 4.2). We do not know what role Torres played in the planning of the performance beyond that of composing the Latin text. In the prologue, he tells us that "este festín se libró á mi cuydado" (this dance was undertaken under my care).[5] Here *libró* (from *librar*) seems to refer to Torres' writing of the libretto for the performance, in accordance with the second definition Cobarrubias gives *librar*: "remitir con escritura ... alguna partida" (to render something in writing). Accordingly, I would like to suggest that Torres was not the principal organizer of the dance, but rather that he was sought out by the main organizers, the women of Mexico City's Black community, for his knowledge of Latin and theology, which he taught at the university.[6] As a cleric, however, Torres may have been the women's spiritual advisor, especially if they belonged to a religious confraternity, as I contend; therefore, he may have been asked to compose the Latin text for the performance, working with the women as they choreographed their dance under his care.

In the following sections, I analyze both the women's performance and the text that describes it. While in her reading of this text and performance, Linda Curcio-Nagy assigns agential actions to colonial authorities, sustaining that "the performance of the Afro-Mexican women before Villena illustrates how city councilmen and court artists may have

---

[5] Torres, *Festín*, fol. 1v.   [6] Hernández Reyes, "*Festín*," 343.

FESTIN

HECHO POR LAS

Morenas Criollas de la muy noble, y muy leal Ciudad
de Mexico.

AL RECEBIMIENTO, Y ENTRADA
del Excellentifsimo Señor Marques de Villena,
Duque de Efcalona, Virrey de efta
Nueua Efpaña.

COMPVESTO POR NICOLAS DE TORRES,
Y
DEDICADO A DON ENRIQVE PACHECO Y
Auila, Cauallero de la Orden de Santiago, Capitan
de la Guardia de fu Excellencia, y Sargento
mayor defte Reyno.

Con licencia en Mexico, en la Imprenta de Francifco
Robledo, en la calle de S. Francifco, año 1640.

FIGURE 4.2 Title page of *Festín*. Courtesy of the University of Salamanca, Spain

manipulated performances to create their image of the perfect vassal," I foreground the women's agency, reading the performance along the continuum of the festive culture studied in this book thus far.[7] I argue, first,

[7] Curcio-Nagy, *Great Festivals*, 59.

that it was the women who exercised agency in shaping the performance: from choosing the theme, to choreographing their dance, to making – and paying for – all the necessary preparations. I contend that this leadership illustrates the social power Afro-Mexican women wielded in the seventeenth century. Given the sociohistorical context, I suggest that these women represented a religious confraternity, to which they belonged and which paid for the material used in the performance. Thus, rather than perform vassalage to colonial domination, the Black dancers performed their agency, or capacity for negotiating their identity within the colonial structure. Finally, I propose that the women's confraternity or Afro-Mexican confraternities in general may have had a hand in the publication of *Festín*, sponsoring it so that their performance and they themselves, as one of the dancers put it, would "viviré á la fama" (live in fame).[8] This would make it the first known example of this kind of sponsorship in the Iberian Atlantic, though not the only, as I discuss in the last section. This chapter is the first analysis of this text from an Afro-centric perspective.

The chapter is divided into six sections. The first looks at viceregal entries in colonial Mexico City to illustrate the kind of festival within whose contours the women's performance took place. The second section discusses the Queen of Sheba's biblical story and its afterlife in Western culture to underscore the symbolism the women may have drawn on, as well as to explain Torres' and his world's ambivalence to the women's performance. The third section looks at the Black female presence in colonial Mexico City to show Afro-Mexicanas' place in colonial society. The fourth section discusses Afro-Mexicanas' role in confraternities to demonstrate the likelihood that the women represented one or more Afro-Mexican brotherhoods. I then turn to *Festín* to analyze how the women performed Afro-Mexican creole culture and subjectivity. I conclude the chapter by pondering the possibility that the women or the larger Black community they may have represented sponsored the publication of *Festín*. The aim of this chapter, then, is to showcase the height of Afro-Mexican creole culture and subjectivities as symbolized through the women's performance.

Festín was first published as a four-folio quarto pamphlet and was then – in the same year of 1640 – incorporated into a Sammelband, or multi-text volume, of all the texts composed and subsequently printed for the viceroy's arrival. It is within this compilation that most of these texts are to be found

---

[8] Torres, *Festín*, fol. 4v.

today. The first text in the Sammelband is its most famous, and the one that gives its name to the whole volume, the account by Cristóbal Gutiérrez de Medina, the viceroy's almoner, of the viceroy's journey from Spain to Mexico, *Viage de tiera, y mar (Journey by Land and Sea)* (also published 1640).[9] Other texts include a description of the ephemeral triumphal arch built for the entry, a book of virtues (*Zodiaco*), a panegyric poem (*loa*), a quatrain (*redondillas*), and an account (*Relación*) written by doña María de Estrada de Medinilla, a wealthy white lettered Mexicana (all published 1640). *Festín* is the final text in the collection of seven distinct works. It is hard to tell whether this position reflects *Festín*'s original valuation, yet this position seems significant, especially from a racial point of view.

Despite its rearmost position in the Sammelband, *Festín* merits our attention because it reveals how Afro-Mexican women adapted to colonial society and culture. Like the 1610 celebration of the beatification of Ignatius of Loyola discussed in Chapter 3, it reveals how Novohispanic Black creoles adapted and mixed African festive practices with baroque festival culture and Amerindian traditions. This is underscored by the women's choice to reenact the Queen of Sheba's visit to King Solomon, a story they learned through European sources. Albeit mediated by Torres' narrative, *Festín* still reveals how knowledgeable the women were of Hispanic baroque festive practices. Finally, *Festín* is a unique text in the early modern Iberian Atlantic, where few sources paid sustained attention to a Black performance and, by extension, to Black cultural agency. While Afro-Mexicans indubitably took part in many viceregal entries, *Festín* is the only text that documents Afro-Mexicans' participation in these events; it is therefore a valuable tool for understanding the types of performances Afro-Mexicans staged on civic occasions.

I would like to take the Queen of Sheba's journey as a metaphor of the women's – and, by extension, Afro-Mexicans' – cultural journey, not from Africa to the Americas, but from Africans to Afro-Mexicans. One element of the women's performance incorporated aspects of the foundational myth of the Virgin of Guadalupe, emphasizing not only the women's

[9] The Real Academia Española copy of the Sammelband only includes the first folio of *Festín* as the first folio of the collection. In 1947, the Mexican scholar Manuel Romero de Terreros published a modern edition, *Viaje del Virrey Marquéz de Villena*, based on the copy at the Nettie Lee Benson Latin American Collection at the University of Texas at Austin, that only includes Gutiérrez de Medina's text. Besides the Real Academia Española and the Benson copies, I consulted the copies at the University of Salamanca, the Hispanic Society of America, Yale University, and the British Library. The Benson's copy of *Festín* does not contain the author's name, dedication, or prologue.

piety but, more importantly, their Mexicanness as well. As we saw in Chapter 1, the earliest textual evidence of Blacks performing "with king and queen" was most likely performed by foreign-born *ladinos* in Mexico City in 1539. From 1608 onward, we have evidence of creoles performing with a king and/or queen, but often African-born individuals were selected for these royal roles. By 1640, all the performers are creoles – that is, Afro-Mexicans. I therefore posit that this performance marks the maturation of Afro-Mexican's creole cultural consciousness, or strong sense of belonging to the Mexican cultural landscape. It also expresses Afro-Mexican subjectivities, especially female subjectivities, or the ways the women understood and saw themselves and imagined their socio-symbolic belonging.

From 1521 (the Spanish foundation of Mexico City) to 1640 (the women's performance), Blacks in Mexico had gone from Africans and *ladinos* to Afro-Mexicans, and as increasingly integrated members of society, staked a claim to inclusion in its cultural life. In this sense, the women's performance was meant to mirror the Queen of Sheba's journey to Jerusalem to see King Solomon, where she found Judaism, Christianity's theological precursor, as well as the viceroy's voyage from Spain to Mexico, and more importantly, Afrodescendants' own passage from Africans to (Afro-)Mexicans.

In *Festín*, we move from the city streets to the viceregal palace and an audience of Mexico City's religious and secular elite. It was this rarefied context that allowed for *Festín*'s sophisticated structure, use of allegory, and language. At a metaphorical level, this move from the streets to the palace also marks Afro-Mexicans' move from the periphery to the center of colonial Mexican culture. Interestingly enough, while in the biblical story it is the Queen of Sheba who travels to see Solomon, here it is the inverse: the viceroy/Solomon travels to receive the women's/queen's gifts. The women portray themselves (or are portrayed) as native to Mexico, with the viceroy as the incoming foreigner, whom the women receive. As the hosts, the women are a priori placed in a position of power. Moreover, the women's leadership in the performance could indicate that while men may have wielded more power in Afro-Mexican communities and festive practices in earlier years, as suggested by the texts explored in the foregoing chapter, Afro-Mexicanas now occupied the leadership roles. This would add Afro-Mexico to what is known of Black confraternal communities and their festive traditions elsewhere in the diaspora, namely that Black festive queens wielded more power than their male counterparts, as noted in Chapter 1.

VICEREGAL ENTRIES IN MEXICO CITY

Viceregal entries – colonial festivals staged for the arrival of a new viceroy – were among Mexico City's largest festivals, normally lasting anywhere between two and six months. Originally a modest ceremony in the sixteenth century, the celebration became ever more lavish in the seventeenth.[10] In 1603, for example, festivities marking the arrival of viceroy don Juan de Mendoza y Luna, the third Marquis of Montesclaros (r. 1603–7) cost the city 36,800 pesos; in 1624, the arrival of don Rodrigo Pacheco y Osorio de Toledo, the third Marquis of Cerralvo (r. 1624–35), totaled 20,000 pesos; and in 1640, Villena's entry exceeded a staggering 40,000 pesos.[11] These costs normally surpassed the city's annual revenue, listed as 16,500 pesos in 1620.[12] This conveys the importance colonial authorities gave to these festivals, supplementing city funds with loans and even with their own money.[13] Doubtless, as with regal entries in Europe, the local elites aimed at impressing and thereby ingratiating themselves with the new viceroy. As Curcio-Nagy points out in her study of these festivities, they were also meant to distract and entertain the masses: *panem et circenses* (bread and circuses).[14] In its preparatory discussions of the 1640 entry, for example, the *cabildo* remarked that a second reason for the entry was, "divertir al pueblo de trabajos y desconsuelos que ha tenido en perdidas y otros çucesos" (distract the people from the difficulties and sadness they have endured from losses and other events).[15] Droughts, which had spiked to four in the previous decade, may have been one of the difficulties to which the *cabildo* was referring.[16]

According to Curcio-Nagy, a typical viceregal entry included poetry recitals, banquets, *moros y cristianos* performances, crimson velvet ropes demarking the procession route, a canopy embroidered with silver or gold thread for the viceroy, a ceremonial presentation of the key to the city, and formal oaths of fealty by city officials at the triumphal arches constructed for the event.[17] Other typical elements of these celebrations can be found in the preparations made by the *cabildo* for the 1640 entry. The *cabildo*

---

[10] See Curcio-Nagy, *Great Festivals*, 18–19.

[11] *Actas de cabildo*, 15:196, 25:184, 32:82. In 1640, the *cabildo* cited 1603 as the model they wished to follow (ibid., 32:77).

[12] Ibid., 23:170.

[13] In 1640, for example, the city borrowed 36,600 pesos against its wine tax (ibid., 32:77).

[14] Curcio-Nagy, *Great Festivals*.   [15] *Actas de cabildo*, 32:77.

[16] Mendoza, Velasco, and Jáuregui, "Historical Droughts."

[17] Curcio-Nagy, *Great Festivals*, 19.

bought the "el mejor caballo de braso" (best walking horse) and ordered for it "una silla ricamente bordada de oro con todas la guarniciones y almartagaletix de tela rica" (a saddle with rich gold embroidery and all the trimmings and rich fabric).[18] The viceroy was to enter the city astride this magnificent steed accompanied by "ocho lacayos españoles" (eight Spanish servants).[19] The cabildo even detailed how city officials were to be dressed:

Las cuales dichas vestiduras han de ser. Ropones de tiersopelo carmesi de castilla. Alforrados de tela blanca y naranjada calzon y ropilla de terciopelo liso aforrados en la mesma tela acuchillado grande manga de la mesma tela. Media amarilla ó naranjada que diga con la tela. Gonas de terciopelo plumas de los colores de los cabos. Ligas con puntas de oro bolillas bordadas de oro.[20]

The said vestments should be a red Castilian velvet cape with white and orange lining. Velvet breeches and shirts with big sleeves of the same fabric. Yellow or orange stockings. Velvet hats with colorful feathers. Sock garters with gold tassels and gold borders.

These liveries were the height of baroque fashion and denoted the high status of the officials who welcomed the viceroy. The festivities in the streets also included *corridas* (bullfights), fireworks, and masquerades. As all these details suggest, the 1640 entry was one of the most lavish the city had witnessed, lasting four months. Its magnitude had no precedent in Mexico City, and was perhaps only surpassed by the celebrations in 1680 for don Tomás de la Cerda y Aragón, the third Marquis of la Laguna (r. 1680–6), for which Sor Juana Inés de la Cruz and don Carlos de Sigüenza y Góngora designed one triumphal arch each.[21]

The women's dance, a private event performed in the great hall of the viceregal palace, is not discussed in these plans. This suggests that the *cabildo* did not hire the women, but rather that the women planned their dance, preparing it and procuring all the necessary materials, and more importantly, that they may have proposed the dance themselves. The *cabildo* was the principal planner of the entry, but not all performances were sponsored by it. As we saw in the previous chapter, all sectors of society were invited and encouraged to contribute to public festivals in Mexico City. And as evidenced by the other texts in the Sammelband, other entities offered the new viceroy tributes as well. For example, the *audiencia*, archbishop, Feliciano de la Vega y Padilla (r. 1638–40), Jesuits,

---

[18] Ibid.; *Actas de cabildo*, 32:83–4.   [19] *Actas de cabildo*, 32:84.   [20] Ibid., 32:85.
[21] See Inés de la Cruz, *Neptuno alegórico*; Sigüenza y Góngora, *Teatro de virtudes*; Arenal, "Sor Juana's Arch"; García, "Saldos del criollismo."

and Franciscans each sponsored *loas*, or panegyric poems. Like the *cabildo*, these entities sought to enter the viceroy's good graces and secure his favor during his reign. The women and, by extension, Mexico City's Black community would have been motivated by the same desire. In a world where they were presented in the most negative of terms, Afro-Mexicans more than any other group would want to make a good impression on this or any incoming viceroy as it ensured their survival in a sometimes violently hostile environment.

A TRANSCULTURAL JOURNEY OF THE IMAGINATION FROM SHEBA TO MEXICO

The choice of the biblical figure of the Queen of Sheba – whether it was Nicolás de Torres' or the female performers' – was significant in many ways. She represented a powerful Black figure that linked the women of Mexico City to Christianity from antiquity, arguing for a long Christian lineage, or unbroken *limpieza de sangre*. The women must have known about the queen through sermons. Indeed, preachers always sought to offer Black parishioners Black holy figures as examples to follow. As an independent Black monarch, the Queen of Sheba may have very well represented lost (through the enslavement of their forebears) and desired sovereignty for the women. As Kim F. Hall has observed, "although sexuality plays a part in her story, she does hint at a more liberating history. To put it bluntly, she is a Black woman with a brain. Her wisdom is a key part of her story and relations with Solomon."[22] Therefore, the Queen of Sheba's reputation as a strong ruler could imply the strategic choice the women may have made in selecting her, whether they chose her independently or did so in conjunction with Torres. They could have performed as a nondescript African queen or the story of princess Iphigenia's conversion to Christianity, both common figures from the repertoire of Afro-baroque culture. Instead, they chose a significant Black woman presented on equal terms to the Israelite King Solomon, to drive home their message of their sociopolitical agency, no doubt. Through their depiction of the Queen of Sheba the women affirmed themselves as historical subjects, descended, like Solomon, from saintly royalty. This section, then, seeks to trace the queen's cultural journey from Sheba to Mexico in order to illustrate that the women likely possessed the knowledge that would have poised them to select the queen for their

[22] Hall, "Object into Object?" 359.

performance. I propose that in doing so, they sought to draw a parallel between the Queen of Sheba's sovereignty and their own cultural journey of integration from *boçales* and *ladinas* to *criollas*. At the same time, the Queen of Sheba's afterlife in the European imagination can help us understand Torres' ambivalent language about the women's performance. This ambivalence seems to suggest that Torres was only a half-willing contributor to the women's act.

Recent scholarship asserts that the Queen of Sheba, though disputed as a historical figure, would likely have hailed from the region around the Red Sea, a pivotal center of the ancient world's spice trade, though there is no consensus on exactly which of the ancient kingdoms of the region would have been her home state. There are, however, two prevailing hypotheses: one, put forward by Harry St. John Bridger Philby, asserts that she was from the southern corner of the Arabian Peninsula (in present-day Yemen); another, proposed by Nicholas Clapp, holds that she hailed from northeastern Africa (in present-day Ethiopia).[23] The women's performance and Torres' text followed the second hypothesis, which is the one that has prevailed in the West since the first century CE, beginning with the Judeo-Roman historian Josephus, who wrote in his *Antiquities of the Jews* that

[T]here was then a woman queen of Egypt and Ethiopia; she was inquisitive into philosophy, and one that on other accounts also was to be admired. When this queen heard of the virtue and prudence of Solomon, she had a great mind to see him. ... Accordingly, she came to Jerusalem with great splendor and rich furniture; for she brought with her camels laden with gold, with several sorts of sweet spices, and with precious stones.[24]

Both from Josephus' and the biblical perspectives, the Queen of Sheba makes a diplomatic visit to Solomon out of the pursuit of wisdom, in order to engage in a colloquy with the Israelite king and "to test him with hard questions" on his faith.[25] Impressed with Solomon's wisdom and the wealth of his kingdom, she is inspired to convert. In both accounts, she offers unbounded riches of gold, precious stones, and costly spices. In the exegesis, she also offers her own beautiful body – that other account on which she was to be admired. We will see how the Afro-Mexican women played with this sexual subtext in their performance, which constituted a

---

[23] Philby, *The Queen of Sheba*, 43–76; Clapp, *Sheba*, 221–87. The New American Bible (NAB) follows Philby's hypothesis (1 Kings 10:1). See also Goldenberg, *The Curse of Ham*, 18–19.
[24] 8.6.5.   [25] NAB, 1 Kings 10:1.

bold move for a population already perceived as excessively sexualized. Furthermore, it is the lack of geographical specificity (in antiquity as well as early modernity; see Chapter 3) about Africa that allowed the women – descended from West and Central Africans – to claim the queen as their forebear. This indicates how Afro-Mexicans were able to avail themselves of the tropes of the exotic genre and use them to their advantage, as proposed in the previous chapter.[26]

Josephus may have influenced medieval scholars, such as St. Bernard of Clairvaux and even St. Thomas Aquinas, who held that the bride in Song of Songs (also known as Song of Solomon) was the Queen of Sheba.[27] Leading them to this conclusion was 1:5:

> I am Black *and* lovely,
> daughters of Jerusalem,
> dark like the tents of Kedar,
> like the tent curtains of Solomon.[28]

From this interpretation arose the notion that the Queen and Solomon were lovers. In the fourth century, St. Jerome translated "Black *and* lovely" in the Hebrew original (Torah: [*shchure ani* (=and) *u·naue*]; Septuagint: μέλαινά εἰμι καὶ (=and) καλή [*mélainé eìmi kaì kalé*]) as "*nigra* sed [=but] *formosa*" [Black *but* beautiful], which became the dominant European view of Black femininity and Blackness in general and persisted at the time of the women's performance. Jerome's Judeo-Christian-inflected semantic shift from the augmentative conjunction (*and*) to the contradictory one (*but*) presupposed a negative view of Blackness, as if it were inimical to physical (*formositas*) and spiritual (*pulchritas*) beauty.[29] From this perspective, Blackness was conceived a priori as antithetical to Western notions of beauty. This is, for example, how Bernard of Clairvaux describes it in his exegetical sermon: "sponsa, cum pulchritudine utique compositionis, naevo non carere nigredinis" (the bride, despite the gracefulness of her person, bears the stigma of dark skin).[30]

---

[26] See Mason, *Infelicities.*   [27] Clapp, *Sheba*, 26–7.

[28] NIV; my emphasis. Translation modified in accordance with the literal meaning of the original (see the Interlinear Bible). According to the NAB, Kedar was "a Syrian desert region whose name suggests blackness" (Song 1:3). The same Bible adds, "tents were often made of black goat hair" (ibid.).

[29] The Queen of Sheba is also mentioned in Matthew 12:42 and Luke 11:31, where is she called "the Queen of the South."

[30] St. Bernard, *Sermones in Cantica*, 25, 3.

Christian legend holds that the Queen of Sheba, persuaded by Solomon's wisdom and faith, converted after their theological discussion. As such, she mothered a people who worshiped the "true" Abrahamic God from antiquity, and who welcomed the "good news" (Christianity) when the Apostle Matthew brought it to them. Along with other Black saints, the Queen of Sheba must have been offered as a model to Afro-Mexicans and was indeed included in Alonso de Sandoval's collection of Black saints. Both the story of the Queen of Sheba and the Church's interpretation of her as a proto-Christian saint must have been well known to Afro-Mexicans.

As a biblical feminine Black figure, then, the Queen of Sheba held both positive and negative signifiers. On one hand, for medieval Christian scholars, just as Solomon prefigured Christ, the African queen prefigured the Black magus Balthazar (see Figure 4.3), who witnessed and paid tribute to the Savior at his birth.[31] As such, she was seen as a non-Hebrew (i.e., Gentile) pre-Christian holy woman. On the other hand, as attested by medieval manuscripts such as Hans Vintler's fifteenth-century *Die Pluemen der Tugent* (*Flower of Virtue*), her Blackness – understood as a mark of sin in the High Middle Ages – was interpreted as an ominous sign of sinful baseness, and she herself as a temptress (see Figure 4.4).[32] Vintler depicts the Queen of Sheba as having seduced Solomon to worship the devil, rather than having been convinced by his wisdom and faith in the Abrahamic God. Here the queen's Blackness, seen as evil, constitutes a danger that can corrupt even the wisest of holy men. More than a reference to the biblical story, Vintler's image, and the medieval view on the Queen, extracted her from the biblical context and used her Blackness as a symbol of evil, incarnated in the Black female body.

---

[31] In the Middle Ages, Christian authors endeavored to add Africans into the "economy of salvation." As part of these efforts, one of the three magi, who had been conceived as white until that point, became Black (see Kaplan, *The Rise of the Black Magus*). At first, both Balthazar and Gaspar were represented as Black in different texts and images, albeit not in the same text or image. Eventually Balthazar exclusively came to be represented as Black. Balthazar became important for Afrodescendants, especially for their king and queen performances. While in the Portuguese Empire, the feast of Our Lady of the Rosary was when Black confraternities elected their king and queen, in the Spanish Empire, as I noted in Chapter 1, it was the feast of the Epiphany (January 6), which is part the Church's Christmas season; hence, why in Mexico City in 1608, the king and queen were elected on Christmas Eve, the beginning of the Christmas season. Recall that in Mexico City in 1608, the celebrants supposedly agreed to return to the house on January 6. Given this tradition in the Spanish Empire, Torquemada thought the events had taken place on January 6 (*Monarchia indiana*, 1:759).

[32] See Heng, *The Invention of Race*, 181–256.

FIGURE 4.3 Giulio Clovio, *Adoration of the Magi* and *Solomon Adored by Sheba*. Rome, 1546. *Farnese Hours*, fols. 38v–39 r. Courtesy of the Morgan Library and Museum, New York

Medieval ambivalence toward the Queen of Sheba is best illustrated in Conrad Kyeser's mid-fifteenth-century treatise on military technology, *Bellifortis (Strong in War)*. Visually, the Queen of Sheba is depicted as a strong ruler, standing erect, a crown on her head, a scepter in her left hand and an orb in her right (Figure 4.5). Blonde locks descend beyond her shoulders. The accompanying text, however, communicates a different message.

> Sum regina Sabba clarior ceteris et venusta
> Pulchra sum et casta stat speculum pictore sculptum
> In quo contemplantur juvenes quecumque volunt
> Et in visu tacta fune retro follis absconsa
> Per aerem subito movet fuliginem ore
> Astans nisi similis pelle colore stabit.[33]

---

[33] Kyeser, *Bellifortis*, fol. 122r. English in Bowersox, "Blackening the Queen of Sheba."

FIGURE 4.4 Hans Vintler, *The Queen of Sheba and Solomon Worshiping a Demon*, Tyrol, ca. 1410. In *Die Pluemen der Tugent*, fol. 6 r. Courtesy of the Austrian National Library, Austria

> I am the Queen of Sheba, more famous than others, and attractive:
> I am beautiful and chaste. There is a mirror in my chest,
> In which young men may behold whatever they wish.
> While one of them views it, he pulls a rope, the bellows are compressed,
> And darkness suddenly bursts forth from my mouth into the air:
> Then he stands before me with a similar skin, similar in color.

While "beautiful and chaste," the queen's "darkness" "suddenly bursts forth" from her mouth and turns young men Black like her. Little attention is paid to her chastity in the text. Instead, the text focuses on the

FIGURE 4.5 Conrad Kyeser, *The Queen of Sheba*, in *Bellifortis*, fol. 122 r, detail. Bohemia, ca. 1450. Courtesy of the Göttingen State and University Library, Germany

wickedness her Blackness signifies and its potential for contagion. Her beauty is a mirror that attracts and transfixes young men so she can turn them Black. Her Blackness is thus conceived as a deceptive, corruptive force. Her body is dark because it holds in a destructive force that she can release at any moment. The bellows were often associated with the devil, who was believed to use them to blow wicked thoughts into the ears of the unsuspecting, as in Dürer's *The Dream of the Doctor* (ca. 1498). It's appearance here is significant; it is the instrument the queen uses to propel her evil out into the world, as it does the devil's wicked temptations.

In Kyeser's image, then, the queen's body is weaponized as racialized evil. The implications for medieval conceptions of race are enormous. As in Sandoval's understanding of Blackness discussed in Chapter 2, the queen's Blackness is "innate and intrinsic," extending beyond her skin to the essence of her being. The implication is that her evilness, and that of her whole race, is immutable but, more importantly, that this Blackness is a dangerous weapon capable of tainting the entire human race. If in 1612, Black male bodies were seen as a threat to "white" female bodies as demonstrated in the second chapter, here Black female Being (understood as body and soul) is seen as a threat to "white" male Being, and by extension, the body politic.

We will see how this medieval ambivalence toward the Queen of Sheba permeated the subtext of the women's performance and the narrative that describes it, as it must have the lives of Afro-Mexican women in the seventeenth century. Torres, for example, feels the need to defend his subject matter to his readers, and his ambivalence about the women's performance is palpable throughout the text. In the prologue, he justifies his part in the performance by appealing to its high purpose: to pay homage to the viceroy, whom he describes as "la mayor grandeza que ha visto esta Monarquia" (the greatest majesty New Spain has seen).[34] Villena, King Philip III's cousin thrice removed, was the first Spanish American viceroy who was a Grandee of Spain and a duke. Given this noble intent, Torres asserts that he could not help making himself vulnerable to scorn for his part in the performance:

Lector amigo, ruego á Dios que lo seas: y mas oy, quando con el desaliño de mis obras te descubro el cuerpo, para que executes con la murmuracion tu encubierta venganza. Yo te busco, yo te doy ocasion; aprovechate pues la tienes: mas solo te advierto, atiendas à mi assumpto: pues guiado de un amoroso aplauso, me entregué al suplicio de tu correcion. ... Yo me obligué al riesgo: y assi dirás que fue errar por mi gusto.[35]

Reader, I pray to God you are a friend, especially today when I expose myself with my work, giving you occasion to carry out your hidden vengeance with your gossip. I seek you out, I give you occasion; take advantage of the opportunity. I only ask you to pay attention to my subject, for guided by loving praise,

[34] Torres, *Festín*, fol. 2r.   [35] Ibid., fol. 1v.

I submitted myself to your scorn. . . . I committed myself to the risk, but you will say I erred of my own volition.

What else could compel Torres to defend himself in this fashion if not the fraught nature of his subject matter: a highly sexualized dance performed by Black women?

The Queen of Sheba is therefore a perfect racial signifier; Christian authors' ambivalence toward her reflects their uneasiness about race vis-à-vis religion. Since in this period, "religion did the work of race," Blacks' Christianity sometimes upended Iberian notions of race.[36] Blacks could not be seen as the Other through religion, which may be why Iberians developed a biological theory of race early on.

Torres' ambivalence about the Queen of Sheba, understood as a representation of colonial racial and sexual ideology, mirrors colonial authorities' apparent vacillation toward Afro-Mexican festive practices. As I have shown thus far, Afro-Mexicans' festive traditions were welcomed by colonial authorities when performed in the name of empire but prosecuted when done outside officially sanctioned events. As with the figure of the Queen of Sheba, as a feminine body, this irresolution reflects a desire to control Afro-Mexicans' lives in the same way authorities sought to control women's bodies and restrict their movement through sumptuary laws and other mechanisms. Yet in both cases they failed at controlling either bodies or practices.

Perhaps also influenced by Josephus or his sources, Ethiopia, home to one of the oldest Christian communities in the world, claimed the Queen of Sheba as its own from early on. The fourteenth-century Ethiopian text *Kebra Nagast* (*The Glory of Kings*), for example, asserts that the rulers of Ethiopia were the direct descendants of Solomon and the Queen of Sheba.[37] We cannot know for sure, however, whether the women or Torres were aware of this tradition. It is more likely that they were drawing from the Christian tradition summarized previously, as most Afro-Mexicans descended from West and Central Africans.[38] The women were Ethiopians inasmuch as they were Africans, for as I noted in Chapter 2 for Sandoval, Ethiopia was understood not as just part of Africa but rather as a metonym for Africa itself.

The women must have heard about the Queen of Sheba in many sermons. In his treatise, discussed in Chapter 2, for example, Sandoval

---

[36] Holt, *The Problem of Race*, 42.   [37] Clapp, *Sheba*, 221.
[38] Velázquez Gutiérrez, *Mujeres*, 67–77.

listed the Queen of Sheba among a group of "illustrious holy Africans."[39]
Of her, Sandoval writes: "Y para excelencia desta Reina, y fundamento de
sus grandezas, basta lo que Christo dize della" (and for this queen's
excellence and basis of her greatness what Jesus says of her is enough).[40]
In the gospels, Jesus says: "At the judgment the Queen of the South will
arise with this generation and condemn it, because she came from the ends
of the earth to hear the wisdom of Solomon; and there is something greater
than Solomon here."[41] For Jesus' contemporaries, the south meant Egypt
and the land to its south, ancient Nubia, which they called the land of
Kush, the patriarch of the Black race.[42] Sandoval adds: "En genero de
sabiduria, fue esta Reina de muy gran nombre y en santidad, que es la
sabiduria de mucho mayor" (this queen was renowned for wisdom and
holiness, which is the true and much greater wisdom).[43] "Santidad"
(holiness), especially for Afrodescendants, in Sandoval's time was understood as acceptance of one's condition.[44] Thus, Torres is able to neutralize
the queen's testing of Solomon in his text and emphasize instead their
wisdom in recognizing the viceroy's power.

AFRO-MEXICAN WOMEN IN MEXICO CITY IN THE FIRST
HALF OF THE SEVENTEENTH CENTURY

The women's participation in the festivities for the entry of the new
viceroy attests to the social agency Black women wielded in seventeenth-
century Mexico City. Torres' full description of the women corroborates
their influential sociopolitical status: "Negras, Estrellas, que produzidas
en este Indiano suelo, solicitavan la predominancia de su influencia"
(Black stars from American soil who demanded the preeminence of their
native land).[45] This select group of Mexico City's Black community, then,
was made up of native-born women, *morenas criollas*. The text, if not the
women themselves, sought to elevate the women to the same fame of the
Americas. The text then inscribes the women's performance within
the contemporary discourse of the greatness of the Americas.
Alternatively, the text could already be recognizing the women's preeminence. This would not be without precedent in the Spanish Empire. For

---

[39] Sandoval, *Un tratado*, Book 2, chap. XXXII.   [40] Ibid., 217.
[41] Matthew 12:42; also Luke 11:31.   [42] See Goldenberg, *The Curse of Ham*, 17–25.
[43] Sandoval, *Un tratado*, 218.
[44] See Vieira, *Sermões*; Bristol, *Christians, Blasphemers, and Witches*, 23–62.
[45] Torres, *Festín*, fol. 2r.

example, on July 21, 1623, the Council of the Indies issued a real *cédula* in Philip III's name ordering the "preeminencias" of "morenos libres" who serve the crown be observed: "que se mire por el tratamiento de los morenos libres, y guarden sus preeminencias" (my officials should ensure the good treatment of free *morenos* and see to it that their privileges [*preeminencia*] be honored).[46] While there was a concrete law protecting a specific group of *morenos, preeminecnia* – as *Festín* shows – was a highly symbolic word used to mark the status of individuals or things. *Festín* could be recognizing the women's socio-symbolic prestige.

As detailed in Chapter 2, in the aftermath of the supposed 1612 plot, the Audiencia issued a set of "Nuevas ordenanças de negros" (New Ordinances for Blacks). Ordinance number four prohibited Black women from wearing expensive clothes and jewelry:

Que ninguna negra ni mulata, libre ni cautiva, pueda traer, ni traiga, ninguna joya de oro, ni plata, ni perlas, ni vestido de seda de Castilla, ni mantos de seda, ni pasamanos de oro ni de plata, so pena de cien azotes y de perdimiento de los tales vestidos, joyas, perlas y demás, aplicado según de suso.[47]

No Black or mulatta woman, free or in captivity, can wear gold or silver jewelry, pearls or clothes of Castilian silk, silk mantles, or sleeves with gold or silver borders, on pain of 100 lashes and the confiscation of their clothes, jewelry, pearls and the rest.

This was not the first time colonial law had barred Afrodescendants from wearing fine clothes. As early as the New Laws of 1542, the Spanish Empire had criminalized Blacks' consumption of what were considered luxury items, although these were central to Afro-Mexicans' festive performances, as explored in the previous chapter and in this chapter. In the *Recopilación de las leyes de los reynos de las Indias* (*Recompilation of the Laws of the Indies*), a code of colonial laws published in 1681, we find the following provision, originally issued by Philip II (r. 1556–98) on February 11, 1571:

Ninguna negra libre, ó esclava, ni mulata, trayga oro, perlas, ni seda; pero si la negra, o mulata libre fuere casada con Español, pueda traer unos zarcillos de oro, con perlas, y una gargantilla, y en la saya un ribete de terciopelo, y no pueda traer, ni traygan mantos de burato, ni de otra tela, salvo mantillas, que lleguen poco mas abaxo de la cintura, pena de que les quiten, y pierdan los joyas de oro, vestido de seda, y manto que traxeren.[48]

---

[46] In *Recopilación*, 7:5:10.

[47] In Lucena Samoral, *Regulación de la esclavitud*, 157; English in Germeten, *Black Blood Brothers*, 60.

[48] *Recopilación*, 7.5.33.

No Black or mulatta woman, slave or free, should wear gold, pearls, or silk, except if she is married to a Spaniard, she may wear gold earrings, with pearls, and a choker, and a silk hem on her skirt, but may not wear, nor should wear linen mantles, or of any other fabric, except shawls, which may go down to the waist more or less, under penalty that they will be to lose and have taken from them any gold jewelry, silk dresses, and mantle they should be wearing.

Such laws, which were issued on a regular basis, came in response to Afrodescendants' use of such luxuries.[49] For example, in 1625, only thirteen years after the supposed Black conspiracy of 1612, Englishman Thomas Gage (ca. 1603–56), at the time a Dominican friar (later a proponent of the Black Legend), was scandalized by the clothes and jewels on Black women in the streets of Mexico City:

> A Blackamoor or tawny young maid and slave will make hard shift, but she will be in fashion with her neck-chain and bracelets of pearls, and her ear-bobs of some considerable jewels. The attire of this baser sort of people of Blackamoors and mulattoes (which are of a mixed nature, of Spanish and Blackamoors) is so light, and their carriage so enticing that many Spaniards even of the better sort (who are too prone to venery) disdain their wives for them.[50]

Both the 1612 ordinance and Gage's text are marked by negative views on Afro-Mexicans, yet both texts bear witness to the fact that Black women in Mexico City had the capital to buy clothes and jewelry the cost of which could surpass what some Spaniards could afford. As Rebecca Earle has noted, the visual nature of race meant that a Black woman in fine clothing belonged to a different racial group than a Black woman in rags.[51] Colonial officials may have been anxious that by dressing in rich attire, Afro-Mexicanas, especially mulattas, would pass as *españolas* (female Spaniards) or white female Novohispanic *criollas*.[52]

A 1711 image, *Appearance of a Mulatta, Daughter of Black Woman and Spaniard*, attributed to Manuel de Arellano (1662–1722), considered one of the oldest *casta* paintings in existence, may bear further witness to Afro-Mexicans' sartorial agency.[53] The painting shows a young mulatta wearing an elegant white dress (known as a *manga* [sleeve]) with rich lace and a great deal of jewelry, including what look like diamond earrings, a

---

[49] See Walker, *Exquisite Slaves*, 43–96; Earle, "Luxury, Clothing and Race."

[50] Gage, *The English–American*, fol. 56. Gage wrote the account of his American travels after he had returned to Protestantism as an anti-Hispanic propagandist text.

[51] Earle, "Luxury, Clothing and Race."

[52] See Walker, *Exquisite Slaves*, 43–96; Earle, "Luxury, Clothing and Race."; Meléndez, "Visualizing Difference"; Terrazas Williams, "Finer Things."

[53] See Katzew, "Rendering of a Mulato."

FIGURE 4.6 Attributed to Manuel de Arellano, *Appearance of a Mulatta, Daughter of Black Woman and Spaniard*, Mexico City, 1711. Courtesy of the Denver Art Museum.

diamond choker, and gold rings, and a beautiful headband with rich lace too (Figure 4.6).[54] A Spanish Capuchin friar, Fray Francisco de Ajofrín (1719–89), who traveled to Mexico City in 1763, described Afro-Mexicanas' sartorial customs in similar terms:

El traje de las negras y mulatas es una *soya de embrocar* (a modo de una basquiña pequeña de seda, con sus corchetes de plata, y por ruedo una buena cinta o listón), la cual traen sobre la cabeza o sobre los hombros, sacando la cabeza por lo angosto o cintura de la saya; traen sus guardapiés que llaman *enaguas*, de tela de China, con flecos de Holanda o encajes ricos, y su calzado honesto.[55]

[54] The arrival of Viceroy Fernando de Alencastre (r. 1711–16) in 1711, the year Arellano may have painted the mulatta, has led Ilona Katzew to wonder if it was part of a series of paintings for the festivities staged for the viceroy's arrival: "The Invention of Casta Painting."

[55] Ajofrín, *Diario*, 1:84.

Black and mulattas wear a dress (like a short silk *basquiña* [i.e., a type of skirt], with its silver corsets, and a good belt or cincture), which goes up to their head or over their shoulder; and they wear silk [*tela de China*] petticoats with fine linen or cotton tassels [*flecos de Holanda*] or rich lace [*encajes*], and their shoes are simple.

These texts and this image show that Black women were indeed buying and wearing expensive fabric, as we see in the performance. As Tamara J. Walker has observed apropos Afro-Limeños, in colonial Latin America, "elegant clothing was also a tool that enslaved [and free/d] men and women [of African descent] used to negotiate their status, express their ideas about masculinity and femininity, and attend to conceptions of belonging in ways that not only reflected but also challenged the dominant norms."[56] By staging this performance in the context of these prohibitions, the women put this agency into practice, claiming honor and belonging within Mexican society through their splendid costumes.

Nevertheless, given the repressive sociohistorical context, it is noteworthy that these women were able to perform their dance before the highest authority in the land: the viceroy. Besides the fact that such sumptuary restrictions were relaxed in times of public rejoicing, such as the arrival of a new viceroy, as Herman Bennett has argued,

[A]s Africans labored in the urban milieu, they acquired the cultural insight necessary to navigate the colonial labyrinth. With a Christian-inflected cultural and legal consciousness, urban slaves and servants pressed for autonomy – time and mobility to interact with friends and familiars.[57]

In their performance, these women make manifest just such a cultural and legal consciousness, autonomy, and mobility. Membership in a religious confraternity would have allowed the women to detach themselves from the negative view of their counterparts, as well as to bring together the funds required to purchase the material used in the performance. It is likely that the women belonged to one or more Afro-Mexican confraternities, which would have allowed them to mobilize collective resources. This hypothesis is supported by the fact that confraternities were the main form of organization for Catholics in early modernity, and Blacks in the Catholic world were no exceptions. Blacks (and Indigenous groups) in fact used confraternities in more strategic ways than Europeans.

---

[56] Walker, *Exquisite Slaves*, 18.   [57] Bennett, *Africans*, 2.

MADRES Y HERMANAS: WOMEN IN AFRO-MEXICAN CONFRATERNITIES

Women had their own confraternities and also took on important roles in all-Black confraternities, especially as alms collectors, caregivers, and mourners.[58] As Germeten notes,

Afromexican confraternities needed women's organizational skills and resources to fulfill charitable goals. Women served important symbolic and actual functions in Black and mulatto confraternities. . . . In a social context in which life expectancy for slaves was very low, African women were able to provide other slaves with much-needed charity. The confraternities of slaves and Africans in the seventeenth century provided the precious benefit of health care and burial, and women helped fund and lead these confraternity activities.[59]

But women were not mere aides-de-camp among Afro-Mexican confraternities. As Germeten notes, women "were even among confraternity founders."[60] In the first quarter of the seventeenth century, for example, Black women in Mexico City founded the all-female confraternity of St. Iphigenia.[61] In this confraternity, women were the officers and decided most if not all confraternal matters.[62] Women also held leadership roles in confraternities founded by men, where they were known as *madres* or mothers.[63] This reflects Black women's leadership roles in their microcommunities.

While similar to women's roles in Indigenous-membership confraternities, Afro-Mexican women's leadership in Black confraternities stands in stark contrast to the roles available to women in Spanish confraternities in seventeenth-century Mexico City. As Germeten observes, "Spanish women, in contrast, expressed their piety in more private ways. Wills of wealthier women in seventeenth-century Mexico City, who were generally Spanish, show high level devotion to confraternities, although men were always the founders, leaders, procession participants, or alms-collectors."[64] As Germeten further points out, while Spanish women could attain religious authority by becoming nuns, Black women, who were generally not allowed to become nuns, attained this spiritual authority through their leadership in confraternities.[65] This resonated with the

---

[58] Germeten, *Black Blood Brothers*, chapter 2; Santana, "Mulheres negras."
[59] Germeten, *Black Blood Brothers*, 41.   [60] Ibid., 43.
[61] Besides Germeten, see Castañeda García, "La devoción a santa Ifigenia."
[62] Spiritual directors often influenced confraternities' decisions, which they had to approve anyway.
[63] Germeten, *Black Blood Brothers*, 54.   [64] Ibid., 41.   [65] Ibid., 41–2.

African world they or their forebears knew, particularly in the Kongo and Angola, "which were characterized by a matrilineal kinship system and public leadership roles for women."[66] As Germeten adds, in these African societies, women "were priestesses and holy visionaries."[67] Thus, removed from their ancestral homelands, Afro-Mexican women found in confraternities ways to continue these roles in ways that were acceptable to the Spanish theocracy, especially the Inquisition.

While I agree with Germeten in seeing African roots in Afro-Mexican women's leadership in confraternities, I also see a second factor that she does not mention, namely that Black women enjoyed greater mobility than men, and again, than their white female counterparts.[68] Free Afro-*Mexicanas* outnumbered their male counterparts; these women also enjoyed greater access to property.[69] Employed as domestic servants, women were often used as messengers and sent on errands. (María Elisa Velázquez has documented the presence of these women in Mexican households: Figure 4.7.) In a world where propriety dictated that Spanish women remain at home, Spanish women used Afro-Mexican women as their emissaries, for notions of decency did not place the same restrictions on Black female bodies.[70] Furthermore, more Black women than men were self-employed vendors in the streets of seventeenth-century Mexico City, where they moved with relative ease. Also, as self-employed merchants, Black women had more independence as to what to do with their time. Black men, most of whom were employed as journeymen or coachmen, were perpetually tethered to a worksite or an employer.

As Germeten suggests, "it is possible that the leadership roles of women in Afromexican confraternities were consistent or carried over to other aspects of social life."[71] No doubt, then, as we see in the women's performance, Afro-Mexican *madres* and *hermanas* (female confraternity members and leaders, also *cofradas*) took leadership roles in Afro-Mexican festive life, designing and making costumes for kings and queens, princesses and princes, dukes and duchesses, pages, the king's guard, and all the other roles represented in their performances. But again, they did not only carry out behind-the-scenes labor for these performances but rather also participated in them in private gatherings, on the streets, and in

---

[66] Ibid., 45.   [67] Ibid. See Thornton, *The Kongolese Saint Anthony.*

[68] Germeten, *Black Blood Brothers*, 43; Velázquez Gutiérrez, *Mujeres*; Sierra Silva, *Urban Slavery*, 144–200.

[69] Terrazas Williams, "My Conscience Is Free and Clear"; Velázquez Gutiérrez, *Mujeres*, 278. See also Jouve Martín, *The Black Doctors of Colonial Lima*, xviii.

[70] See Van Deusen, *Recogimiento.*   [71] Germeten, *Black Blood Brothers*, 48.

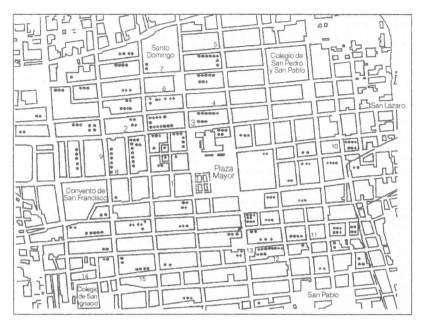

FIGURE 4.7 Dwellings of Black women in Mexico City, 1580–1753. From Velázquez Gutiérrez, *Mujeres*, 278. Reproduced with the author's permission

the halls of power of Mexico City. *Madres* and the spouses of the confraternities' male leaders were usually elected queens, princesses, and for other ceremonial female noble titles, as documented in judge López de Azoca's 1609 report discussed in Chapter 2.[72] A confraternity, moreover, was one of the few institutions available to Afro-Mexicans that would have allowed them to bring together the funds to purchase the material used in the performance.[73] If the 1612 prohibition on expensive fabric was still in effect in 1640, a confraternity would have been a better candidate for an exemption, or perhaps could pay a fine for violating it. Or, as the repeated reports of travelers could suggest, there was less control over the continuously proscribed women's dress in law than authorities wanted. It is even possible that a whole group of Afro-Mexican confraternities came

---

[72] See Walker, "The Queen of *los Congos*."

[73] Nicole von Germeten found that, of 440 Black seventeenth-century Mexico City testators, "36 percent mentioned membership in one or more confraternities," showing that a great number of the city's Black population – many who left no will – belonged to confraternities (*Black Blood Brothers*, 94).

together to sponsor the performance in the hope of currying favor with the new viceroy. Perhaps, like the Queen of Sheba, Mexico City's Black community hoped to attain "everything [they] desired and asked for" from the viceroy.[74]

Furthermore, as Curcio-Nagy points out, Mexico City "was home to at least one Afro-Mexican female dance troupe that often danced in the Corpus Christi procession at the behest of city councilmen."[75] This troupe was identified by Maya Ramos Smith in her history of dance during the colonial period.[76] Perhaps the women who performed before the viceroy belonged to this troupe or another about which we do not yet know. This is not incompatible with confraternity membership. A dance troupe could be part of a confraternity or have its own confraternity, availing itself of that corporate agency to bring together the resources it needed to perform its cultural function. This multilayered form of agency – simultaneous membership in different institutions – was very common among colonial Afro-Mexicans and illustrates the varied strategies colonial Afrodescendants employed to garner and deploy agency and express subjectivities.

THE QUEEN OF SHEBA'S MANIFOLD BODY: PERFORMING SEXUALITY, CULTURAL IDENTITY, AND POWER BEFORE THE VICEROY

The women's performance took the form of what was known at the time as a "danza hablada" (literally, spoken dance). *Autoridades* defines "danza hablada" as a dance performance "compuesta de personages vestidos al proposito de alguna historia" (composed of characters dressed for the purpose of representing some story).[77] This may very well be the form taken by the 1539 performance in celebration of the True of Nice (see Chapter 1). This form underscores the Afro-creole culture this performance put on display, as it incorporated elements of European festival culture. The same dictionary defines "festín" as "festejo particular que se hace en alguna casa, concurriendo mucha gente a divertirse con báiles, música, y otros entretenimientos" (a private party in some house attended by many people, who attend to enjoy themselves with dances, music, and

---

[74] See 1 Kings 10:13.   [75] Curcio-Nagy, *Great Festivals*, 58.
[76] Ramos Smith, *La danza en México*, 36.
[77] *Autoridades* 3:5. I cite from *Autoridades* because Cobarrubias' *Tesoro* does not account for different types of *danzas*.

other forms of entertainment).[78] Thus, the women's performance was a "festín" (literally, small fiesta) insofar as it took place in the viceroy's home, palace that it was. Dalia Hernández Reyes has suggested that the women's performance may have taken the form of a *sarao*, which *Autoridades* defines as "junta de personas de estimacion y gerarchía, para festejarse con instrumentos, y báiles cortesanos" (a gathering of people of esteem and hierarchy celebrated with courtly instruments and dances).[79] While the women's performance did take place within a courtly context before an audience of "people of esteem and hierarchy," it is unlikely, in my view, that they would have performed a European-inflected courtly dance, since there already was a long-standing tradition of "bailes de negros" (Black dances) in the Iberian world as explored in Chapter 3. Moreover, *saraos* would not become popular until the next century.

The dance drew heavily on the performative aspects of the biblical account of the Queen of Sheba's visit to Solomon, thus it serves us well to recall it:

The Queen of Sheba, having heard of Solomon's fame, came to test him with subtle questions. She arrived in Jerusalem with a very numerous retinue, and with camels bearing spices, a large amount of gold, and precious stones. . . . Then she gave the king one hundred and twenty gold talents, a very large quantity of spices, and precious stones. *Never again did anyone bring such an abundance of spices as the Queen of Sheba gave to King Solomon. . . . King Solomon gave the Queen of Sheba everything she desired and asked for*, besides such presents as were given her from Solomon's royal bounty.[80]

The emphasized text provides us, on one hand, an idea of what the women hoped to replicate in their performance, and on the other, an idea of what they may have wished to gain by it for Mexico City's Black community. As Torres puts it in the prologue, "sirvame à mi de amparo, si à ellas de agradicimiento" (may the dance bring me protection as it will the women the viceroy's gratitude).[81]

In the performance, each of the ten dancers personified the Queen of Sheba. In this manner, they multiplied the body of the queen into a manifold body that embodied the polysemy of their performance. The first dancer, the leader of the troupe ("La Capitana"), carried a rich banner made of silver silk fabric ("lama de plata"). Each of the dancers and all the furniture used in the performance were dressed with this shiny,

---

[78] Ibid., 3:740.   [79] Ibid., 6:47, Hernández Reyes, "*Festín*," 346.
[80] NAB, 1 Kings 10:1–13; my emphasis.   [81] Torres, *Festín*, fol. 1v.

expensive fabric, also known as *restaño* and *glassé*, from the French.[82] If the 1612 prohibition on opulent clothing and jewelry was still in effect, how did the women managed to acquire this luxury fabric? That prohibition being in place, it may have been relaxed for this occasion. Also, membership in a confraternity may have exempted the women from this bar, as I suggested previously. In any event, the women's use of this costly fabric highlights the kind of sartorial agency Afro-Mexicans could display in their lives (as Gage's text and the Audiencia's ordinance attest) and performances.

On one side of the banner was painted the coat of arms of the Marquis of Villena (Figure 4.8). On the other side was painted the meeting of Solomon and the Queen of Sheba:

Hazia ygualdad á sus espaldas en Regio Trono el Rey Salomon, no con menos ornato, tan amante como agradecido a los dones, que postrada á sus pies le ofrecía la Reyna Sabbà.[83]

On the back, with no less ornament, Solomon upon a regal throne, so loving and grateful for the gifts which the Queen of Sheba, prostrate at his feet, offered him.

The accompanying text bridges the image with the women's performance:

> Sabbá su cetro enagena
> Por prudente á Solomon,
> Y oy con toda su nacion,
> Se le rinde al de Villena.[84]

> The Queen of Sheba
> Ceded her throne to wise
> Solomon, and today, with
> All her nation, to Villena.

The image and text establish the allegorical context of the performance. The text draws a parallel between Solomon and Villena, and therefore a bridge between allegory and reality, to the present, where the Queen of Sheba's "whole nation" ("toda su nacion") – which in antiquity and early modernity, referred to ethnic group (see Chapter 2) – pays homage to the viceroy.[85] Thus, as they did with the Queen of Sheba, the women mimetically extended their bodies to represent Mexico City's entire Black

---

[82] *Autoridades* 5:599 and 4:53. See Meléndez, "Visualizing Difference."

[83] Torres, *Festín*, fol. 2r.   [84] Ibid.

[85] *Autoridades* defines "nacion" as "La colección de los habitadores en alguna Provincia, Pais o Reino" (the collectivity of the inhabitants of some province, nation or kingdom) (4:644).

FIGURE 4.8 Coat of Arms of the marquis of Villena in Cristóbal Gutiérrez de Medina, *Viage*. Courtesy of the University of Salamanca, Spain

community ("toda su nacion"). The repeated use of "nacion," as well as "Guinea" (one of the several names for Africa at the time) and "estirpe" (forebears), could even suggest that the women intended to represent *all* African people.[86] In this fashion, the women could have conceived of themselves as belonging to an imagined pan-African community.[87] This

[86] Torres, *Festín*, fols. 3–4.

[87] In his study *Imagined Spiritual Communities in Britain's Age of Print*, Joshua King "resist[s] Anderson's implication that imagining national communities is an essentially secular activity coordinated with the decay of religious forms" (4; see Anderson, *Imagined Communities*, 11–12, 22–36). Although King's study, like Anderson's, focuses on the nineteenth century, they

claim could be supported by the fact that they were a group of Novohispanic creole Black women performing themselves as the biblical Queen of Sheba. As stated in Chapter 1, they saw themselves as members of a global diasporic community, and here they make explicit claims of belonging to that community. In *New World Drama*, Elizabeth M. Dillon distinguishes between the ontic – embodied or material – and mimetic – referential or immaterial – features of performance.[88] Here, as in other parts of the performance, the women embody what they represent, merging the ontic with the mimetic. This embodiment of Sheba was only possible thanks to the women's ethnic identity, which was an a priori condition of their performance.[89] In this way, to borrow a phrase from Dillon, they "performed *themselves* as a people."[90]

Furthermore, as Hall has noted, "being liminal figures . . . queens could be identified with 'land,' 'people,' 'nation,' their liminality serving the very principle of identity – of the invulnerability rather than the vulnerability of the realm."[91] Thus, rather than suggesting a submissive nation, as has been proposed, the women represent – that is, intend to represent – a strong people, even if deferential to imperial power. Yet, even if the women meant to represent an imagined pan-African community, their most effective representation is that of their local community, which they hoped to benefit with their performance. At the beginning of the viceroy's reign, their performance is deployed to ingratiate Mexico City's Black population to the source of colonial power. To this end, the women perform within a rhetoric of love, patriotic love for the viceroy and everything he represents. This rhetoric of love has been seen as a sign of "total submission," yet a close analysis of the performance reveals that the women deployed this deferential rhetoric in a strategic manner, which they hoped would earn them the viceroy's goodwill.

can be applied to Black confraternities, which were conscious of belonging to networks of communities with common roots in Africa. Moreover, as both King and Anderson contend, print allowed dispersed people to imagine themselves as a community. Festival accounts like *Festín*, may have allowed Blacks to imagine themselves as a community in Mexico City and beyond.

[88] Dillon, *New World Drama*, 50.

[89] What I mean to suggest here is that all ethnic performance necessarily has ethnicity as an a priori condition.

[90] Dillon, *New World Drama*, 4; my emphasis. While later in the colonial period Black groups identified themselves according to their African geographical origin (*congos*, *angolas*, etc.), at this point they were all agglomerated into one large group (Velázquez Gutiérrez, *Mujeres*, 67–77).

[91] Hall, "Object into Object," 359.

As one woman danced, the nine other women held "tarjas" (placards) with painted "emblemas" (allegories) and Latin text explaining them, which they presented to the viceroy "hincadas de rodillas" (on their knees).[92] (This text is included in its entirety in Spanish in *Festín*.) These allegories mixed the biblical account of the encounter between the Queen of Sheba and Solomon with the viceroy's and the women's own background – that is, their cultural heritage. I concentrate on those examples that are pertinent to my discussion. (Other parts played with the viceroy's identity and heritage.) Hispanic baroque festivals communicated their message through emblems, and the women's use of them, whether they did so at Torres' suggestion or because they were familiar with them, underscores their capacity to mobilize the tropes and conventions of Hispanic baroque festive culture.[93] Here the women engage in the kind of symbolic exchange central to creolization.[94]

The third dancer carried a placard with an allegory of love, a major theme in the performance, as noted earlier. Like most of the text, the accompanying text plays with the concepts of light vis-à-vis whiteness and darkness vis-à-vis Blackness, where Villena is the sun and the dancer is a dark cloud ("negra nube"), made bright ("luciente") by the viceroy. In a highly eroticized tone, Villena's light ("arrebol") penetrates the dancer ("negra nube") like a bright sun ("luciente sol"):

> Y en regiones estrañas,
> Adora tu arrebol
> Mi negra nube, por luciente sol.[95]
>
> And in strange regions,
> My dark cloud adores
> Your light for bright sun.

This play with light/whiteness and darkness/Blackness is highly significant. The women work to invert the traditional conception of these ideas. Where darkness/Blackness represents evil/impurity, the women seek to elevate themselves and through them their "nation" above the traditional valuation of Blackness/impurity. Their cloudiness/darkness is purified by the love for and light of the sun/viceroy. Their affection, they contend, is superior to all others. This is doubly significant. This superior love, philos, is above the sexual love of eros. The women's performance, then, while

---

[92] Torres, *Festín*, fol. 2r.
[93] See Arellano and Pereira, *Emblemática y religión*; Mínguez, *Emblemática y cultura simbólica*.
[94] See my discussion of creolization in the Introduction.   [95] Ibid., fols. 2v–3r.

not devoid of sexuality, is not meant as a mere sexual performance. After all, they represent a wise queen who understood herself as an equal to Solomon. Second, that superior affection is meant to suggest that they are the most loyal subjects in the realm. By declaring such a devotion, they are certainly positioning themselves as the worthiest of the viceroy's favor. This calculated play with these opposites underscores the women's strategic choices throughout the performance. They use the language that would place them in the highest esteem before the viceroy. Counter to Iberian racial ideology, they propose that a person's true self is within and that a Black person can be more loyal. In other words, to paraphrase Martin Luther King Jr., they propose that skin color does not determine a person's character.

The verses also seem to recall the language often found in contemporary mystical texts, where the soul is a debased thing that seeks out the light of Christ's love. Indeed, as Nora E. Jaffary has studied, mysticism underwent a sort of democratization in early modernity, and colonial Latin America was no exception, as many laypeople were attracted to its allure. These quasi-mystics became known as *alumbrados* (literally, illumined, in the theological sense of the term), "whose piety emphasized internal prayer and meditation."[96] *Festín*'s similarities with mystical language could be Torres' and/or the women's doing, as both or either Torres and the women could have been attracted to mysticism, employing mystical language here to express patriotic love in the sensual manner common of mystic language, which often modeled itself on the Song of Songs, as in St. John of the Cross' (1542–91) *Cántico espiritual* [*Spiritual Canticle*] (1577). In fact, imitating Song of Songs, stanza thirty-three of St. John's poem reads:

> No quieras depreciarme
> que, si color moreno en mí hallaste,
> ya bien puedes mirarme
> después que me miraste,
> que gracia y hermosura en mi dejaste.[97]

> Despise me not,
> For, if you found Blackness in me,
> You can look at me again
> After looking at me once,
> For you left grace and beauty in me.

---

[96] Jaffary, *False Mystics*, 3; see esp. 1–18 and 47–78.
[97] Version B edited by María de Jesús Mancho Duque.

We can see here how similar *Festín*'s poetic lines are to John's. But in comparison to the biblical text, John's stanza says something different, because in the biblical text the bride does not say "color moreno en mí hallaste" (you found Blackness in me) but rather affirms that she is "Black and beautiful." John's text is a poetical exegesis of Song of Songs 5:1. Finally, the women could have been inspired by Black mystics like the Afro-Peruvian Úrsula de Jesús (1604–66), whose fame was widespread at the time of the women's performance.[98]

The same dancer then perfumed the viceroy with aromatic African incense (*pebete de Guinea*), declaring that although she was not white, her love was so true that it surpassed whiteness:

> Recibe de Guinea
> Este pebete, que en tu luz humea,
> Que aunque el blanco color se me limite,
> Si lo yguala á mi amor, no le compite.[99]

> Receive from Africa
> This incense, which rises up to your light,
> And though white skin is denied me,
> My love cannot compare.

The intended message here is that the women's affection elevates them to the level of the viceroy's light. Nonetheless, this highly sexualized scene is puzzling. As noted previously, from medieval times, the Queen of Sheba was seen as a temptress. Thus the women – and Torres – are able to engineer this highly erotic scene without offending the viceroy's and Novohispanic society's sense of decency. They are able to temper its eroticism by transferring it onto the queen. Moreover, the women's purpose of performing loyalty functioned as an acceptable signifier that permitted this highly erotic embodiment of patriotic love – that is, love of land, king, and his representatives: in other words, the women's declared affection for the viceroy and everything he stood for – the Spanish king and his empire. Fully aware of the Queen of Sheba's ambivalent reputation vis-à-vis her sexuality, and playing with it, we can affirm with Linda Walsh Jenkins, then, that the women's performance was "'authentically female,' 'replete with female signs' and based on a 'bio-grammar' derived from 'experiences [their] body [had] known on the basis of [race and] gender.'"[100]

---

[98] See De Jesús, *The Souls of Purgatory*.   [99] Ibid., fol. 3r.
[100] Jenkins, "Locating the Language of Gender Experience," 6–8.

The fourth dancer carried a placard with an image of a black hand charm: "una mano en forma de higa de azabache" (Figure 4.9).[101] The women offered it to the viceroy to "ward off the effects of the evil eye" ("mal de ojo")[102]:

> Si el azabache obliga
> A que á tu gentileza sirva de higa,
> Recibe por despojo
> La de mi mano contra el mal de ojo.[103]

FIGURE 4.9 Jet black hand charm. Courtesy of Xacopedia

[101] Ibid.   [102] Curcio-Nagy, *Great Festivals*, 60.   [103] Torres, *Festín*, fol. 3r.

If my darkness forces me
To serve as the charm of your kindness,
Take as spoil of war
My hand's charm against the evil eye.

Thought to be "a symbol of fertility from Africa," the black hand charm had been popular in Europe, especially the Iberian Peninsula, since antiquity.[104] This African charm became the symbol of the Black Power movement, to evoke a familiar image. Here, the women reappropriate it as an African symbol and use it to represent their affection for the viceroy. Apropos the women's performance, Curcio-Nagy has argued that "[i]n the end, the women appeared as loyal and submissive, accepting of their subordinate social and legal position in the colonial hierarchy."[105] Yet the agency exercised in this and other parts of the performance seems to disprove this assessment. If the women appeared submissive at other moments, this one suggests an affirmation of their cultural identity and heritage as well as their sociopolitical capital. With the black hand charm, they present themselves as possessors of ancestral knowledge that can keep the viceroy safe from harm. Power here is inverted: the lord is protected by his subjects rather than vice versa. As Jouve Martín has emphasized in response to Curcio-Nagy, "we would be wrong if we saw these festivities only as forms of subordination and acculturation. They were at the same time means by which members of different social groups actively sought to redress or redefine their position in colonial society."[106] And in so doing, they defined their own creole culture.

The use of this charm is also significant because it contrasts sharply with colonial authorities', particularly the Inquisition's, response to Afro-Mexicans' use of African or even Indigenous medical practices. As Sara Vicuña Guengerich points out, "Africans and their descendants used a variety of charms, talismans, and rituals to bring themselves luck and to protect themselves from various maladies; hence, their practices were suspected of being the work of the devil."[107] Indeed, according to Bennett, about 50 percent of all Mexican Inquisition cases were brought against Afro-Mexicans.[108] Many of these cases were brought against Afro-Mexicanas accused of practicing sorcery (*hechicería*) or witchcraft

---

[104] Curcio-Nagy, *Great Festivals*, 60. This charm is very popular in the Caribbean, where it is placed on newborn infants to protect them from the "evil eye."
[105] Curcio-Nagy, *Great Festivals*, 62.   [106] Jouve Martín, "Public Ceremonies," 194.
[107] Guengerich Vicuña, "The Witchcraft Trials of Paula de Eguiluz," 176.
[108] Bennett, *Africans*, 9.

(*brujería*).[109] Reading these cases, however, one can see that most of the time these women were merely practicing herbal medicine and love magic. For example, between 1623 and 1630, María Jerónima, a free (creole) *mulata* from Mexico City, was tried by the Inquisition for sorcery.[110] María Jerónima was a midwife, and her neighbor, an Arara (Dahomeyan) slave named Maria, found her practices suspicious and denounced her to the Inquisition.[111] According to Maria's testimony, when attending to her patients, María Jerónima would mix some things ("menudencias") in a pot. In 1630, María Jerónima was found guilty and sentenced to be exiled from the Americas (for Brazil was also under Spanish rule at this time) in perpetuity ("perpetuamente"). María Jerónima's case points to the suspicion with which colonial authorities regarded Afro-Mexicanas' herbal medicine practices. This is perhaps why the women in the performance chose an African charm that was also common among Iberians, who most likely had forgotten its African origin, but which the Inquisition and the Church still saw as superstition.

The fifth dancer carried a placard with the most enigmatic image of the performance: "Hazia gala de ostentacion el quinto lugar un Sol que haziendo oriente de unas rosas, dexava examinar sus luces de los desvelos de un aguila" (In fifth place, there came a bright sun, who was the light of some roses, allowing an eagle to examine them).[112] This could be another mystical image, where the women are the mystical roses illumined by God's light, the sun. In this sense, the image may have mingled Christian and Nahua theology, alluding specifically to Huitzilopochtli, the Nahua sun god, and the eagle, which denotes Mexico's Aztec past. In this manner, the image is drawn from Mexico's cultural landscape. The roses could also symbolize the Virgin of Guadalupe, who first appeared amid roses to the Indigenous man Juan Diego, according to legend. In the context of the performance, the viceroy is the eagle who studies the women, and the sun could signify the Spanish monarch or

---

[109] See Bristol, *Christian, Blasphemers, and Witches*; Few, *Women Who Live Evil Lives*. On the difference between sorcery and witchcraft for purposes of the Spanish Inquisition, see Vicuña Guengerich, "Paula de Eguiluz."

[110] "Processo criminal contra Maria Geronyma, mulata libre," Mexico City, 1623–30, HL, Mexican Inquisition Papers, Series II, Box 6, HM35165. It is interesting that María Jerónima was denounced by an African-born slave. This could point to other motives, as well as to how fast enslaved Africans learned to navigate colonial society, learning to use its state control apparatuses, such as the Inquisition, to their advantage.

[111] In *Hall of Mirrors*, Laura A. Lewis discusses a case where a Black woman, Ana María, accused another, Adriana, before the Inquisition for being a sorcerer just because Adriana refused Ana María lodging in her inn (1–3).

[112] Torres, *Festín*, fol. 3v.

empire, whom the viceroy represents. Both the women/roses and the viceroy/ eagle then are under the Spanish sun. The women thus invoke a transhispanic symbol of power, for the eagle symbolized both Aztec and Spanish imperial power. This assertion of their Mexicanness underscores and serves as a metaphor of a matured creole Afro-Mexican performative culture. As noted earlier, the women merge the ontic with the mimetic to represent themselves as true Mexicans. Unlike in the performance studied in the previous chapters, they no longer look to Africa, but rather to Mexico for symbolic language to articulate their identities. They represent and embody an African queen, but an African queen who foreshadowed their own cultural journey, now fulfilled. The image could also connect to the next part of the performance, where the women allude to the viceroy as a new Hercules expanding the limits of the known world.

But first, the accompanying text plays with the concepts of light and darkness again. The women tell the viceroy that they are not afraid of his gaze: "No turba gran señor mi negra tinta/ Tu vista clara en mi nacion sucinta" (Your bright gaze, my lord,/ Does not disturb my Black nation).[113] In another play with the concept of Blackness, they then ask the viceroy not to doubt their love and loyalty because of the color of their skin: "No quede, no, señor, mi amor dudoso,/ No viva por ser negro escrupuloso" (Let not my love, my lord, live in doubt,/ Or be scrupulous for my being Black).[114] In this scene, then, the women again assert that their race is capable of supreme love and loyalty, countering the anti-Black narrative that was the currency of the era.

The seventh dancer carried a placard that represented Hercules. This symbolized both Spain and the viceroy as the king's representative in New Spain. The theme of this placard was "Go no further" (*Non plus ultra*), alluding to Hercules setting the limits of the ancient world at the Strait of Gibraltar (the two columns which were incorporated into Spain's coat of arms). In the accompanying text, setting a new limit of the Iberian world, to which the women belonged, the viceroy sets Hercules' columns in New Spain:

> Por mares de explendor navegué estrellas,
> con fuertes remos fatigué la espuma,
> Las Provincias ocultas heri á huellas,
> Las regiones del viento bordé en pluma,
> Por fixar estas dos columnas bellas,
> Y en el Indiano suelo.[115]

---

[113] Ibid. "Tinta," literally ink.   [114] Ibid.   [115] Ibid.

Through splendid sea I sailed under the stars,
Fought the mighty waves,
Traveled through dark regions,
Flew over the wind
To set up these two beautiful columns
On American soil.

Rather than view this as a mimetic act of delimiting possession, I see a possible parallel between the viceroy's Herculean gesture and the women's performance. Like the viceroy's symbolic delimitation of the new Iberian world, the women's performance of the Queen of Sheba's journey could recall the Middle Passage, where and despite which, through Herculean feats of endurance, enslaved Africans held on to their cultural heritage.

The following dancer personified Fortune. Fortune is represented by the moon, which also represents womanhood. In his description, Torres asks, in the narrative portion of the text, "si ay seguridad en palabras mugeriles" (whether a woman's word can be trusted), which illustrates his uneasiness with the women's performance, or women in general, and places him in a long tradition of male clerics (beginning with St. Paul, of course: "Let your women keep silence in the churches" [*mulier tacere in ecclesia*]) uneasy with women's speech.[116] However, the women counter this negative view by asking, in the accompanying text, "si puede aver en amor/ alguna negra ventura" (whether there could be in love any dark fortune).[117] Like the promise to protect the viceroy with the black hand charm, here the women promise to protect him from Fortune's whims. They assure him that their affection and loyalty will keep him safe: "como Luna é de adoraros/ porque la vuestra Vi-llena" (I shall adore thee like the Moon/ For thine I saw full).[118] The Spanish plays with the verb to see ("ver," past tense "vi"), the adjective full ("llena"), and the viceroy's title as marquis, Vi-llena. In the end, however, the women's affection was unable to protect the viceroy, whose tenure was cut short because of his relation to the duke of Braganza, who led Portugal's separation from Spain the same year Villena arrived in New Spain. The all-too-powerful bishop of Puebla, Juan de Palafox y Mendoza (r. 1640–55), who disliked the viceroy, successfully campaigned with Philip III to have Villena recalled to Spain in 1642, where he was later named viceroy of Navarre.[119]

---

[116] Ibid.; KJV, 1 Corinthians 14:34. See Ibsen, *Women's Spiritual Autobiography*, 1–18.
[117] Fol. 4r.   [118] Ibid.
[119] See Romero de Terreros in Gutiérrez de Medina, *Viaje*, viii; Israel, *Razas*, 212–19; Hernández Reyes, "*Festín*," 340n3.

Finally, the diverging voices in this section (Torres' attitude and the women's response) could underscore the women's role in shaping the performance and its text. The text could reflect Torres' desire to reproduce Catholic discourse about female Blackness and female bodies in general and the women's opposing desire to assert their sociopolitical agency and affirm the prowess of their gender to express their empowered Black womanhood.

The final dancer represented a resurrecting phoenix, a symbol of rebirth since antiquity. According to Torres, this is also a symbol of the House of Villena. Phoenixes were also a common feature of the catafalques built for Iberian elites in early modernity.[120] Moreover, in ancient mythology, the phoenix came from Africa.[121] Thus, once more, the women's performance makes visible the transregionality of an ostensibly European symbol. In the accompanying text, a parallel is drawn between the phoenix and the women. In the closing verses of the poem, the Black poetic voice says that, like a phoenix, she will live in fame in the viceroy's flames: "Donde mi amor ordena,/ que me entregue à las brasas de Villena" (My love compels me/ To surrender to Villena's flames).[122] Here the viceroy becomes the fire where the phoenix dies and rises again – another erotic undertone in this very sexually charged text and performance. In the concluding lines of the poem, which may be the most beautiful verses in the whole account, there is a further play on the concept of darkness. Here the poetic voice describes herself as "carbon con alma" (coal with a soul), similar to the bride in Song of Songs, as if saying "I am Black *and* lovely."[123] She, then, is ignitable (coal), but even before she is set aflame by the viceroy's fire (another mystical image), she already possesses a soul – that is, she is a human being, a Christian, in the language of the epoch. Theologically, she and the viceroy are made of the same ontic substance – God's breath. She is both moon and phoenix, a moving and changing thing (moon/woman) with the Christlike power to resurrect (phoenix). Like a phoenix, she will die in the viceroy's fire so that she and her race ("estirpe") can live in fame:

> Siendo carbon,
> Ya de mi estirpe injuria, ó ya borron,

---

[120] See Arbury, "Spanish Catafalques"; Orso, *Art and Death at the Spanish Habsburg Court*; Scott, "The Catafalques of Philip II."

[121] Pliny, *Natural History*, 10.2.   [122] Torres, *Festín*, fol. 4v.

[123] Ibid. This same phrase, "carbon con alma," appears in Claramonte's *El negro* (ca. 1602), published in Barcelona in 1638. Perhaps Torres was familiar with this text.

> Pues ardiendo en tu llama,
> Carbon con alma viviré á la fama.[124]

> Being black as coal,
> Of my race a slander, or an ink blot,
> Burning in your flame,
> Coal with a soul, I will live in fame.

Here the viceroy is mimetically made to represent Solomon as the prefiguration of Christ, who will raise the women's whole nation from the dead on the Last Day. The performance, therefore, was not devoid of theological implications – certainly Torres' doing. However, as much as this may have been Torres' intervention, most of the text suggests that the women were responsible for the greater part of the performance, which availed itself of African elements with which Torres may have not been familiar, such as the incense or black hand charm, though the latter had been thoroughly Iberianized. This resurrection can also serve as a metaphor of the women's cultural identity. They were born on American soil and built a creole identity that has regenerated African elements.

The women too could be prefiguring a future, a bright future for their race. Recall that the performer calls herself "Ya de mi estirpe injuria, ó ya borron" (Of my race a slander, or an ink blot). As a Black woman, she could be a transgressor to her race, a doubly negative force, Black and female, like the Queen of Sheba was seen the Middle Ages. Or, alternatively, she could be a "borron" of her race. I translated "borron" as "ink blot," but that is not its only meaning. As "ink blot," "borron" is synonymous with "transgression." At the time of the women's performance, "borron" also meant "la priméra idéa de los Pintóres, en que están como en bosquéjo y confusas algunas partes de la pintúra" (painters' first idea, where some parts of the painting are present); in other words, "borron" means sketch (*bosquéjo*).[125] Thus the women see themselves as a sketch, or first iteration, of their race, of a future the viceroy/Solomon/Christ will help them (the descendants of the Queen of Sheba) achieve. Therefore, "fama" (fame) also acquires a theological meaning here: salvation. The women thus articulate a utopic/Christian Afrofuturism. The women's love, their faith, will save their whole race. Yet, while Torres, like the missionaries of his time, envisions for the women a future where they are free of the colonial condition in the afterlife,

---

[124] Ibid. The idea of "borron" also appears in Claramonte's *El negro*, further supporting the possibility that Torres was drawing from this text, or that this idea was commonplace in the Iberian world.

[125] *Autoridades* 1:657.

Afro-Mexicans desired this liberty in life, a desire compatible with the building of God's kingdom here on earth. Perhaps the women, and Afrodescendants by extension, had a better understanding of the Gospel than Torres; an understanding *avant la lettere*, of a future where the Gospels' promise of equality ("Love your neighbor as yourself") is fulfilled.[126] Finally, recall that there is also a biblical basis for the Queen of Sheba's presence as a judge in the end times: "At the judgment the Queen of the South will arise with this generation and condemn it."[127] This active role is erased in Torres' imagining of the resurrection of the dead. The women/coal lie passively as they await the viceroy/phoenix's flames. Yet the women's performance exceeds the passivity Torres wants to ascribe to them.

VIVIR A LA FAMA: FROM PERFORMANCE TO PRINT

Festín is dedicated to Enrique Pacheco y Ávila, Knight of the Order of St. James, Captain of the Viceroy's Guard, and Sergeant Major of the Viceroyalty, but it would not be surprising if the women sponsored its publication. This would not be the only example of a group of people of African descent in the early modern Iberian world sponsoring the publication of an account of a festival in which they had played a major role. As Lisa Voigt has analyzed, in 1734, the members of a Black confraternity of the Rosary in Ouro Preto, Minas Gerais, Brazil, sponsored the publication of an account of a festival in which they had played a leading role. The Blacks of Ouro Preto had housed the Eucharist in their church while the city's parish church (*igreja matriz*) was being built. When the church was completed, a great Eucharistic festival took place. The Blacks then sponsored the publication of Simão Ferreira Machado's *Triunfo eucharistico* (*Eucharistic Triumph* English in Voigt, *Spectacular Wealth*, 142;) (Lisbon, 1734), which describes the great pomp that characterized the transfer of the Eucharist from their church to the new church in May of the previous year (Figure 4.10). In the dedication of the account to the Virgin Mary, the members of the confraternity explain what compelled them to sponsor the publication of the account. After speaking about their affection for Mary, the members – speaking through their lettered representative, like Mexico's women did through Torres – turn to the reasons for wanting the account published:

Do mesmo nosso afeto nasceu o desejo, de que tão grande solenidade se publicasse, porque a notícia tem estímulos para o exemplo; e dilatando mais a

---

[126] See Matthew 22:39.   [127] Matthew 12:42; also Luke 11:31.

TRIUNFO
EUCHARISTICO
EXEMPLAR DA CHRISTANDADE LUSITANA
em publica exaltaçaõ da Fé na folemne Trasladaçaõ
DO DIVINISSIMO
SACRAMENTO
da Igreja da Senhora do Rofario, para hum novo Templo
DA SENHORA DO PILAR
EM
VILLA RICA,
CORTE DA CAPITANIA DAS MINAS.
Aos 24. de Mayo de 1733.
DEDICADO A' SOBERANA SENHORA
DO ROSARIO
PELOS IRMÃOS PRETOS DA SUA IRMANDADE,
e a inftancia dos mefmos expofto á publica noticia
Por SIMAM FERREIRA MACHADO
natural de Lisboa, e morador nas Minas.
LISBOA OCCIDENTAL,
NA OFFICINA DA MUSICA, DEBAIXO DA PROTECCAÕ
dos Patriarchas Saõ Domingos, e Saõ Francifco.
M.DCC.XXXIV.
Com todas as licenças neceffarias.

FIGURE 4.10 Title page of *Triunfo eucharisto*, Lisbon, 1734. Courtesy of the Biblioteca Nacional de Portugal

veneração, e glória de vosso Santíssimo Filho, também dilata este motivo de vosso agrado. Esta consideração nos obrigou a solicitar esta pública escritura, em que sempre o nosso afeto esteja referindo em *perpétua lembrança*, e continua narração *aos presentes, e futuros* toda a ordem de tão magnífica solenidade.[128]

The desire was born from our same affection, that such a great solemnity be published, because the news can stimulate by example; and disseminating more the veneration and glory of your Holy Son, this motive of your pleasure will also be

---

[128] Machado, *Triunfo Eucharisto*, s/f; *English in Voigt*, Spectacular *Wealth*, 142; my emphasis.

disseminated. This consideration obliged us to solicit this public writing, in which our affection will always be referred in *perpetual memory*, and such magnificent solemnity in all of its order will be continuously narrated to *those in the present and the future.*

As Voigt observes, "[c]learly the brothers see print ('publica escritura') as another means of contributing to the public good."[129] As the last verse of Torres' account may suggest – "Carbon con alma viviré á la fama" – the Afro-Mexican women may have been guided by the same desire to have their "affection ... referred in perpetual memory," thus serving as an example to their contemporaries and future subjects in the Spanish Empire. Moreover, whereas Ouro Preto's festival took place in the city's streets, the women's performance took place indoors, in a hall of the viceregal palace. Thus they had a more pressing reason for wanting Torres' account published, for only New Spain's elites had been privy to their performance. Perhaps, parallel to what Voigt suggests about *Triunfo eucharistico*, the women "sponsored the publication of a public record of the events, making sure that their festive contribution was more enduring than the festival itself."[130]

In 1747, thirteen years after Ouro Preto, another Black confraternity from Salvador, colonial Brazil's capital until 1763, sponsored the publication of a sermon preached during their celebration of their patron saint, then Blessed (now Saint) Gonzalo Garcia, José dos Santos Cosme e Damião's *Sermam de S. Gonsalo Garcia*. While the members of this confraternity dedicated the prologue to their benefactor, they were no doubt driven to sponsor the publication of that sermon by the same reasons their Ouro Preto's counterparts were – that is, for "perpetual memory" of their devotion to "those in the present and the future," recognizing the endurance and reach of the printed word. We cannot doubt that their Mexican counterparts were motivated by the same reasons. And given the difficulty of publishing something in colonial Latin America, this desire to produce a public record underscores Afro-Latinos' cultural consciousness and awareness of the value of the public archive as a post-factum tribunal on their lives. Through these kinds of records, Afro-Latinos sought to deposit a positive image of themselves in this archive. The women's possible sponsoring of the publication of *Festín* would not be unique in the Iberian Atlantic, and as the publications of such documents were normally sponsored by those who stood to gain

[129] Ibid.   [130] Ibid., 146.

most from them, it would not be far-fetched to entertain that the women sponsored the publication of *Festín*.

This would contrast sharply with the Anglo-Atlantic, for example. Discussing Orlando Patterson's concept of "slavery as social death" with respect to print technology's documentary power to create public memory, Elizabeth Dillon suggests that, while plantation slavery did not mean the social death of slaves, "the social life that emerged in the shadow of such technologies was marked by the structural violence visited on New World Africans by slavery," which, according to Dillon, kept them away from the print public sphere.[131] In other words, while slaves still managed to create a meaningful social existence for themselves in the plantation system, that system did not give them access to print technology as a form of self-representation. The examples cited here show that that was not always the case in the Iberian world.[132]

In sum, then, both the women's performance and Torres' text constitute an invaluable testament to Afro-Mexican women's social and cultural agency in colonial Mexico, especially seventeenth-century Mexico City. Not only did they manage to perform before the highest authority in the land, but they may have also sponsored the publication of the text that immortalized their performance – to borrow Torres' allegory, a Herculean feat given the oppressive sociohistorical context in which they lived. In their performance, the women put in motion their cultural awareness. They selected a legendary feminine figure that allowed them to perform their sexuality within an acceptable signifier – loyalty to the viceroy and everything he represented. Their dance included cultural elements that underscored their Black creole identity – a fusion of African, European, and American cultural elements such as the black hand charm, the phoenix, and the eagle. In the end, then, the women did not perform vassalage, as Curcio-Nagy contends, but rather sexuality, cultural identity, and power – demonstrating through it all their knowledge of Hispanic baroque culture.

---

[131] Dillon, *New World Drama*, 19.

[132] I do not mean to suggest that the women were enslaved – they most likely were free – but rather that in the Iberian world, Blackness did not necessarily imply exclusion from print technology, as it did in the early modern Anglo Atlantic, as Dillon points out. Joanna Brooks has shown that, akin to Black confraternities in the Iberian world, in the early republican United States, secret societies "provided key institutional venues for black entry into the public sphere of print" ("Early American Public Sphere," 82; see Voigt, *Spectacular Wealth*, 193n51). For a Latin American example of what Brooks calls "black counter-publicity," see José Piedra, "Literary Whiteness and the Afro-Hispanic Difference" ("Early American Public Sphere," 75).

Festín is far removed from the tension between Blacks and Europeans that surround the texts discussed in previous chapters. Indeed, no Black revolts or plots were recorded in New Spain during this period.[133] We may wonder, then, if the women would have been able to perform before the viceroy had that not been the case. The examples from 1539 and 1610 – regarding the 1537, 1608, and 1612 perceived plots – suggest that they would.[134] The (apparent) absence of the cloud of suspicion hanging over the women's performance makes their dance a unique example of harmonious master–subject relations in the Americas, while also showing the agency the women exercised in their performance. In the end, then, *Festín* illustrates what agency Afro-Mexican women wielded in the seventeenth century, as well as how Novohispanic creoles adapted African festive practices to baroque culture. *Festín* stands as a final testament of the performative Black creole culture Afro-Mexicans (and by extension colonial Afro-Latin Americans) developed in the diaspora.

[133] Blacks participated in the 1692 revolt, which was initiated and led by members of the Indigenous population. This revolt was chronicled by Carlos de Sigüenza y Góngora in his *Alboroto y motín* (1692).

[134] These examples, more importantly, reveal colonial attitudes toward these performances (see Chapter 2 here).

Conclusion

Where Did the Black Court Go?

Festín is the last text we have about Afro-Mexican festive kings and queens, in public or otherwise. Thus, it marks the culmination of the representation if not of this performance in colonial Mexico City. In 1539, the Black king and queen probably performed in a muddy square. By 1610, that square was cobbled and flanked by majestic public buildings: the cathedral, the *ayuntamiento*, or city hall, the archbishop's residence, and viceregal palace. While many Blacks worked as servants in the viceregal palace, one can imagine how many looked at it from the *plaza mayor* and wondered if they would ever do anything important within its halls. In 1640, a select group of Afro-Mexicanas performed as the Queen of Sheba in its throne room. From 1539 to 1640, Afro-Mexicans moved ever closer to the center of power through this performative genre, though not without setbacks as we saw in Chapter 2. Thus the festivals studied in this book evince not only the evolution of Afro-Mexican culture but also the development of Afro-Mexican sociopolitical action.

Yet one must wonder what became of Afro-Mexican festive kings and queens after 1640. Afro-Mexican festive culture and Black confraternities certainly did not disappear. Neither did New Spain's Black population decrease. According to Bennett, while the slave population declined, the free Black population experienced continual growth, reaching approximately 624,000 or 10 percent of the total population in 1810, the beginning of the end of colonial rule and the start of Mexican independence.[1] So it is hard to explain colonial sources' increased silence about Afro-Mexican festive culture, particularly festival kings and queens, after

[1] Bennett, *Africans*, 1.

1640. We know that Black confraternities remained active in Mexico City at least until independence, and more likely until the anticlerical reforms of 1850, which abolished all religious institutions. For example, a 1706 *memorial* of all of the confraternities in Mexico City listed nine Afro-Mexican *cofradías* (see Table 3.1).[2] These confraternities were active in Mexico City in 1794, when another *memorial* was done.[3] As for festive Black kings and queens, most of the information we have about them from other geographies (Brazil, River Plate, Panama, Peru, New Orleans, New England, and the Caribbean) comes from the eighteenth century. In New Orleans, the practice became today's Mardi Gras Indians.[4] In Brazil and Panama, Black kings and queens are performed pretty much as they were in the colonial period.[5]

Perhaps Mexico City's growing anti-Black animus finally managed to exclude Afro-Mexicans from public festivals. This would constitute an erasure *avant la lettre*, of the sort carried out by white *criollos* after independence as they sought to cast a new national narrative of *whiteness*.[6] While Hernández Cuevas and others argued that Mexico's Black past was erased through the implementation of *mestizaje* as the official state ideology after the Mexican Revolution, the erasure of Afro-Mexican festive culture from the colonial archive after 1640 would demonstrate that *criollos* began excluding Afro-Mexicans from the official discourse before independence.[7] Afro-Mexicans, for example, seem to have been excluded from the well-documented 1680 entry of Tomás de la Cerda y Aragón (see Chapter 4). And Linda A. Curcio-Nagy's study of Novohispanic viceregal entries only offers the example of the Black performance analyzed in Chapter 4 of this book. An alternative answer, however, could be that Afro-Mexican culture became increasingly Mexican, erasing racial lines. Although race remained a great source of anxiety for colonial authorities, the colonial encounter connected colonial subjects in culturally intimate ways. It would have been at this intimate level that the three cultures would merge. A 1702 Inquisition case might suggest this.

On October 16, 1699, in a letter written by her confessor on her behalf, María López de Avilés, an American-born Spanish creole resident of

---

[2] "Memorial de todas las cofradías."   [3] "Censo de todas las cofradías."
[4] See Dewulf, *From the Kingdom of Kongo*.
[5] See Kiddy, *Blacks of the Rosary*; Lund Drolet, *El ritual congo*.
[6] See Reid Andrews, *Afro-Latin America*.
[7] Hernández Cuevas, *African Mexicans*; Sue, *Land of the Cosmic Race*.

Mexico City, informed the Inquisition that she had been told by one Lucas Mercado that a certain mulatto named Isidro de Peralta "hazia en su casa cierta fiesta, o celebridad, a que concurrian variedad de hombres de todas especie" [*sic*] (held a certain fiesta, or ceremony, in his house, which was attended by a variety of men of all kind).[8] In his own testimony, Lucas Mercado testified that

[A]bra como un año, poco mas, o menos, q[ue] este [declarante] tubo noticia y supo q[ue] en la Calle de las Cuadrillas, en una casa q[ue] no save como se nombra el dueno principal de ella, se juntavan diferentes personas y las mas negros y mulatos, y en ella en una sala en q[ue] estava un altar con la ymagen de s[a]n Agustin, uno de ellos en si mesmo haze suva [*sic*] a un puesto como Pulpito, y en el Predicava a los demas, como un cuarto de ora, mas o, menos, y todos estavan callando mientras Predicava, y acavado el sermon, merendavan, hera por la tarde, y por la mañana almorzavan.[9]

[A] year or so ago this witness had news that on Cuadrillas Street, in a house whose owner's name he does not know, [he] met different people, most of them Blacks and mulattoes, in a room where there was an altar of an image of Saint Augustine, and one of them [i.e., of the Blacks] [went] up to a pulpit and preached for about an hour, while all listened attentively, and after the sermon, if it was afternoon, they would have a snack, or if it was morning, they would have lunch.

Mercado added that "el dia de la fiesta del s[an]to depues de ella uvo comida esplendida en di[c]ha casa para los d[ic]hos Congregantes, o, Religiosos y Convidados á costa de los q[ue] llaman sus priores" (on the feast day of their patron saint [i.e., Saint Augustine] [August 28], after the ceremony, there was a splendid meal in the said house for those gathered, at the expense of those they call their priors).[10] Another witness, Juan Pérez de Villagomez, testified that "en d[ic]ha sala, a lo ultimo de ella, estavan unos musicos y dos morenillos de avito colorado q[ue] cantavan y tocavan en d[ic]ha fiesta, y q[ue] según lo q[ue] entendio havia de durar por todo el dia" (in the back of said room [where Isidro preached and they ate] there were some musicians and two Black boys with red robes singing and playing music in the said fiesta, and from what he understands, it [the fiesta] was to last another day).[11] This same witness also declared that Isidro's house was not the only place where this took place, but rather that

---

[8] "El señor fiscal del Santo Oficio contra Ysidro de Peralta," insert, fol. 1r. For a close analysis of this case, see Farman Sweda, "Black Catholicism."

[9] "El señor fiscal del Santo Oficio contra Ysidro de Peralta," fol. 4v.

[10] Ibid., fols. 6v–7r. Feast days taken from *Missale romanum ex decreto sacrosancti concilii tridentini restitutum*, 1634.

[11] "El señor fiscal del Santo Oficio contra Ysidro de Peralta," fol. 9r.

"al modo de la junta q[ue] lleva referida ay otras en diferentes casas y varrios de la ciudad con nombre de Religion" (of the kind of meetings he has referred to there are others in different houses and neighborhoods in this city that they call confraternities).[12]

In his witness testimony, Gabriel Sanabria testified that in these meetings, "vio q[ue] hizieron la ceremonias y exercieron como se hazen en la Terz[e]ra Orden de s[a]n Fran[cis]co" (he saw that they [the Blacks] performed the ceremonies and exercises carried out by the Third Order of Saint Francis). According to most of the witnesses, these ceremonies and exercises consisted of a sermon, reading from "un libro de devocion como mas de media ora ... y a lo ultimo se rezava el rosario" (a devotion book for more than half an hour ... and at the end they would pray the rosary). Another witness, José de Santa María, testified that the mulatto Francisco de Ugalde, who was a "master of music" (*maestro de música*) at his parish (not identified) was among those gathered, and that Isidro was "el yventor y solicitador de las Religiones" (the founder and convener of these confraternities).[13] These four witnesses, perhaps without knowing it, in fact were referring to some of the Black *cofradías* active in Mexico City at the time (see Table 5.1).

All of these confraternities were Black, except for that of the Most Blessed Sacrament, and had existed in Mexico City since the sixteenth century, as discussed in Chapter 1. The Most Blessed Sacrament was among Mexico City's oldest and most prestigious confraternities, making its inclusion in the case surprising.

TABLE 5.1 *Confraternities referenced by the witnesses*

CONFRATERNITY	LOCATION
Saint Ephigenia	Merdecerian convent
Saint Benedict and the Coronation of Christ	Franciscan convent
Saint Nicholas of Toletino	Augustinian convent
Most Blessed Sacrament	Cathedral

SOURCE: "El señor fiscal del Santo Oficio contra Ysidro de Peralta, mulato, por fundar a su modo una religion de san Agustin," Mexico City, 1699, HL, Mexican Inquisition Papers, Series II, Box 6, HM35168, insert

---

[12] Ibid., fol. 9r–9v.   [13] Ibid., fols. 16v–17r.

It appears that Isidro was the *mayordomo* (leader) of the confraternity of Saint Nicholas of Toletino, on whose feast day (September 10) its members would process through the streets of Mexico City. Apparently, in 1699 and in other years, they did this without permission. In fact, this confraternity, one of Mexico City's oldest Black sodalities, was accused of the same offense in 1600 by the diocesan prosecutor for supposedly establishing "una cofradia de disciplina con la cual salieron el juebes santo ... asotandose en forma de prosesion ... llevando estandarte ... sin tener para ello licencia del prelado ni de ministro de su nombre" (a penitent confraternity that came out in procession on Maundy Thursday with its standard and flagellating themselves without having permission from the bishop or a minister in his name).[14] As Nicole von Germeten has discussed, many Afro-Mexican *cofradías* were penitent societies that would process through the streets of Mexican cities and towns during Holy Week, flagellating themselves, for which reason they were known as blood brotherhoods (*cofradías de sangre*).[15] But here, as in other instances, we see colonial authorities singling out Black confraternities for behaving "como los demas" (like the other) "disciplinantes" (penitents), as Viceroy Enríquez put in his 1572 report.[16]

The most serious charge against Isidro and his companions, however, was made by María López de Avilés, who told her confessor that "juntos todos la d[ic]ha casa, empiezan la d[ic]ha fiesta como quienes quieren celebrar la Missa, y despues de varias ceremonias quando llegan al Evangelio, dizen una oracion del santo, segun parece en romance, y otra en latin" (all gathered in the said house, they begin the said ceremony like those who want to say Mass, and after some rituals, when they come to the Gospel, they say a prayer to the saint [Saint Augustine], it seems in Spanish, and another in Latin).[17] These were serious accusations in a society where the Inquisition was charged with upholding orthodoxy and regularly punished those who violated it with public penance and exile. Yet the Inquisition only charged Isidro and his companions of establishing a confraternity and processing through the streets as one without ecclesiastical permission. Isidro's companions, twenty-two persons "de todas especies" (of all kind) were arrested as accomplices (see Table 5.2).

[14] "Contra algunos mulatos que han fundado cofradia y salido en procesion sin licencia," Mexico City, 1600, AGN, BN, vol. 810, exp. 28, fol. 1r.

[15] Germeten, *Black Blood Brothers*, 23–37.

[16] "Carta del virrey Martín Enríquez," fol. 1v.

[17] El señor fiscal del Santo Oficio contra Ysidro de Peralta, fol. 1r–v.

TABLE 5.2 *Persons arrested in Isidro's case*

NAME		RACE	AGE
1.	Alfonso de Pamplona	Mulatto	18
2.	Domingo Felix	Spaniard	20
3.	Manuel Rodríguez	Spaniard	20
4.	Juan Elijo	Mulatto	20
5.	Blas Román	Negro	
6.	Diego de la Villa	Mestizo	22
7.	Pascual Antonio Hernández	Mestizo	
8.	Isidro de Lora	Mulatto	40
9.	Martín López Guerreo	Mulatto	
10.	Miguel Rámirez	Spaniard	20
11.	Ramón de la Candelaria	Spaniard	17
12.	Francisco de Zalazar	Mulatto	21
13.	Juan Felix	Mestizo	21
14.	Nicolás de la Cruz	Spaniard	23–24
15.	Juan Paez	Spaniard	
16.	Juan Antonio Francisco	Mulatto	21–22
17.	Balthasar de los Reyes	Mulatto	22
18.	Juan Baptista	Mulatto	24
19.	Sebastián Gertrudis		
20.	María de la Encarnación	Mulatta	
21.	Catalina de la Rosa	Mulatta	
22.	Ana Maria	Mulatta	

SOURCE: "Autos contra diferentes personas que formavan nueba religion de san Agustin," Mexico City, 1702, HL, Mexican Inquisition Papers, Series II, Box 6, HM35169, sf

When the case went before the Inquisition in 1702, the different confraternities' spiritual directors (an Augustinian monk for that of Saint Nicholas of Tolentino, a Franciscan monk for that of Saint Benedict, a Mercedarian monk for that of Saint Iphigenia, and a priest from the Cathedral for that of the Most Blessed Sacrament) all testified in favor of the accused.[18] Based on this favorable testimony and the facts of the case, the inquisitor concluded that what Isidro and his companions were doing "no resulta cosa de heregia, ni sabor de ella, y que solo pareze haver sido una devoçion yndiscreta" (it is not nor does it look heretical, but only seems to have been an indiscreet devotion), highlighting that Afro-Mexicans' confraternal gatherings and fiestas were "cosa mui corriente y husada en esta ciudad" (a very common and habitual thing in this city).[19]

[18] "Autos contra diferentes personas," sf.   [19] Ibid., sf.

Isidro's case shows Spanish creoles and mestizos engaging in devotion under the leadership of a mulatto. This illustrates the intergroup interactions that took place in colonial society at the quotidian level. The clerics' and the Inquisition's endorsement of Isidro's leadership among Mexico City's confraternities is significant; it means that Church authorities recognized that Afro-Mexicans could lead others in their devotional life, even if their neighbors would not recognize it. This speaks volumes about interethnic relations in colonial Mexico City and underscores the effects of creolization. If the second scenario I proposed is true, Isidro's case shows that Afro-Mexican culture became increasingly integrated into the broader Novohispanic culture. Indeed, as Krystle Farman Sweda's analysis of this case shows, and scholars such as Joan Cameron Bristol, Matthew Restall, Pablo Sierra Silva, and Patrick Carroll, to name a few, have demonstrated, this hypothesis points to the trans-ethnic relations that characterized daily life during the colonial period.[20] This suggests that the intolerance we saw in Chapter 2 did not ultimately prevail, though the Inquisition case shows that suspicions lingered. Yet the case also demonstrates that Afro-Mexican festive and confraternal practices became more accepted, at least in certain circles. Perhaps this is what an Afro-futuristic horizon looked like for Afro-Mexicans.

Regardless of what we conclude about the post-1640 silence about Afro-Mexicans' festive culture, the performances studied in this book constitute an important early record of Black culture in colonial Mexico, Spanish America, and, ultimately, the Atlantic. They illumine Afrodescendants' festive lives in a period that has received very little scholarly attention in Black studies. The texts discussed in the foregoing chapters showed how festive Black kings and queens took hold and changed during these early years of the diaspora. Studying this tradition in its earliest years, this book invites scholars to further examine the early genealogy of this festive practice in particular and of Afrodescendants' first century in the Americas in general.

More importantly, *Sovereign Joy* seeks to show how diasporic Afrodescendants expressed their collective creole subjectivities through this festive genre. As exposed in the Preface, in a recent piece in *The Atlantic*, Imani Perry asserts that "Blackness is an immense and defiant

---

[20] Farman Sweda, "Black Catholicism"; Bristol "Afro-Mexican Saintly Devotion"; Carroll, "Black–Native Relations" and "Los mexicanos negros"; Restall, *Black Middle*; Sierra Silva, *Urban Slavery*, 144–76.

joy."[21] The performances studied in the preceding chapters demonstrate how Afro-Mexicans and their counterparts in other latitudes joyfully defied a zeitgeist that told them that – as state terror has done since the dawn of the modern era – they did not matter, their lives did not matter. And what is more defiant than to perform as a sovereign people "with their king and queen" in and before such a world?

[21] Perry, "Racism Is Terrible."

APPENDIX
Persons Charged in 1609

NAME	RACE	STATUS	MASTER/ EMPLOYER	OCCUPATION	SUPPOSED ROYAL TITLE	ADDITIONAL INFORMATION
			Apprehended			
1. Martín	Black (*negro*)	Slave	Balthasar Reyes		King	
2. Bernabé	Black	Slave	Cristóbal de Oñate		Count of Monterrey and Captain of the Guard	
3. Juan Biasara	Mulatto	Slave	Martín de Zaro		Queen's Stable Master	
4. Pedro	Black	Slave	Hernando Matias de Rivera		Porter and Queen's Jester	
5. Juan Quelelele	Mulatto	Slave	Cristóbal de Gudiel		Juan of Austria	
6. Diego	Mulatto	Slave	Cristóbal de Gudiel		Duke and the King's Secretary	
7. Domingo Pérez	Mulatto	Free			Transylvanian Prince	Melchiora de Monterrey's brother
8. Juan Payo	Black	Slave	Francisco Payo		Duke	
9. Francisco de Loya	Mulatto	Free	Viceroy	Pastry Chef		The one who crowned the king and queen

#	Name	Color	Status				Notes
10.	Balthasar de Contreras	Mulatto	Free	Juan Cano		Duke of Chacona and Guadalupe	Possibly a musician since *chacona* (*xacona*) is a musical term
11.	Diego Mártinez	Mulatto	Slave	Novice of San Jerómino		Member (*Criado*) of the Royal Household	
12.	Diego Martín	Mulatto	Free		Tailor	Member of the Royal Household	
13.	Sebastián Gómez	Mulatto	Free	Archbishop	Pastry Chef	Member of the Royal Household	
14.	Thomas de Campos	Mulatto	Free			Marquess of Montes Claros and Captain General (*Adelantado*) of Castile	
15.	Martín de Coca	Black	Slave	Apothecary's Daughter		Member of the Royal Household	
16.	Luis	Black	Slave	Gonzalo Gutiérrez		Count of Barajas	
17.	Balthasar de los Reyes	Black	Slave	Cristóbal Osorio		Prince of Portugal	
18.	Juan	Black	Slave	Gaspar Bello de Acuña		Captain General	
19.	Diego de Castro	Black	Freed		Gambling House Owner	Member of the Royal Household	
20.	Jorge de Alvarado	Black	Free		Welder	Member of the Royal Household	
21.	Diego	Black	Free		Cobbler		
22.	Simón Hernández	Mulatto	Slave	Chief Bailiff of the Royal Tribunal			

(continued)

NAME	RACE	STATUS	MASTER/ EMPLOYER	OCCUPATION	SUPPOSED ROYAL TITLE	ADDITIONAL INFORMATION
23. Lázaro de Mendiola	Mulatto	Slave	Chief Bailiff of the Royal Tribunal			Attacked for shouting "Long live King Philip III, Our Lord!"
24. Melchiora de Monterrey, in whose house the Christmas Eve 1609 party was held	Black (*negra*)	Free			Queen	
25. Petrona	Black	Free			Queen's Lady-in-Waiting	
26. Isabel	Mulatta	Free			Duchess	
27. Leonor	Black	Free			Duchess	
28. Juana	Mulatta	Free			Duchess	
29. Juana	Mulatta	Free			Princess	
30. Felipa	Mulatta	Freed			Member of the Royal Household	Leonor's mother
At Large						
31. María de Monterrey	Black	Slave	Geronimo Lopez Osorio		Princess of Portugal	Possibly related to Domingo Pérez and Melchiora
32. Beatriz de los Reyes	Black	Slave	Juan de Basán Velásquez		Duchess	

	Race	Status	Owner	Title	Notes
33. Leonor	Mulatta	Free		Moorish Queen	
34. Isabel	Mulatta	Slave		Queen's Maid	
35. Francisca de Mendoza	Black	Free	Ana de Castilla	Ambassador	
36. Catalina	Mulatta	Freed		Marquess of Ayamonte	
37. Isabel	Mulatta	Freed			
38. Pascual de Torres	Mulatto	Free		Count	Silversmith
39. Antón de Dios	Black	Slave		Queen's Chamberlain	
40. Juan de León	Mulatto	Free	María Viuda de Soto	Prince of Chacano	Possibly a musician, for reasons stated earlier
41. García	Black	Free		Marquess of Portugal and Queen's Servant	Creole
42. Juan Ochoa	Mulatto	Free		Member of the Royal Household	
43. Diego Báez	Mulatto	Free		President of Castile	Rope maker (cordonero)
44. Francisco	Black	Slave		Duke and Marquess of Cañete	
45. An old mulatto	Mulatto	Free			
46. Lázaro de Caçena	Spaniard	N/A			
47. Juan de Páredes	Spaniard	N/A		Count of Fist in Face	
48. Juan Pérez	Mulatto	Free		Dom Sebastian of Portugal	
49. Francisco	Black	Slave	Ana de la Fuente		

SOURCE: "Carta de López de Azoca, alcalde del crimen de la Audiencia de México," Mexico City, February 8, 1609, AGI, Mexico 73, R. 1, N. 4, fols. 5 v–6 v

Bibliography

PRINTED PRIMARY SOURCES

Actas del cabildo de la ciudad de México [1524–1809], edited by Ignacio Bejarano. Mexico City: Aguilar & Hijos, 1889–1911. 54 vols.

Ajofrín, Francisco de. *Diario del viaje que por orden de la sagrada Congregación de Popaganda Fide hizo a América septentrional em el siglo XVIII* [1763–6], edited by Vicente Castañeda y Alcover. Madrid: Real Academia de la Historia, 1958. 2 vols.

Alegre, Francisco Javier. *Historia de la provincia de la Comapñía de Jesús de Nueva España* [1566–1766], edited by Ernest J. Burrus and Feliz Zubillana. Rome: Institutum Historicum S.J., 1956–60. 4 vols.

St. Ambrosde. *De Noe et arca* [4th cent.]. Documenta Catholica Omnia. http://www.documentacatholicaomnia.eu/04z/z_0339-0397__Ambrosius__De_Noe_Et_Arca_Liber_Unus__LT.pdf.html

Antonil, André João. *Brazil at the Dawn of the Eighteenth Century*, translated by Timothy J. Coates. Dartmouth: Tagus, 2012.

    Cultura e opulência do Brasil, por suas drogas, e minas. Lisbon: Deslandesiana, 1711.

Aquinas, Thomas. *Super epistolam ad Romanos* [13th cent.] Documenta Catholica Omnia. http://www.documentacatholicaomnia.eu/04z/z_1225-1274__Thomas_Aquinas__Super_Epistolam_ad_Romanos_Lectura__LT.pdf.html

Augustine. *Confessions* [4th cent.], translated by Carolyn J.-B. Hammond. Cambridge, MA: Harvard University Press, 2014. 2 vols.

Baerle, Caspar van. *The History of Brazil Under the Governorship of Count Johan Maurits of Nassau, 1636–1644*, translated by Blanche T. van Berckel-Ebeling Koning. Gainesville: University Press of Florida, 2011.

    Rerum per octennium in Brasilia et alibi gestarum sub praefectura illustrissimi comitis I. Mauritii Nassaviaeetc. comitis historia. Amsterdam: Silberling, 1660.

Bautista Méndez, Juan. *Crónica de la provincial de Santiago de México de la Orden de Predicadores, (1521–1564),* edited by Justo Alberto Fernández. Mexico City: Porrua, 1993.

Benzoni, Girolamo. *Breve extracto do augustissimo triunfo, que a augusta Braga prepara em obsequio do Santissimo Sancramento.* Coimbra: Colegio das Artes da Companhia de Jesu, 1731.

La historia del mondo nuovo. Venice: Collegio della Illustrissima Signoria di Venezia, 1565.

History of the New World, translated by W. H. Smyth. Boston: Adamant Media Corporation, 2005.

St. Bernard of Clairvaux. *Sermones in Cantica Canticorum* [12th cent.]. Documenta Catholica Omnia. www.documentacatholicaomnia.eu/03d/1090-1153,_Bern ardus_Claraevallensis_Abbas,_Sermones_in_Cantica_Canticorum,_LT.pdf

Calmon, Francisco. *Relação das fautíssimas festas que celebrou a Câmara da Vila de Nossa Senhora da Purificição, e Santo Amaro da Comarca da Bahia pelos augistíssimos desposórios da Sereníssima Senhora Dona Maria, Princesa do Brasil, com o Seréníssimo Senhor Dom Pedro, Infante de Portugal.* Lisbon: Miguel Manescal da Costa, 1762.

Carrió de la Vandera, Alonso. *El lazarillo de ciegos caminantes* [1776], edited by Antonio Lorente Medina. Caracas: Ayacucho, 1985.

Carvajal y Robles, Rodrigo de. *Fiestas de Lima por el nacimiento del principe Baltasar Carlos, Lima, 1632,* edited by Francisco López Estrada. Seville: Escuela de Estudios Hispano-Americanos, 1950.

Cavazzi da Montecuccolo, Giannantonio. *Istorica descrizione de' tre regni Congo, Matamba et Angola, situati nell'Etiopia inferiore occidentale e delle missioni apostoliche esercitatevi da religiosi capuccini.* Bologna: Giacomo Monti, 1687.

C'est la deduction du sumptueux ordre plaisantz spectacles et magniques théâtres dressés et exhibés par les citoiens de Rouen, ville métropolitaine du pays de Normandie a la Sacrée Majesté du Treschristian Roy de France, Henry second leur souverain Seigneur, et à Tres illustre dame, ma Dame Katharine de Medicis, La Royne son épouse. Rouen: Robert le Hoy, 1551.

Chimalpahin, Domingo. *Annals of His Time* [17th cent.], edited by James Lockhart, Doris Namala, and Susan Schroeder. Stanford, CA: Stanford University Press, 2006.

Diario, edited by Rafael Tena. Mexico City: CONACULTA, 2001.

Cobarrubias Orozco, Sebastián de. *Tesoro de la lengua castellana o española.* Madrid: Luis Sánchez, 1611.

Colección de documentos inéditos de la Corona de Aragón, edited by Próspero Bofarull y Mascaré. Barcelona: José Eusebio Monfort, 1851. 8 vols.

Columbus, Christopher. *Diario de a bordo,* [1492], edited by Luis Arranz Márquez. Madrid: Historia 16, 1991.

Consejo Provincial de Lima. *Libros de cabildos de Lima: Libro cuarto, años 1548–1553.* Lima: Impresores San Martín, 1935.

Cruz, San Juan de la. *Cántico espiritual y poesía completa* [16th cent.], edited by Paola Elia, Marías Jesús Machado Duque, and Domingo Ynduráin. Barcelona: Crítica, 2002.

Damião, José dos Santos Cosme e. *Serman de S. Gonsalo Garcia, pregado no terceiro dia do solenissimo triduo, que celebrão os homens pardos de cidade da Bahai na cathedral da mesma cidade.* Lisbon: Miguel Rodrigues, 1747.

Dávila y Padilla, Agustín. *Historia de la fundación y discurso de la provincial de Santiago de México de los Predicadores, etc.* [1596]. Brussels: Ivan de Meerbeque, 1625.

De Jesús, Úrsula. *The Souls of Purgatory: The Spiritual Diary of a Seventeenth-Century Afro-Peruvian Mystic, Úrsula de Jesús* [seventeenth century], edited by Nancy E. van Deusen. Albuquerque: University of New Mexico Press, 2004.

Díaz del Castillo, Bernal. *Historia verdadera de la conquista de la Nueva España (manuscrito "Guatemala")* [1575], edited by José Antonio Barbón Rodríguez. Mexico City: Colegio de México and Universidad Nacional Autónoma de México, 2005.

Diccionario de Autoridades. Madrid: Real Academia Española, 1726–1739.

Duran i Sanpere, Agustí, and Josep Sanabre, eds. *Llibre de les Solemnitats de Barcelona.* Barcelona: Institució Patxot, 1930. 2 vols.

Fernandes, Gaspar. *Cancionero musical,* edited by Aurelio Tello. Havana: Casa de las Américas, 2001.

Figgis, John Neville. *Divine Right of Kings [1896].* London: Forgotten Books, 2019.

Folheto de ambas Lisboas. Lisbon: Oficina de Música, 1730–1.

Franco Silva, Alfonso. *Regesto documental sobre la esclavitud sevillana (1453–1513).* Seville: Universidad de Sevilla, 1979.

Gage, Thomas. *The English–American, His Travail by Sea and Land, or a Survey of the West India's.* London: R. Cotes, 1648.

Gestoso y Pérez, José. *Curiosidades antiguas sevillanas.* Seville: El Universal, 1885.

Los Reyes Católicos en Sevilla (1477–78). Seville: Revista de Tribunales, 1891.

Guerreiro, Afonso. *Das festas que se fizeram na cidade de Lisboa, na entrada del Rey D. Philippe primeiro de Portugal.* Lisbon: Francisco Correa, 1581.

Guimarães, João Ribeiro. *Summario de varia historia: Narrativas, lendas, biographias, descripcões de templos e monumentos, estadisticas, costumes, civis, politicos e religiosos de outras eras.* Lisbon: Rolland & Semoind, 1872. 5 vols.

Gutiérrez de Medina, Cristóbal. *Viage de tierra, y mar, feliz por mar, y tierra, que hizo el Excellentísimo Señor Marqués de Villena, mi señor, yendo por Virrey, y Capitán General de la Nueva España.* Mexico City: Juan Ruiz, 1640.

Viaje del Virrey Marqués de Villena, edited by Manuel Romero de Terreros. Mexico City: Imprenta Universitaria, 1947.

Herodotus. *Histories* [430 BCE], edited by Aubrey De Sélincourt and John Marincola. London: Penguin Books, 2003.

Hippocrates. *Airs Waters Places* [4th cent. BCE]. In *Hippocrates,* vol. 1, edited by William Henry Samuel Jones, Edward Theodore Withington and Paul Potter, Cambridge, MA: Harvard University Press, 1984. 65–138.

The Holy Bible: New International Version. Grand Rapids, MI: Zondervan, 1978.

Icaza, Francisco A. *Conquistadores y pobladores de Nueva España: Diccionario autobiográfico sacado de los textos originales*. Madrid: Imprenta de El Adelantado de Segovia, 1923. 2 vols.

Inés de la Cruz, Sor Juana. *Neptuno alegórico*, edited by Electa Arenal and Vincent Martin. Madrid: Cátedra, 2009.

The Interlinear Bible, edited by Jay P. Green. Grand Rapids, MI: Baker Book House, 1981.

Josephus, Flavius. *The Antiquities of the Jews* [94 CE], translated by William Whiston. Lanham, MD: Start, 2013.

Lucena Salmoral, Manuel, ed. *Regulación de la esclavitud negra en las colonias de América Española (1503–1886): Documentos para su estudio*. Acalá de Henares: University of Acalá/University of Murcia, 2005.

Machado, Simão Ferreira. *Triunfo Eucharistico, Exemplar da Christandade Lusitana na publica exaltaçaõ da Fé na solemne Trasladaçaõ do Divinissimo Sacramento da Igreja da Senhora do Rosario, para hum novo Templo da Senhora do Pilar em Villa Rica, Corte da Capitania das Minas*. Lisbon: Officina da Música, 1734.

Mascarenhas, José Freire Monterroio. *Relaçam da embayxada, que o poderoso rey de Angome, Kiay Chiri Bronco Senhor dos dilatadissimos Sertoens de Guiné Mandou ao Illustrissimo e Excellentissimo Senhor D. Luiz Peregrino de Ataide, etc.* Lisbon: Francisco da Silva, 1751.

Mendoza, Blanca, Victor Velasco, and Ernesto Jáuregui. "A Study of Historical Droughts in Southeastern Mexico." *Journal of Climate* 19.12 (2006): 2916–34.

Mercado, Tomás de. *Summa de tratos, y contratos*. Seville: Hernando Díaz, 1571.

Missale romanum ex decreto sacrosancti concilii tridentini restitutum. Rome: Vatican Press, 1634.

Monumenta mexicana [1571–1605], edited by Felix Zubilaga. Rome: Society of Jesus, 1956–91. 8 vols.

Monumenta missionaria africana [1471–1699], edited by António Brásio. Lisbon: Agência Geral das Colônias, 1951–88. Series 1, 15 vols.

Moreto y Cavana, Augustín. *Loas, entremeses y bailes*, edited by María Luisa Lobato. Kassel: Reichenberger, 2003.

Muñoz, Andrés. *Viaje de Felipe Segundo á Inglaterra* [1554]. Madrid: Sociedad de Bibliófilos Españoles, 1877.

New American Bible. Washington, DC: US Conference of Catholic Bishops, 2002.

Ojea, Fernando. *Libro tercero de la historia religiosa de la Provincia de México de la Orden de Santo Domingo* [1550–76]. Mexico City: Museo Nacional, 1907.

Ortiz de Zuñiga, Diego. *Anales eclesiásticos y seculares de la muy noble y muy leal ciudad de Sevilla que contienen sus más principales memorias desde el año de 1246 hasta el de 1671*. Madrid: Royal Printing Office, 1677.

Paré, Ambroise. *Les oeuvres*. Paris: Veusue Gabriel Buon, 1598.

Pérez de Rivas, Andrés. *Corónica y historia religiosa de la provincia de la Compañía de Jesús en Nueva España* [ca. 1600–50]. Mexico City: Sagrado Corazón, 1896. 2 vols.

Pigafetta, Filippo, and Eduardo Lopes. *Relatione del reame di Congo et delle circonvicine contrade*. Rome: Bartolomeo Grassi, 1591.

Relazione del reame di Congo, edited by Giorgio R. Cardona. Milano: Bompiani, 1978.

Relatione del reame di Congo et delle circonvicine contrade. Fascimile edition. Paris: Hachette/BNF, 2012.

Le royaume de Congo & les contrées environnantes (1591), edited by Willy Bal. Paris: Chandeigne, 2002.

Pliny the Elder. *Natural History* [1st cent. CE], edited by Harris Rackham. Cambridge, MA: Harvard University Press, 1938–63. 10 vols.

Recopilación de leyes de los reynos de las Indias mandadas imprimir y publicar por la Magestad Católica del rey Don Carlos III, Nuestro Señor [1681]. Madrid: Viuda de D. Juanquín Ibarra, 1791.

Relacíon de las fiestas que en la ciudad de Lima se hizieron por la beatificación del bienaventurado Padre Ignacio de Loyola, fundador de la Compañía de Jesús. Lima: Francisco del Canto, 1610.

Relacíon de las fiestas que en la ciudad del Cuzco se hizieron por la beatificación del bienaventurado Padre Ignacio de Loyola, fundador de la Compañía de Jesús. Lima: Francisco del Canto, 1610.

Relación muy verdadera sobre las pazes y concordia que entre Su Magestad y el Christianísimo Rey de Francia passaron, y las fiestas y reçibimiento que se hizo a Su Magestad en la Villa de Aguas Muertas, a XIV y XV de Julio de MDXXXVIII. Madrid: (unknown printer) 1538.

Rikel, Dinisio de. *Compendio breve que trata de la manera de como se han de hazer las processiones.* Mexico City: Juan Cromberger, 1544.

Rivera Cambas, Manuel. *México pintoresco, artístico y monumental.* Mexico City: Imprenta de la Reforma, 1880–3. 3 vols.

Royal Spanish Academy. *Diccionario de Autoridaes.* Madrid: Francisco Relación del Hierro, 1726–39. 6 vols.

Sánchez, Herrero J., and González S. M. Pérez. *CXIX reglas de hermandades y cofradías: Siglos XIV, XV y XVI.* Huelva: Universidad de Huelva, 2002.

Sandoval, Alonso de. *De instauranda aethiopum salute: El mundo de la esclavitud negra en América* (1627), edited by Ángel Valtierra. Bogota: Empresa Nacional, 1956.

Naturaleza, policia sagrada y profana, costumbres y ritos, disciplina y catecismo evangélico de todos etiopes. Seville: Francisco de Lira, 1627.

Tomo primero De instauranda Aethiopum salute: Historia de Aethipia, naturaleza, policia sagrada y profana, costumbres y ritos, disciplina y catecismo evangélico de todos aetíopes, conque se restaura la salud de sus almas. Madrid: Alonso de Paredes, 1647.

Un tratado sobre la esclavitud [1627], edited by Enriqueta Vila Vilar. Madrid: Alianza, 1987.

Treatise on Slavery: Selections from De Instauranda Aethiopum Salute [1627], edited by Nicole von Germeten. Indianapolis: Hackett, 2008.

Sigüenza y Góngora, Carlos de. *Alboroto y motín de México del 8 de junio de 1692: Relación de don Carlos de Sigüenza y Góngora en una carta dirigida al almirante don Andrés de Pez* [1692]. México City: Instituto Nacional de Antropología e Historia, 1932.

Teatro de virtudes [1680], edited by Alejandro Montiel Bonilla. Puebla: Secretaría de Cultura de Puebla, 1999.

Strabo. *Geography* [1st cent. CE], edited by Horace Leonard Jones. Cambridge, MA: Harvard University Press, 1917–35. 8 vols.

Torquemada, Juan de. *Monarchia indiana con el origen y guerras de los indios occidentales, de sus poblaçiones, descubrimiento, conquista, conuersión, y otras cosas marauillosas de la mesma tierra, etc.* [1615]. Madrid: Nicolás Rodríguez Franco, 1723. 3 vols.

Torres, Nicolás de. *Festín hecho por las morenas criollas de la muy noble, y muy leal Ciudad de México al recibimiento, y entrada del Excellentísimo Señor Marqués de Villena, Duque de Escalana, Virrey de esta Nueva España. etc.* Mexico City: Francisco Robledo, 1640.

Vieira, António. *Sermões.* Porto: Lello & Irmão, 1959. 5 vols.

Voragine, Jacobus de. *The Golden Legend or Lives of the Saints* [1501], edited by Frederick S. Ellis. London: Temple Classics, 1931.

SECONDARY SOURCES

Adorno, Rolena. *Guaman Poma: Writing and Resistance in Colonial Peru.* Austin: University of Texas Press, 2000.

Polemics of Possession in Spanish American Narrative. New Haven, CT: Yale University Press, 2014.

Aguirre Beltrán, Gonzalo. *Cuijila: Esbozo etnográfico de un pueblo.* Mexico City: Fondo de Cultura Económica, 1989.

El negro esclavo en Nueva España. Mexico City: Fondo de Cultura Económica, 1989.

La población negra de Mexico, 519–1810: Estudio etnohistórico [1946]. Mexico City: Fondo de Cultura Económica, 1989.

Alegría, Ricardo E. *Juan Garrido, el Conquistador Negro en las Antillas, Florida, México y California, c. 1503–1540.* San Juan: Centro de Estudios Avanzados de Puerto Rico y El Caribe, 1990.

Alenda y Mira, Jenaro. *Relaciones de solemnidades y fiestas públicas de España.* Madrid: Sucesores de Rivadeneyra, 1903.

Alencastro, Luiz Felipe de. *O trato dos viventes: Formação do Brasil no Atlântico Sul, séculos XVI e XVII.* Sao Paulo: Companhia das Letras, 2006.

Alkmim, Tania. "Falas e cores: Um estudo sobre o português de negros e escravos no Brasil do século XIX." In *História da língua nacional,* edited by Laura do Carmo and Ivana Stolze Lima. Rio de Janeiro: Casa de Rui Barbosa, 2008. 247–64.

Alves, Marieta. *Mestres ourives de ouro e prata da Bahia.* Salvador: Museu do Estado, 1962.

Anderson, Benedict. *Imagined Communities: Reflections on the Origin and Spread of Nationalism.* London: Verso, 1991.

Andrés-Gallego, José, and Jesús M. García. *La Iglesia y la esclavitud de los negros.* Pamplona: Universidad de Navarra, 2002.

Arbury, Andrew S. "Spanish Catafalques of the Sixteenth and Seventeenth Centuries." PhD thesis. University of Michigan, 1993.

Araújo, Emanoel. *A mão afro-brasileira: Significado da contribuição artística e histórica.* Sao Paulo: Técnica Nacional de Engenharia, 1988.

Arellano, Ignacio. "América en las fiestas jesuitas: celebraciones de San Ignacio y San Francisco Javier." *Nueva Revista de Filología Hispánica* 56.1 (2008): 53–86.

Estructuras dramáticas y alegóricas en los autos de Calderón. Pamplona: Kassel, 2001.

Arellano, Ignacio, and Ana M. Pereira. *Emblemática y religión en la península ibérica (Siglo de Oro).* Pamplona: University of Navarra, 2010.

Arenal, Electa. "Sor Juana's Arch: Public Spectacle, Private Battle." In *Crossing Boundaries: Attending to Early Modern Women,* edited by Jane Donawerth and Adele Seeff. Cranbury, NJ: Associated University Presses, 2000. 173–94.

Armenteros Martínez, Iván. "La esclavitud en Barcelona a fines de la Edad Media (1479–1516): El impacto de la primera trata atlántica en un mercado tradicional de esclavos." PhD thesis, Universitat de Barcelona, 2012.

"De hermandades y procesiones: La cofradía de esclavos y libertos negros de Sant Jaume de Barcelona y la asimilación de la negritud en la Europa premoderna (siglos XV–XVI)." *Clio: Revista de Pesquisa Histórica* 29.2 (2012). http://hdl.handle.net/10261/65499

Atkins, Jennifer. *New Orleans Carnival Balls: The Secret Side of Mardi Gras, 1870–1920.* Baton Rouge: Louisiana State University Press, 2017.

Baker, Geoffrey. "The Resounding City." In *Music and Urban Society in Colonial Latin America,* edited by Geoffrey Baker and Tess Knighton. Cambridge: Cambridge University Press, 2011. 1–20.

Bakhtin, Mikhail M. *Rabelais and His World,* translated by Hélène Iswolsky. Bloomington: Indiana University Press, 1984.

Barranco, Marga G., and Aurelia Martín Casares. "The Musical Legacy of Black Africans in Spain: A Review of Our Sources." *Anthropological Notebooks* 2 (2009): 51–60.

Bastide, Roger. *African Civilisations in the New World,* translated by Peter M. Green. New York: Harper & Row, 1972.

Bauer, Ralph, and Joseé A. Mazzotti. *Creole Subjects in the Colonial Americas: Empires, Texts, Identities.* Chapel Hill: University of North Carolina Press, 2012.

Becco, Horacio J. *El tema del negro en cantos, bailes y villancicos de los siglos XVI y XVII.* Buenos Aires: Ollantay, 1951.

Bennett, Herman L. *African Kings and Black Slaves: Sovereignty and Dispossession in the Early Modern Atlantic.* Philadelphia: University of Pennsylvania Press, 2019.

Africans in Colonial Mexico: Absolutism, Christianity, and Afro-creole Consciousness, 1570–1640. Bloomington: Indiana University Press, 2003.

Colonial Blackness: A History of Afro-Mexico. Bloomington: Indiana University Press, 2009.

Bernand, Carmen. *Negros esclavos y libres en las ciudades hispanoamericanas.* Madrid: Fundación Histórica Tavera, 2010.

Bernasconi, Robert, and Tommy L. Lott, eds. *The Idea of Race*. Indianapolis, IN: Hackett, 2000.

Bettelheim, Judith. "Carnaval of Los Congos of Portobelo, Panama: Feathered Men and Queens." In *African Diasporas in the New and Old Worlds: Consciousness and Imagination*, edited by Geneviève Fabre. Amsterdam: Rodopi, 2006. 187–309.

Bindman, David, Henry L. Gates, and Karen C. C. Dalton. *The Image of the Black in Western Art*. Cambridge, MA: Harvard University Press, 2010. 5 vols.

Blumenthal, Debra. "*La Casa dels Negres*: Black African Solidarity in Late Medieval Valencia." In *Black Africans in Renaissance Europe*, edited by Thomas F. Earle and Kate J. P. Lowe. Cambridge: Cambridge University Press, 2005. 225–46.

Borges, Célia Maia. *Escravos e libertos nas irmandades do Rosário: Devoção e solidariedade em Minas Gerais, séculos XVIII e XIX*. Juiz de Fora: Editora Universidade Federal Juiz de Fora, 2005.

Borucki, Alex. *From Shipmates to Soldiers: Emerging Black Identities in the Río de la Plata*. Albuquerque: University of New Mexico Press, 2015.

Borucki, Alex, David Eltis, and David Wheat, eds. *From the Galleons to the Highlands: Slave Trade Routes in the Spanish Americas*. Albuquerque: University of New Mexico Press, 2020.

Boschi, Caio César. *Os leigos e o poder: Irmandades leigas e política colonizadora em Minas Gerais*. Sao Paulo: Ática, 1986.

Bowersox, Jeff, and Astrid Khoo. "Blackening the Queen of Sheba (ca. 1402–1405)." Black Central Europe. https://blackcentraleurope.com/sources/1000-1500/blackening-the-queen-ofsheba-before–1405

Bowser, Frederick P. *The African Slave in Colonial Peru, 1524–1650*. Stanford, CA: Stanford University Press, 1974.

Boxer, Charles R. *The Dutch in Brazil, 1624 to 1654*. Oxford: Clarendon, 1957.

Brásio, António. *Os prêtos em Portugal*. Lisbon: Agência Geral das Colónias, 1944.

Braun, Harald, and Magallón J. Pérez. *The Transatlantic Hispanic Baroque: Complex Identities in the Atlantic World*. Farnham: Ashgate, 2014.

Brewer-García, Larissa. *Beyond Babel: Translations of Blackness in Colonial Peru and New Granada*. Cambridge: Cambridge University Press, 2020.

"Hierarchy and Holiness in the Earliest Colonial Black Hagiographies: Alonso de Sandoval and His Sources." *William and Mary Quarterly* 76.3 (2019): 477–508.

Bristol, Joan C. "Afro-Mexican Saintly Devotion in a Mexico City Alley." In *Africans to Spanish America: Expanding the Diaspora*, edited by Sherwin K. Bryant, Rachel S. O'Toole, and Ben Vinson III. Urbana: University of Illinois Press, 2014. 114–35.

Christians, Blasphemers, and Witches: Afro-Mexican Ritual Practices in the Seventeenth Century. Albuquerque: University of New Mexico Press, 2007.

Bristol, Michael D. *Carnival and Theater: Plebian Culture and the Structure of Authority in Renaissance England*. New York: Methuen, 1985.

Brooks, Joanna. "The Early American Public Sphere and the Emergence of a Black Print Counterpublic." *William and Mary Quarterly* 62.1 (2005): 67–26.

Buisseret, David, and Steven G. Reinhardt. *Creolization in the Americas*. College Station: Texas A&M University Press, 2000.

Burns, Kathryn. "Unfixing Race." In *Histories of Race and Racism: The Andes and Mesoamerica from Colonial Times to the Present*, edited by Laura Gotkowitz. Durham, NC: Duke University Press, 2012. 57–71.

Camacho Martínez, Ignacio. *La hermandad de los mulatos de Sevilla: Antecedentes históricos de la Hermandad del Calvario*. Seville: Ayuntamiento de Sevilla, 2001.

Camba Ludlow, Úrsula. *Imaginarios ambiguos, realidades contradictorias: Conductas y representaciones de los negros y mulatos novohispanos, siglos XVI y XVII*. Mexico City: Colegio de México, 2008.

Campt, Tina. *Listening to Images*. Durham, NC: Duke University Press, 2017.

Cañizares-Esguerra,Jorge. "New World, New Stars: Patriotic Astrology and the Invention of Indian and Creole Bodies in Colonial Spanish America, 1600 –1650." *American Historical Review* 104.1 (1999): 33–68.

Cantor, Norman F., and Michael S. Werthman. *Renaissance, Reformation, and Absolutism, 1450–1650*. New York: Thomas Y. Crowell, 1972.

Carew, Jan R. *Fulcrums of Change*. Trenton, NJ: Africa World Press, 1988.

Carrera, Magali M. *Imagining Identity in New Spain: Race, Lineage, and the Colonial Body in Portraiture and Casta Paintings*. Austin: University of Texas Press, 2003.

Carroll, Patrick J. "Black–Native Relations and the Historical Record in Colonial Mexico." In *Beyond Black and Red: African–Native Relations in Colonial Latin America*, edited by Matthew Restall. Albuquerque: University of New Mexico Press, 2005. 245–67.

"Mandinga: The Evolution of a Mexican Runaway Slave Community, 1735 –1827." *Comparative Studies in Society and History* 19.4 (1977): 488–505.

"Los mexicanos negros, el mestizaje y los fundamentos olvidados de la 'raza cósmica': Una perspectiva regional." *Historia Mexicana* 44.3 (1995): 403–38.

Castañeda García, Rafael. "La devoción a santa Ifigenia entre negros y mulatos de Nueva España, siglos XVII y XVIII." In *Esclavitud, mestizaje y abolicionismo en los mundos hispánicos*, edited by Aurelia Martín Casares. Granada: Universidad de Granada, 2015. 151–72.

"Devociones y construcción de identidades entre los negros y mulatos de la Nueva España (s. XVIII)." In *Imagen y poder: VI Encuentro Internacional sobre Barroco*, edited by Norma Campos Vera. La Paz: Fundación Visión Cultural, 2012. 241–47.

"Modelos de santidad: Devocionarios y hagiografías a San Benito de Palermo en Nueva España." *Historia Moderna* 38.1 (2016): 39–64.

"Santos negros, devotos de color: Las cofradías de San Benito de Palermo en Nueva España (identidades étnicas y religiosas, siglos XVII–XVIII)." In *Devoción, paisanaje e identidad: Las cofradías y congregaciones de naturales en España y en América (siglos XVI–XIX)*, edited by Óscar Álvarez Gila, Alberto Angulo Morales, and Jon Ander Ramos Martínez. Bilbao: Universidad del País Vasco, 2014. 145–64.

Castellano, Juan R. "El negro esclavo en el entremés del Siglo de Oro." *Hispania* 44.1 (1961): 55–65.

Castro Henriques, Isabel. *Os africanos em Portugal: História e memória: séulos XV–XXI*. Lisbon: Mercado de Letras, 2011.

Caviness, Madeline Harrison. "From the Self-Invention of the Whiteman in the Thirteenth Century to the Good, the Bad, and the Ugly." *Different Visions* 1 (2008). chrome-extension://efaidnbmnnnibpcajpcglclefindmkaj/viewer.html?pdfurl=https%3A%2F%2Fdifferentvisions.org%2Fwp-content%2Fuploads%2Fsites%2F1356%2F2020%2F03%2FIssue-1-Caviness-2.pdf&clen=2446492&chunk=true

Chasteen, John C. *National Rhythms, African Roots: The Deep History of Latin American Popular Dance*. Albuquerque: University of New Mexico Press, 2004.

Chávez Bárcenas, Ireri. "Villancicos de Navidad y espiritualidad postridentina en Puebla de los Ángeles en el siglo XVII." In *El villancico en la encrucijada: Nuevas perspectivas en torno a un género literario-musical (siglos XV–XIX)*, edited by Esther Borrego Gutiérrez and Javier Marín-López. Kessel: Reichenberger, 2019. 233–58.

Chiles, Katy L. *Transformable Race: Surprising Metamorphoses in the Literature of Early America*. Oxford: Oxford University Press, 2014.

Clapp, Nicholas. *Sheba: Through the Desert in Search of the Legendary Queen*. New York: Houghton Mifflin, 2001.

Cohen, Theodore W. *Finding Afro-Mexico: Race and Nation After the Revolution*. Cambridge: Cambridge University Press, 2020.

Coromines, Joan. *Diccionario crítico etimológico castellano e hispánico*. Madrid: Gredos, 1991. 6 vols.

Cope, R. Douglas. *The Limits of Racial Domination: Plebeian Society in Colonial Mexico City, 1660–1720*. Madison: University of Wisconsin Press, 1994.

Cortés, Vicenta. *La esclavitud en Valencia durante el reinado de los Reyes Catolicos (1479–1516)*. Valencia: Excmo. Ayuntamiento, 1964.

Cortés López, Jorge Luis. *La esclavitud negra en la España peninsular del siglo XVI*. Salamanca: Universidad de Salamanca, 1989.

Los origines de la esclavitud negra en España. Salamanca: Mundo Negro and University of Salamanca, 1986.

Cooper, Jean C. *An Illustrated Encyclopaedia of Traditional Symbols*. London: Thames & Hudson, 1978.

Craft, Renée Alexander. "'¡Los Gringos Vienen!' (The Gringos Are Coming!): Female Respectability and the Politics of Congo Tourist Presentations in Portobelo, Panama." *Transforming Anthropology* 16.1 (2008): 20–31.

When the Devil Knocks: The Congo Tradition and the Politics of Blackness in Twentieth-Century Panama. Columbus: Ohio State University Press, 2015.

Cunha, Maria Clementina Pereira. *Ecos da folia: Uma história social do carnaval carioca entre 1880 e 1920*. Sao Paulo: Companhia das Letras, 2001.

Curcio-Nagy, Linda A. "Giants and Gypsies: Corpus Christi in Colonial Mexico City." In *Rituals of Rule, Rituals of Resistance: Public Celebrations and Popular Culture in Mexico*, edited by William H. Beezley, Cheryl English Martin, and William E. French. Wilmington: Scholarly Resources, 1994. 1–26.

The Great Festivals of Colonial Mexico City: Performing Power and Identity. Albuquerque: University of New Mexico Press, 2004.

Cushing Flint, Shirley. "Treason or Travesty: The Martín Cortés Conspiracy Reexamined." *Sixteenth Century Journal* 39.1 (2008): 23–44.

Davies, Sureka. *Renaissance Ethnography and the Invention of the Human: New Worlds, Maps, and Monsters.* Cambridge: Cambridge University Press, 2016.

Dean, Carolyn. "Copied Carts: Spanish Prints and Colonial Peruvian Paintings." *Art Bulletin* 78.1 (1996): 98–110.

Inka Bodies and the Body of Christ: Corpus Christi in Colonial Cuzco, Peru. Durham, NC: Duke University Press, 1999.

Delaigue, Christine, and Aurelia Martín Casares. "The Evangelization of Freed and Slave Black Africans in Renaissance Spain: Baptism, Marriage, and Ethnic Brotherhoods." *History of Religions* 52.3 (2013): 214–35.

Delgado, Richard, and Jean Stefancic. *Critical Race Theory: An Introduction.* New York: New York University Press, 2017.

Deusen, Nancy van. "The 'Alienated' Body: Slaves and Castas in the Hospital de San Bartolomé in Lima, 1680 to 1700." *The Americas* 56.1 (1999): 1–30.

Between the Sacred and the Worldly: The Institutional and Cultural Practice of Recogimiento in Colonial Lima. Stanford, CA: Stanford University Press, 2002.

Devisse, Jean, and Michel Mollat. "The African Transposed." In *The Image of the Black in Western Art*, vol. 2, edited by David Bindman, Henry L. Gates, and Karen C. C. Dalton. Cambridge, MA: Harvard University Press, 2010. 185–279.

Dewulf, Jeroen. *From the Kingdom of Kongo to Congo Square: Kongo Dances and the Origins of the Mardi Gras Indians.* Lafayette: University of Louisiana at Lafayette Press, 2017.

Díaz, María Elena. "Writing Royal Slaves into Colonial Studies." In *Repensando el pasado, recuperando el futuro: Nuevos aportes interdisciplinarios para el estúdio de la América colonial*, edited by Verónica Salles-Reese. Bogotá: Pontificia Universidad Javeriana, 2005. 253–70.

Dillon, Elizabeth M. *New World Drama: The Performative Commons in the Atlantic World, 1649–1849.* Durham, NC: Duke University Press, 2014.

Donnelly, John Patrick, and Michael W. Maher, eds. *Confraternities and Catholic Reform in Italy, France, and Spain.* Kirsville, MO: Thomas Jefferson University Press, 1999.

Earle, Rebecca. "Luxury, Clothing and Race in Colonial Spanish America." In *Luxury in the Eighteenth Century: Debates, Desires and Delectable Goods*, edited by Maxine Berg and Elizabeth Eger. Houndmills: Palgrave, 2003. 219–27.

Earle, Thomas F., and Kate J. P. Lowe. *Black Africans in Renaissance Europe.* Cambridge: Cambridge University Press, 2005.

Edwards, Erika D. *Hiding in Plain Sight: Black Women, the Law, and the Making of a White Argentine Republic.* Tuscaloosa: University of Alabama Press, 2020.

Eliav-Feldon, Miriam, Benjamin H. Isaac, and Joseph Ziegler. *The Origins of Racism in the West.* Cambridge: Cambridge University Press, 2015.

Evans, William McKee. "From the Land of Canaan to the Land of Guinea: The Strange Odyssey of the Sons of Ham." *American Historical Review* 85.1 (1980): 15–43.

Eze, Emmanuel C., ed. *Race and the Enlightenment: A Reader*. Malden, MA: Blackwell, 2009.

Fanon, Frantz. "The Fact of Blackness." In *Black Skin, White Masks*, translated by Charles Lam Markmann. New York: Grove Press, 1967. 109–40.

Farman Sweda, Krystle. "Black Catholicism: The Formation of Local Religion in Colonial Mexico." PhD thesis, The Graduate Center, CUNY, 2020.

Fernández-Armesto, Felipe. *The Canary Islands After the Conquest: The Making of a Colonial Society in the Early Sixteenth Century*. Oxford: Clarendon, 2003.

Feros, Antonio. *Speaking of Spain: The Evolution of Race and Nation in the Hispanic World*. Cambridge, MA: Harvard University Press, 2012.

Ferrão, Cristina, José P. M. Soares, Ernst van Boogaart, Rebecca P. Brienen, and Dante M. Teixeira. *Dutch Brazil*. Petropolis: Index, 2002.

Few, Martha. *Women Who Live Evil Lives: Gender, Religion, and the Politics of Power in Colonial Guatemala, 1650–1750*. Austin: University of Texas Press, 2003.

Florentino, Manolo. "Slave Trading and Slave Traders in Rio De Janeiro, 1790–1830." In *Enslaving Connections: Changing Cultures of Africa and Brazil during the Era of Slavery*, edited by José C. Curto and Paul E. Lovejoy. Amherst, NY: Humanity Books, 2004. 57–79.

Fogelman, Patricia, and Marta Goldberg. "'El rey de los congos': The Clandestine Coronation of Pedro Duarte in Buenos Aires, 1787." In *Afro-Latino Voices: Narratives from the Early Modern Ibero-Atlantic World, 1550–1812*, edited by Kathryn Joy McKnight and Leo J. Garofalo. Indianapolis, IN: Hackett, 2009. 155–73.

Fonseca, Jorge. *Escravos e senhores na Lisboa quinhentista*. Lisbon: Colibri, 2010.

Religião e liberdade: Os negros nas irmandades e confrarias portuguesas (séculos XV a XIX). Lisbon: Humus, 2016.

Foucault, Michel. *Discipline and Punish: The Birth of the Prison*, edited by Allan Sheridan. New York: Vintage, 1977.

"Nietzsche, Genealogy, and History." In *The Foucault Reader*, edited by Paul Rabinow. New York: Vintage, 2010.

Security, Territory, and Population, edited by Michel Senellart. New York: Picador, 2009.

Society Must Be Defended, edited by David Macey. London: Penguin, 2004.

Fracchia, Carmen. *"Black but Human": Slavery and the Visual Arts in Hapsburg Spain, 1480–1700*. Oxford: Oxford University Press, 2019.

Fra-Molinero, Baltasar. *La imagen de los negros en el teatro del siglo de oro*. Madrid: Siglo XXI, 1995.

Franco Silva, Alfonso. *La esclavitud en Sevilla y su tierra a fines de la Edad Media*. Seville: Seville Provincial Government, 1979.

Fredrickson, George M., *Racism: A Short History*, edited by Albert Camarillo. Princeton, NJ: Princeton University Press, 2015.

Fromont, Cécile. *The Art of Conversion: Christian Visual Culture in the Kingdom of Kongo*. Charleston: University of North Carolina Press, 2014.

"Dancing for the King of Congo from Early Modern Central Africa to Slavery-Era Brazil." *Colonial Latin American Review* 22.2 (2013): 184–208.

"Envisioning Brazil's Afro-Christian *Congados*: The Black King and Queen Festival Lithograph of Johann Moritz Rugendas." In *Afro-Catholic Festivals in the Americas: Performance, Representation, and the Making of Black Atlantic Tradition*, edited by Cécile Fromont. College Park: Pennsylvania State University Press, 2019. 117–39.

Fryer, Peter. *Rhythms of Resistance: African Musical Heritage in Brazil*. Middletown, CT: Wesleyan University Press, 2000.

Fuente, Alejandro de la. "Afro–Latin American Art." In *Afro–Latin American Studies: An Introduction*, edited by Alejandro de la Fuente and George Reid Andrews. Cambridge: Cambridge University Press, 2018. 438–85.

Fuentes, Marisa J. *Dispossessed Lives: Enslaved Women, Violence, and the Archive*. Philadelphia: University of Pennsylvania Press, 2016.

García, Pablo. "Saldos del criollismo: El *Teatro de virtudes politicas* de Carlos de Sigüenza y Góngora a la luz de la historiografía de Fernando de Alva Ixtlilxóchitl." *Colonial Latin American Review* 18.2 (2009): 219–35.

García Ayluardo, Clara. "Confraternity, Cult and Crown in Colonial Mexico City 1700–1810." PhD thesis, History, University of Cambridge, 1989.

García de León, Antonio. *Fandango: El ritual del mundo jarocho a través de los siglos*. Mexico City: Scheidegger & Spiess, 2009.

Garofalo, Leo. "The Shape of a Diaspora: The Movement of Afro-Iberians to Colonial Spanish America." In *Africans to Spanish America: Expanding the Diaspora*, edited by Sherwin K. Bryant, Rachel S. O'Toole, and Ben Vinson III. Urbana: University of Illinois Press, 2014. 27–49.

Gerhard, Peter. "A Black Conquistador in Mexico." *Hispanic American Historical Review* 58.3 (1978): 451–59.

Germeten, Nicole von. *Black Blood Brothers: Confraternities and Social Mobility for Afro-Mexicans*. Gainesville: University Press of Florida, 2006.

"Black Brotherhoods in Mexico City." In *The Black Urban Atlantic in the Age of the Slave Trade*, edited by Jorge Cañizares-Esguerra, Matt D. Childs, and James Sidbury. Philadelphia: University of Pennsylvania Press, 2013. 248–68.

"Colonial Middle Men? Mulatto Identity in New Spain's Confraternities." In *Black Mexico: Race and Society from Colonial to Modern Times*, edited by Ben Vinson III and Matthew Restall. Albuquerque: University of New Mexico Press, 2009. 136–54.

"Juan Roque's Donation of a House to the Zape Confraternity, Mexico City, 1623." In *Afro-Latino Voices: Narratives from the Early Modern Ibero-Atlantic World, 1550–1812*, edited by Kathryn Joy McKnight and Leo J. Garofalo. Indianapolis, IN: Hackett, 2009, 83–103.

Gharala, Norah L. A. *Taxing Blackness: Free Afromexican Tribute in Bourbon New Spain*. Tuscaloosa: University of Alabama Press, 2019.

Gil, Fernando. *Primeras "doctrinas" del nuevo mundo: Estudio histórico-teológico de las obras de Fray Juan de Zumárraga (1548)*. Buenos Aires: PUCA "Santa María de los Buenos Aires," 1993.

Gilroy, Paul. *The Black Atlantic: Modernity and Double Consciousness.* Cambridge, MA: Harvard University Press, 1993.

Githiora, Chege J. *Afro-Mexicans: Discourse of Race and Identity on the African Diaspora.* Trenton, NJ: Africa World Press, 2008.

Goldenberg, David M. *The Curse of Ham: Race and Slavery in Early Judaism, Christianity, and Islam: Race and Slavery in Early Judaism, Christianity, and Islam.* Princeton, NJ: Princeton University Press, 2004.

Gómez, Ximena. "*Nuestra señora*: Confraternal Art and Identity in Early Colonial Lima." PhD thesis, University of Michigan, 2019.

Gonzalbo Aizpuru, Pilar. *Vivir en Nueva España: Orden y desorden en la vida cotidiana.* Mexico City: Colegio de México, 2009.

Gonzalbo Aizpuru, Pilar, and Solange Alberro. *La sociedad novohispana: Estereotipos y realidades.* Mexico City: Colegio de México, 2013.

González de León, Félix. "Hermandades y cofradías de negros en la Sevilla del XVI." *Alma Mater Hispalense.* http://personal.us.es/alporu/histsevilla/cofra dias_negros_sevilla.htm

González Díaz, Antonio Manuel. *La esclavitud en Ayamonte durante el Antiguo Régimen.* Huelva: Diputación Provincial de Huelva, 1997.

Graeber, David, and Marshall Sahlins. *On Kings.* Chicago: Hau Books, 2017.

Graubart, Karen B. "'*So color de una cofradía*': Catholic Confraternities and the Development of Afro-Peruvian Ethnicities in Early Colonial Peru." *Slavery & Abolition* 33.1 (2012): 43–64.

Grenham, T. G. "Interculturation: Exploring Changing Religious, Cultural, and Faith Identities in an African Context." *Pacifica Brunswick East.* 14: 191–206.

Gruesser, John C. *Confluences: Postcolonialism, African American Literary Studies, and the Black Atlantic.* Athens: University of Georgia Press, 2005.

Gual Camarena, Miguel. "Una cofradía de negros libertos en el siglo XV." *Estudios de Edad Media de la Corona de Aragón* 5 (1952): 457–66.

Guengerich Vicuña, Sara. "The Witchcraft Trials of Paula de Eguiluz, a Black Woman, in Cartagena de Indias, 1620–1636." In *Afro-Latino Voices: Narratives from the Early Modern Ibero-Atlantic World, 1550–1812,* edited by Kathryn Joy McKnight and Leo J. Garofalo. Indianapolis, IN: Hackett, 2009. 175–93.

Gutiérrez Rodríguez Encarnación and Shirley A. Tate, eds. *Creolizing Europe: Legacies and Transformations.* Liverpool: Liverpool University Press, 2015.

Hahn, Thomas. *Race and Ethnicity in the Middle Ages.* Durham, NC: Duke University Press, 2001.

Hall, Kim F. "Object into Object? Some Thoughts on the Presence of Black Women in Early Modern Culture." In *Early Modern Visual Culture: Representation, Race, Empire in Renaissance England,* edited by Peter Erickson and Clark Hulse. Philadelphia: University of Pennsylvania Press, 2000. 346–79.

Things of Darkness: Economies of Race and Gender in Early Modern England. Ithaca, NY: Cornell University Press, 1995.

Hall, Stuart. "*Creolité* and the Process of Creolization." In *Creolizing Europe: Legacies and Transformations,* edited by Encarnación Gutiérrez Rodríguez and Shirley A. Tate. Liverpool: Liverpool University Press, 2015. 12–25.

Harpster, Grace. "The Color of Salvation: The Materiality of Blackness in Alonso de Sandoval's *De instauranda aethiopum salute.*" In *Envisioning Others: Race, Color, and the Visual in Iberia and Latin America*, edited by Pamela A. Patton. Leiden: Brill, 2016. 83–110.

Harris, Max. *Aztecs, Moors, and Christians: Festivals of Reconquest in Mexico and Spain*. Austin: University of Texas Press, 2000.

Haynes, Stephen R. *Noah's Curse: The Biblical Justification of American Slavery*. Oxford: Oxford University Press, 2007.

Heng, Geraldine. *The Invention of Race in the European Middle Ages*. Cambridge: Cambridge University Press, 2019.

Henriques, Isabel Castro. *A herença africana em Portugal*. Lisbon: CTT, 2009.

Hering Torres, Max Sebastián, María Elena Martínez, and David Nirenberg, eds. *Race and Blood in the Iberian World*. Berlin: Lit, 2012.

Hernández Cuevas, Marco Polo. *African Mexicans and the Discourse on Modern Nation*. Dallas, TX: University Press of America, 2004.

Hernández Reyes, Dalia. "*Festín de las morenas criollas*: Danza y emblemática en el recibimiento del Virrey Marqués de Villena." In *Dramaturgia y espectáculo teatral en el época de los Austrias*, edited by Judith Farré Vidal. Pamplona: University of Navarre, 2009. 339–57.

Hewson, Martin. "Agency." In *Encyclopedia of Case Study Research*, vol. 1, edited by Albert J. Mills, Elden Wiebe, and Gabrielle Durepos. Thousand Oaks, CA: Sage, 2009. 13–17.

Heywood, Linda M. "The Angolan-Afro-Brazilian Cultural Connections." In *From Slavery to Emancipation in the Atlantic World*, edited by Sylvia R. Frey and Betty Wood. London: Routledge, 1999. 9–23.

Heywood, Linda M., ed. *Central Africans and Cultural Transformations in the American Diaspora*. Cambridge: Cambridge University Press, 2002.

Heywood, Linda M., and John Thornton. *Central Africans, Atlantic Creoles, and the Foundation of the Americas, 1585–1660*. Cambridge: Cambridge University Press, 2007.

Hill, Ruth. *Hierarchy, Commerce and Fraud in Bourbon Spanish America: A Postal Inspector's Exposé*. Nashville, TN: Vanderbilt University Press, 2005.

Holt, Thomas. *The Problem of Race in the 21st Century*. Cambridge, MA: Harvard University Press, 2002.

Howard, Philip A. *Changing History: Afro-Cuban Cabildos and Societies of Color in the Nineteenth Century*. Baton Rouge: Louisiana State University Press, 1998.

Ibsen, Kristine. *Women's Spiritual Autobiography in Colonial Spanish America*. Gainesville: University Press of Florida, 1999.

Ireton, Chloe. "'They Are Blacks of the Caste of Black Christians': Old Christian Black Blood in the Sixteenth and Early Seventeenth-Century Iberian Atlantic." *Hispanic American Historical Review* 97.4 (2017): 579–612.

Isaac, Benjamin H. *The Invention of Racism in Classical Antiquity*. Princeton, NJ: Princeton University Press, 2006.

Israel, Jonathan I. *Razas, clases sociales y vida política en el México colonial, 1610–1670*. Mexico City: Fondo de Cultura Económica, 1997.

Jaffary, Nora E. *False Mystics: Deviant Orthodoxy in Colonial Mexico*. Lincoln: University of Nebraska Press, 2008.

Jenkins, Linda W. "Locating the Language of Gender Experience." *Women & Performance* (1984): 5–20.

Johnson, Jessica M. *Wicked Flesh: Black Women, Intimacy, and Freedom in the Atlantic World*. Philadelphia: University of Pennsylvania Press, 2020.

Jones, Nicholas R. "Sor Juana's Black Atlantic: Colonial Blackness and the Poetic Subversions of *Habla de Negros*." *Hispanic Review* 86.3 (2018): 265–85.

Staging Habla de Negros: Radical Performances of the African Diaspora in Early Modern Spain. University Park: Pennsylvania State University Press, 2019.

Jordan, Gschwend A., and Kate J. P. Lowe, eds. *The Global City: On the Streets of Renaissance Lisbon*. London: Paul Holberton, 2015.

Jordan, Winthrop. *White Over Black: American Attitudes toward the Negro, 1550–1812*. Baltimore, MD: Penguin, 1968.

Jouve Martín, Ramón José. *The Black Doctors of Colonial Lima: Science, Race, and Writing in Colonial and Early Republican Peru*. Montreal: McGill-Queen's University Press, 2014.

"Death, Gender, and Writing: Testaments of Women of African Origin in Seventeenth-Century Lima, 1651–1666." In *Afro-Latino Voices: Narratives from the Early Modern Ibero-Atlantic World, 1550–1812*, edited by Kathryn Joy McKnight and Leo J. Garofalo. Indianapolis, IN: Hackett, 2009. 105–25.

Esclavos de la ciudad letrada: Esclavitud, escritura y colonialismo en Lima (1650–1700). Lima: Instituto de Estudios Peruanos, 2005.

"Public Ceremonies and Mulatto Identity in Viceregal Lima: A Colonial Reenactment of the Fall of Troy (1631)." *Colonial Latin American Review* 16.2 (2007): 179–201.

Kaplan, Paul H. D. *The Rise of the Black Magus in Western Art*. Ann Arbor: University of Michigan Research Press, 1985.

Katzew, Ilona. "The Invention of Casta Painting: Race and Science in the Age of Enlightenment," Whitney Humanities Center, Yale University, February 26, 2019. https://whc.yale.edu/videos/invention-casta-painting-race-and-science-age-enlightenment

"Manuel de Arellano, 'Rendering of a Mulato (*Diceño de mulata*).'" In *Painting a New World: Mexican Art and Life 1521–1821*, edited by Donna Pierce, Rogelio Ruiz Gomar, and Clara Bargellini. Denver, CO: Denver Art Museum, 2004. 194.

"White or Black? Albinism and Spotted Blacks in the Eighteenth-Century Atlantic World." In *Envisioning Others: Race, Color, and the Visual in Iberia and Latin America*, edited by Pamela A. Patton. Leiden: Brill, 2016. 142–86.

Kennedy, Rebecca F., C. Sydnor Roy, and Max L. Goldman, eds. *Race and Ethnicity in the Classical World: An Anthology of Primary Sources in Translation*. Indianapolis, IN: Hackett, 2013.

Kidd, Colin. *The Forging of Races: Race and Scripture in the Protestant Atlantic World, 1600–2000*. Cambridge: Cambridge University Press, 2006.

Kiddy, Elizabeth W. *Blacks of the Rosary: Memory and History in Minas Gerais, Brazil*. University Park: Pennsylvania State University Press, 2005.

"Congados, Calunga, Candombe: Our Lady of the Rosary in Minas Gerais, Brazil." *Luso-Brazilian Review* 37.1 (2000): 47–61.

"Who Is the King of Kongo? A New Look at African and Afro-Brazilian Kings in Brazil." In *Central Africans and Cultural Transformations in the American Diaspora*, edited by Linda M. Heywood. Cambridge: Cambridge University Press, 2002. 153–82.

King, Joshua. *Imagined Spiritual Communities in Britain's Age of Print*. Columbus: Ohio State University Press, 2015.

Klein, Herbert S., and Francisco Vidal Luna. *Slavery in Brazil*. Cambridge: Cambridge University Press, 2010.

Lahon, Didier. "Esclavage, confréries noires, sainteté noire et pureté de sang au Portugal (XVIe et XVIIIe siècles)." *Lusitania Sacra* 2.15 (2003): 119–62.

"Esclavage et confréries noires au Portugal durant l'Ancien Régime (1441 –1830). PhD thesis, Sorbonne, 2010.

"O escravo africano na vida económica e social portuguesa do Antigo Regime." *Africana Studia* 7 (2004): 73–100.

"Da redução da alteridade a consagração da diferença: As irmandades negras em Portugal (séculos XVI–XVIII)." *Projeto História* 44 (2012): 53–83.

Landers, Jane. "Founding Mothers: Female Rebels in Colonial New Granada and Spanish Florida." *Journal of African American History* 98.1 (2013): 7–23.

Landers, Jane, and Barry M. Robinson, eds. *Slaves, Subjects, and Subversives: Blacks in Colonial Latin America*. Albuquerque: University of New Mexico Press, 2006.

Lane, Jill. *Blackface Cuba, 1840–1895*. Philadelphia: University of Pennsylvania Press, 2005.

Lara, Silvia Hunold. "Uma embaixada africana na América portuguesa." In *Festa, cultura e sociabilidade na América portuguesa*, vol. 1., edited by István Jancsó and Iris Kantor. Sao Paulo: Hucitec, 1002. 151–65.

Fragmentos setecentistas: escravidão, cultura e poder na América portuguesa. Sao Paulo: Companhias das Letras, 2007.

Larkin, Brian. "Confraternities and Community: The Decline of the Communal Quest for Salvation in Eighteenth-Century Mexico City." In *Local Religion in Colonial Mexico*, edited by Martin Austin Nesvig. Albuquerque: University of New Mexico Press, 2006. 189–214.

Leonard, Irving A. *Baroque Times in Old Mexico: Seventeenth-Century Persons, Places, and Practices*. Ann Arbor: University of Michigan Press, 1971.

Lewis, Laura A. *Hall of Mirrors: Power, Witchcraft, and Caste in Colonial Mexico*. Durham, NC: Duke University Press, 2006.

Lipski, John M. *A History of Afro-Hispanic Language: Five Centuries, Five Continents*. Cambridge: Cambridge University Press, 2010.

Lockhart, James. *Spanish Peru: 1532–1560: A Social History*. Madison: University of Wisconsin Press, 1994.

Lopes Don, Patricia. "Carnivals, Triumphs, and Rain Gods in the New World: A Civic Festival in the City of México-Tenochtitlán in 1539." *Colonial Latin American Review* 6.1: 17–40.

Love, Edgar F. "Negro Resistance to Spanish Rule in Colonial Mexico." *Journal of Negro History* 52.2 (1967): 89–103.

Lovejoy, Paul J. "Transatlantic Transformations: The Origins and Identities of Africans in the Americas." In *Africa, Brazil, and the Construction of Trans-Atlantic Black Identities*, edited by Barry Boubacar, Elisee A. Soumonni, and Livio Sansone. Trenton, NJ: Africa World Press, 2008. 81–111.

Lowe, Kate J. P. "The Global Population of Renaissance Lisbon: Diversity and Its Entanglements." In *The Global City: On the Streets of Renaissance Lisbon* edited by Gschwend A. Jordan and Kate J. P. Lowe. London: Paul Holberton, 2015. 56–75.

"The Lives of African Slaves and People of African Descent." In *Revealing the African Presence in Renaissance Europe*, edited by Joaneath A. Spicer. Baltimore, MD: Walters Art Museum, 2012.

"'Representing' Africa: Ambassadors and Princes from Christian Africa to Renaissance Italy and Portugal, 1402–1608." *Transactions of the Royal Historical Society* 17 (2007): 101–28.

"The Stereotyping of Black Africans in Renaissance Europe." In *Black Africans in Renaissance Europe*, edited by Thomas F. Earle and Kate J. P. Lowe. Cambridge: Cambridge University Press, 2005. 17–47.

"Visual Representations of an Elite: African Ambassadors and Rulers in Renaissance Europe." In *Revealing the African Presence in Renaissance Europe*, edited by Joaneath A. Spicer and Natalie Z. Davis. Baltimore, MD: Walters Art Museum, 2012. 99–115.

Lowe, Lisa. *Intimacies of Four Continents*. Durham, NC: Duke University Press, 2015.

Lugo-Ortiz, Agnes, and Angela Rosenthal. *Slave Portraiture in the Atlantic World*. Cambridge: Cambridge University Press, 2016.

Lund Drolet, Patricia. *El ritual congo del noroeste de Panamá: Una estructura afro-americana expresiva de adaptation cultural*. Panamaa City: Instituto Nacional de Cultura, 1987.

Mancuso, Lara. *Cofradías mineras: Religiosidad popular en México y Brasil, siglo XVIII*. Mexico: Colegio de México, 2007.

Martín Casares, Aurelia. "Free and Freed Black Africans in Granada in the Time of the Spanish Renaissance." In *Black Africans in Renaissance Europe*, edited by Thomas F. Earle and Kate J. P. Lowe. Cambridge: Cambridge University Press, 2005. 247–60.

Martín Casares, Aurelia, and Marga G. Barranco. "Popular Literary Depictions of Black African Weddings in Early Modern Spain." *Renaissance and Reformation* 31.2 (2008): 107–21.

Martínez, María E. "The Black Blood of New Spain: *Limpieza de Sangre*, Racial Violence, and Gendered Power in Early Colonial Mexico." *William and Mary Quarterly* 61.3 (2004): 479–520.

Genealogical Fictions: Limpieza de Sangre, Religion, and Gender in Colonial Mexico. Stanford, CA: Stanford University Press, 2013.

Martínez Ferrer, Luis, "Pedro López y los negros y mulatos de la ciudad de México (1582–1597)." In *Socialización y religiosidad del médico Pedro López*

(1527–1597): De Dueñas (Castilla) a la ciudad de México, edited by Luis Martínez Ferrer and María Luisa Rodríguez-Sala. Mexico City: Universidad Nacional Autónoma de México, 2013. 179–216.

Masferrer León, Verónica Cristina. "Por las ánimas de negros bozales: Las cofradías de personas de origen africano en la ciudad de México (siglo XVII)." *Revista Cuicuilco* 18.51 (2011): 83–103.

Mason, Peter. *Infelicities: Representations of the Exotic*. Baltimore, MD: Johns Hopkins University Press, 1998.

Mazzotti, José A. *The Creole Invention of Peru: Ethnic Nation and Epic Poetry in Colonial Lima*. Amherst, NY: Cambria Press, 2019.

Mbembe, Achille. "Afropolitanism." *Nka* 46 (2020): 56–61.

McCoskey, Denise E. *Race: Antiquity and Its Legacy*. London: I. B. Tauris, 2012.

McKinley, Michelle A. *Fractional Freedoms: Slavery, Intimacy, and Legal Mobilization in Colonial Lima, 1600–1700*. Cambridge: Cambridge University Press, 2018.

Meléndez, Mariselle. *Deviant and Useful Citizens: The Cultural Production of the Female Body in Eighteenth-Century Peru*. Nashville, TN: Vanderbilt University Press, 2011.

Raza, género e hibridez en el Lazarillo de ciegos caminantes. Chapel Hill: University of North Carolina Department of Romance Languages, 1999.

"Visualizing Difference: The Rhetoric of Clothing in Colonial Spanish America." In *The Latin American Fashion Reader*, edited by Regina A. Root. London: Bloomsbury, 2020. 17–30.

Mello e Souza, Marina. "The Construction of a Black Catholic Identity in Brazil: Saints and *Minkisi*. A Reflection of Cultural Miscegenation." In *Africa, Brazil, and the Construction of Trans-Atlantic Black Identities*, edited by Barry Boubacar, Elisee A. Soumonni, and Livio Sansone. Trenton, NJ: Africa World Press, 2008, 255–68.

Reis negros no Brasil escravista: história da festa de coroação de rei congo. Belo Horizonte: Editora Universidade Federal de Minas Gerais, 2002.

Mendes, António de Almeida. "The Foundations of the System: A Reassessment of the Slave Trade to the Spanish Americas in the Sixteenth and Seventeenth Centuries." In *Extending the Frontiers: Essays on the New Transatlantic Slave Trade Database*, edited by David Eltis and David Richardson. New Haven, CT: Yale University Press, 2008. 63–94.

Méndez, Juan Bautista. *Crónica de la provincial de Santiago de México de la Orden de Predicadores* [ca. 1521–64], edited by Justo Alberto Fernández F. Mexico: Porrua, 1993.

Merrim, Stephanie. *The Spectacular City, Mexico, and Colonial Hispanic Literary Culture*. Austin: University of Texas Press, 2011.

Miller, Joseph C. "Central Africa during the Era of the Slave Trade, c. 1490s–1850s." In *Central Africans and Cultural Transformations in the American Diaspora*, edited by Linda Heywood. Cambridge: Cambridge University Press, 2002. 21–70.

Mínguez, Víctor. *Emblemática y cultura simbólica en la Valencia barroca: jeroglíficos, enigmas, divias y laberintos*. Valencia: Alfons el Magnanim, 1997.

Mintz, Sidney W., and Richard Price. *The Birth of African-American Culture: An Anthropological Perspective*. Boston: Beacon Press, 2011.

Miranda Nieto, Alejandro. *Musical Mobilities: Son Jarocho and the Circulation of Tradition across Mexico and the United States*. London: Routledge, 2017.

Mondragón Barrios, Lourdes. *Esclavos africanos en la Ciudad de México: El servicio doméstico durante el siglo XVI*. Mexico City: Euram, 1999.

Montgomery, Nick, and carla bergman. *Joyful Militancy: Building Thriving Resistance in Toxic Times*. Chico, CA: AK Press, 2017.

Moore, Rosemary. "Monsters and the Maternal Imagination: The 'First Vision' of Johann Remmelin's 1619 *Catoptrum microcosmicum* Triptych." In *Exceptional Bodies in Early Modern Culture: Concepts of Monstrosity Before the Advent of the Normal*, edited by Maja Bondestan. Amsterdam: Amsterdam University Press, 2020. 59–83.

Morales Folguera, José Miguel. *Cultura simbólica y arte efímero en la Nueva España*. Granada: Government of Andalucia, 1991.

More, Anna H. *Baroque Sovereignty: Carlos De Sigüenza y Góngora and the Creole Archive of Colonial Mexico*. Philadelphia: University of Pennsylvania Press, 2013.

"From Lines to Networks: Carl Schmitt's Nomos and the Early Atlantic System." *Política Común* 5 (2014). https://doi.org/10.3998/pc.12322227.0005.004

Moreno, Isidoro. *La antigua hermandad de "Los Negros" de Sevilla: Etnicidad, poder y sociedad en 600 años de historia*. Seville: University of Seville & Government of Andalucia, 1997.

"Plurietnicidad, fiestas y poder: Cofradías y fiestas andaluzas de negros como modelo para la América colonial." In *El mundo festivo en España y América*. Córdoba: Universidad de Córdoba, 2005. 169–88.

Morgan, Jennifer L. *Laboring Women: Reproduction and Gender in New World Slavery*. Philadelphia: University of Pennsylvania Press, 2004.

Morgan, Ronald J. *Spanish American Saints and the Rhetoric of Identity: 1600–1810*. Tucson: University of Arizona Press, 2002.

Mulvey, Patricia Ann. "Black Brothers and Sisters: Membership in the Black Lay Brotherhoods of Colonial Brazil." *Luso-Brazilian Review* 17.2 (1980): 253–79.

"The Black Lay Brotherhoods of Colonial Brazil: A History." PhD thesis, The Graduate Center, CUNY, 1976.

"Slave Confraternities in Brazil: Their Role in Colonial Society." *The Americas* 39.1 (1982): 39–68.

Mundy, Barbara E. *The Death of Aztec Tenochtitlan, the Life of Mexico City*. Austin: University of Texas Press, 2018.

Navarro García, José Luis. *Historia del baile flamenco*. Sevilla: Signatura Ediciones de Andalucía, 2008.

Naveda Chávez-Hita, Adriana. *Escalvos negros en las haciendas azucareras de Córdoba, Veracruz, 1690–1830*. Veracruz: Universidad Veracruzana, 1987.

Ndiaye, Noémie. "The African Ambassador's Travels: Playing Black in Late Seventeenth-Century France and Spain." In *Transnational Connections in*

Early Modern Theatre, edited by M. A. Katritzky and Pavel Drábek. Manchester: Manchester University Press, 2020. 73–85.

Negrón-Muntaner, Frances. "Decolonial Joy: Theorising from the Art of *Valor y Cambio*." In *Theorising Cultures of Equality*, edited by Suzanne Clisby, Mark Johnson, and Jimmy Turner. New York: Routledge, 2020. 171–94.

Nemser, Daniel. "The Iberian Slave Trade and the Racialization of Freedom." *History of the Present* 8.2 (2018): 117–39.

Infrastructures of Race: Concentration and Biopolitics in Colonial Mexico. Austin: University of Texas Press, 2017.

"Triangulating Blackness: Mexico City, 1612." *Mexican Studies/Estudios Mexicanos* 33.3 (2017): 344–66.

Nesvig, Martin Austin, ed. *Local Religion in Colonial Mexico*. Albuquerque: University of New Mexico Press, 2006.

Ngou-Mve, Nicolás. *El África Bantú en la colonización de México (1595–1640)*. Madrid: Consejo Superior de Investigaciones Científicas, 1994.

"El cimarronaje como forma de expresión del África bantú en la América colonial: elejemplo de Yangá en México." *América Negra* 14 (1997): 27–50.

Lucha y victorias de los esclavos Bantú en México (siglos XVI–XVII): La socialización de los esclavos africanos en Nueva España. Madrid: Agencia Española de Cooperación Internacional para el Desarrollo, 2019.

Nicholson, Helen J. *The Knights Hospitaller*. Woodbridge: Boydell Press, 2003.

Nyquist, Mary. *Arbitrary Rule: Slavery, Tyranny, and the Power of Life and Death*. Chicago: University of Chicago Press, 2015.

Olsen, Margaret M. *Slavery and Salvation in Colonial Cartagena de Indias*. Gainesville: University Press of Florida, 2004.

Orso, Steven N. *Art and Death at the Spanish Habsburg Court: The Royal Exequies for Philip IV*. Columbia: University of Missouri Press, 1989.

Ortiz, Fernando. *Contrapunteo cubano del tabaco y el azúcar*. Havana: Jesús Montero, 1940.

O'Toole, Rachel S. "As Historical Subjects: the African Diaspora in Colonial Latin American History: The African Diaspora in Colonial Latin American History." *History Compass* 11.12 (2013): 1094–1110.

Bound Lives: Africans, Indians, and the Making of Race in Colonial Peru. Pittsburgh: University of Pittsburgh Press, 2012.

Palmer, Colin A. *Slaves of the White God: Blacks in Mexico, 1570–1650*. Cambridge, MA: Harvard University Press, 1976.

Patterson, Orlando. *Slavery and Social Death*. Cambridge, MA: Harvard University Press, 1982.

Pérez Fernández, Rolando Antonio. "El son jarocho como expresión musical afromestiza." In *Musical Cultures of Latin America: Global Effects, Past and Present*, edited by Steven Loza. Berkeley, CA: University of California, 2003. 39–56.

Piedra, José. "Literary Whiteness and the Afro-Hispanic Difference." *New Literary History* 18.2 (1987): 303–332.

Piersen, William D. *Black Yankees: The Development of an Afro-American Subculture in Eighteenth-Century New England*. Amherst: University of Massachusetts Press, 1988.

Philby, Harry St. John Bridger. *The Queen of Sheba*. London: Quartet Books, 1981.

Phillips, William D. *Slavery in Medieval and Early Modern Iberia*. Philadelphia: University of Pennsylvania Press, 2014.

Piper, John. *The Legacy of Sovereign Joy: God's Triumphant Grace in the Lives of Augustine, Luther, and Calvin*. Chicago: Inter-Varsity Press, 2000.

Potter, David. *Renaissance France at War: Armies, Culture and Society, C. 1480 –1560*. Woodbridge: Boydell Press, 2008.

Pratt, Mary Louise. *Imperial Eyes: Travel Writing and Transculturation*. London: Routledge, 2008.

Proctor III, Frank T. *Damned Notions of Liberty: Slavery, Culture, and Power in Colonial Mexico, 1640–1769*. Albuquerque: University of New Mexico Press, 2010.

"Slave Rebellion and Liberty in Colonial Mexico." In *Black Mexico: Race and Society from Colonial to Modern Times*, edited by Ben Vinson III and Matthew Restall. Albuquerque: University of New Mexico Press, 2009. 1–20.

Querol y Roso, Luis. "Negros y mulatos de Nueva España: Historia de su alzamiento en Mexico en 1612." *Anales de la Universidad de Valencia* 12.90 (1935): 3–44.

Rabasa, Jose. *Tell Me the Story of How I Conquered You: Elsewheres and Ethnosuicide in the Colonial Mesoamerican World*. Austin: University of Texas Press, 2014.

Rama, Angel. *La ciudad letrada*. Hanover: Ediciones del Norte, 1984.

The Lettered City. Durham, NC: Duke University Press, 1996.

Ramey, Lynn Tarte. *Black Legacies: Race and the European Middle Ages*. Gainesville: University Press of Florida, 2016.

Ramos Smith, Maya. *La danza en México durante la época colonial*. Mexico City: Alianza, 1990.

Ramsay, Paulette. *Afro-Mexican Constructions of Diaspora, Gender, Identity and Nation*. Kinston: University of the West Indies Press, 2016.

Rarey, Matthew Francis. "Assemblage, Occlusion, and the Art of Survival in the Black Atlantic. *African Arts* 51.4 (2018): 20–33.

Ratner, Carl. "Agency and Culture." *Journal for the Theory of Social Behaviour* 30.4 (2000): 413–34.

Reis, João José. *Death Is a Festival: Funeral Rites and Rebellion in Nineteenth-Century Brazil*. Chapel Hill: University of North Carolina Press, 2003.

Reginaldo, Lucilene. *Os Rosários dos Angolas: Irmandades de africanos e crioulos na Bahia setecenstista*. Sao Paulo: Alameda, 2011.

Reid Andrews, George. *Afro-Latin America: Black Lives, 1600–2000*. Cambridge, MA: Harvard University Press, 2016.

Restall, Matthew. "Black Conquistadors: Armed Africans in Early Spanish America." *The Americas* 57.2 (200): 171–205.

Black Middle: Africans, Mayas, and Spaniards in Colonial Yucatan. Stanford, CA: Stanford University Press, 2013.

Restall, Matthew, ed. *Beyond Black and Red: African–Native Relations in Colonial Latin America*. Albuquerque: University of New Mexico Press, 2005.

Riva Palacio, Vicente. *Los treinta y tres negros*. Mexico City: Fondo de Cultura Económica, 2019.

Röhrig Assunção, Matthias. *Capoeira: A History of an Afro-Brazilian Martial Art*. London: Routledge, 2005.

Rowe, Erin K. "After Death Her Face Turned White: Blackness, Whiteness, and Sanctity in the Early Modern Hispanic World." *American Historical Review* 121.3 (2016): 727–54.

   Black Saints in Early Modern Global Catholicism. Cambridge: Cambridge University Press, 2019.

   "Visualizing Black Sanctity in Early Modern Spanish Polychrome Sculpture." In *Envisioning Others: Race, Color, and the Visual in Iberia and Latin America*, edited by Pamela A. Patton. Leiden: Brill, 2016. 51–82.

Rubial García, Antonio. "La formación de una nueva sensibilidad religiosa en el paso a la Modernidad: Nueva España entre los siglos XVII y XVIII," *Romance Notes* 56.3 (2016): 433–42.

Rubin, Miri. *Corpus Christi: The Eucharist in Late Medieval Culture*. Cambridge: Cambridge University Press, 2004.

Ruiz, Teofilo F. *A King Travels: Festive Traditions in Late Medieval and Early Modern Spain*. Princeton, NJ: Princeton University Press, 2012.

Russell-Wood, Anthony J. R. "Aspectos da vida social das irmandades leigas da Bahia no seculo XVIII." *Universitas* 6–7 (1970): 189–204.

   "Black and Mulatto Brotherhoods in Colonial Brazil: A Study in Collective Behavior." *Hispanic American Historical Review* 54.4 (1974): 567–602.

   The Black Man in Slavery and Freedom in Colonial Brazil. New York: St. Martin's Press, 1982.

Salazar Rey, Ricardo Raúl. *Mastering the Law: Slavery and Freedom in the Legal Ecology of the Spanish Empire*. Tuscaloosa: University of Alabama Press, 2020.

Santana, Analia. "Mulheres negras do Rosário do Pelourinho: memória, identidade e poder." *Seminário Internacional Fazendo Gênero 10 (Anais Eletrônicos)*. Florianópolis, 2013. www.fg2013.wwc2017.eventos.dype.com.br/resources/anais/20/1373235958_ARQUIVO_FazendoGenero10AnaliaSantana.pdf

Santana, Tânia Maria Pinto de. "Nossa Senhora do Rosário no *Santuário Mariano*: Irmandades e devoções negras em Salvador e no Recôncavo Baiano (século XVIII)." *Studia Historica, Historia Moderna* 38.1 (2016): 95–122.

Saunders, A. C. de C. M. *A Social History of Black Slaves and Freedmen in Portugal: 1441–1555*. Cambridge: Cambridge University Press, 2010.

Scarano, Julita. "Black Brotherhoods: Integration or Contradiction?" *Luso-Brazilian Review*. 16.1 (1979): 1–17.

   Devoção e escravidão: A irmandade de Nossa Senhora do Rosário dos Pretos no Distrito Diamantino no século XVIII. Sao Paulo: Companhia Editora Nacional, 1976.

Schwaller, Robert C. "'For Honor and Defence': Race and the Right to Bear Arms in Early Colonial Mexico." *Colonial Latin American Review* 21.2 (2012): 239–66.

   "Géneros de Gente" in Early Colonial Mexico: Defining Racial Difference. Norman: University of Oklahoma Press, 2016.

Scott, John B. "The Catafalques of Philip II in Saragossa." *Studies in Iconography* 5 (1979): 107–34.

Sechrest, Love L. *A Former Jew: Paul and the Dialectics of Race.* New York: T & T Clark, 2009.

Sierra Silva, Pablo Miguel. "The Slave Trade to Colonial Mexico: Revising from Puebla to de los Ángeles, 1590–1640." In *From the Galleons to the Highlands: Slave Trade Routes in the Spanish Americas*, edited by Alex Borucki, David Eltis, and David Wheat. Albuquerque: University of New Mexico Press, 2020. 73–102.

Urban Slavery in Colonial Mexico: Puebla de los Ángeles, 1531–1706. Cambridge: Cambridge University Press, 2019.

Sifford, Elena F. "Mexican Manuscripts and the First Images of Africans in the Americas." *Ethnohistory* 66.2 (2019): 223–48.

Silva Prada, Natalia. *La política de una rebelión: Los indígenas frente al tumulto de 1692 en la Ciudad de México.* Mexico City: Colegio de Mexico, 2007.

Sluyter, Andrew. *Black Ranching Frontiers: African Cattle Herders of the Atlantic World, 1500–1900.* New Haven, CT: Yale University Press, 2012.

Sommer, Doris. "Wiggle Room." In *Cultural Agency in the Americas*, edited by Doris Sommer. Durham, NC: Duke University Press, 2006. 1–30.

Soule, Emily Berquist. *The Bishop's Utopia: Envisioning Improvement in Colonial Peru.* Philadelphia: University of Pennsylvania Press, 2014.

Stallybrass, Peter, and Allon White. *The Politics and Poetics of Transgression.* Ithaca, NY: Cornell University Press, 1986.

Strong, Roy. *Art and Power: Renaissance Festivals, 1450–1650.* Woodbridge: Boydell Press, 2006.

Sturman, Janet L. *The Course of Mexican Music.* New York: Routledge, 2016.

Sue, Christina A. *Land of the Cosmic Race: Race Mixture, Racism, and Blackness in Mexico.* New York: Oxford University Press, 2013.

Sullivan, Edward J. "The Black Hand: Notes on the African Presence in the Visual Arts of Brazil and the Caribbean." In *The Arts in Latin America, 1492–1820*, edited by Joseph J. Rishel and Suzanne L. Stratton-Pruitt. New Haven, CT: Yale University Press, 2006. 39–56.

Sweet, James H. "The Hidden Histories of African Lisbon." In *The Black Urban Atlantic in the Age of the Slave Trade*, edited by Jorge Cañizares-Esguerra, Matt D. Childs, and James Sidbury. Philadelphia: University of Pennsylvania Press, 2013. 233–47.

"The Iberian Roots of American Racist Thought." *William and Mary Quarterly* 54.1 (1997): 143–66.

Recreating Africa: Culture, Kinship, and Religion in the African-Portuguese World, 1441–1770. Chapel Hill: University of North Carolina Press, 2003.

Sweet, John W. *Bodies Politics: Negotiating Race in the American North, 1730–1830.* Philadelphia: University of Pennsylvania Press, 2006.

Tardieu, Jean-Pierre. *Cimarrones de Panamá: La forja de una identidad afroamericana, siglo XVI.* Madrid/Frankfurt: Iberoamericana/Vervuert, 2009.

Resistencia de los negros en el virreinato de México: (Siglos XVI–XVII). Madrid/Frankfurt: Iberoamericana/Vervuert, 2017.

Resistencia de los negros en la Venezuela colonial: representaciones y planteamientos semiológicos. Madrid/Frankfurt: Iberoamericana/Vervuert, 2013.

Tawil, Ezra. *The Making of Racial Sentiment: Slavery and the Birth of the Frontier Romance.* Cambridge: Cambridge University Press, 2006.

Taylor, Chloë. "Race and Racism in Foucault's Collège de France Lectures." *Philosophy Compass* 6.11 (2011): 746–56.

Taylor, Diana. *The Archive and the Repertoire: Performing Cultural Memory in the Americas.* Durham: NC Duke University Press, 2003.

¡Presente! The Politics of Presence. Durham, NC: Duke University Press, 2020.

Terrazas Williams, Danielle. "Finer Things: African-Descended Women, Sumptuary Laws, and Governance in Early Spanish America." *Journal of Women's History* 33.3 (2021): 11–35.

"'My Conscience Is Free and Clear': African-Descended Women, Status, and Slave Owning in Mid-Colonial Mexico." *The Americas* 75.3 (2018): 525–54.

Thompson, Robert Farris. *Flash of the Spirit: African and Afro-American Art and Philosophy.* New York: Random House, 2002.

Thornton, John K. *Africa and Africans in the Making of the Atlantic World, 1400–1680.* Cambridge: Cambridge University Press, 1992.

"Central Africa in the Era of the Slave Trade." In *Slaves, Subjects, and Subversives: Blacks in Colonial Latin America*, edited by Jane G. Landers and Barry M. Robinson. Albuquerque: University of New Mexico Press, 2006. 83–110.

The Kongolese Saint Anthony: Dona Beatriz Kimpa Vita and the Antonian Movement, 1684–1706. Cambridge: Cambridge University Press, 2009.

Thomson, Sinclair. "Was There Race in Colonial Latin America? Identifying Selves and Others in the Insurgent Andes." In *Histories of Race and Racism: The Andes and Mesoamerica from Colonial Times to the Present*, edited by Laura Gotkowitz. Durham, NC: Duke University Press, 2012, 72–94.

Tinhorão, José Ramos. *As festas no Brasil colonial.* Sao Paulo: Editora 34 Ltda., 2000.

Os negros em Portugal: Uma presença silenciosa. Lisbon: Caminho, 1988.

Trambaioli, Marcella. "Apuntes sobre el guineo o baile de negros: Tipologías y funciones dramáticas." In *Memoria de la palabra: Actas del VI Congreso de la Asociación Internacional Siglo de Oro*, edited by María Luisa Lobato and Francisco Domínguez Matito. Madrid/Frankfurt: Iberoamericana/Vervuert, 2004. 1773–83.

Trever, Lisa, and Joanne Pillsbury. "Martínez Compañón and His Illustrated Museum." In *Collecting across Cultures: Material Exchanges in the Early Modern Atlantic World*, edited by Daniela Bleichmar and Peter C. Mancall. Philadelphia: University of Pennsylvania Press, 2013. 236–53.

Trouillot, Michel-Rolph. *Silencing the Past: Power and the Production of History.* Boston: Beacon Press, 2015.

Turino, Thomas, and James Lea. *Identity and the Arts in Diaspora Communities.* Warren, MI: Harmonie Park Press, 2004.

Turner, Sasha. *Contested Bodies: Pregnancy, Childrearing, and Slavery in Jamaica.* Philadelphia: University of Pennsylvania Press, 2017.

Valerio, Miguel A. "Black Confraternity Members Performing Afro-Christian Identity in a Renaissance Festival in Mexico City in 1539." *Confraternitas* 29.1 (2018): 31–54.

"A Mexican *Sangamento*? The First Afro-Christian Performance in the Americas." In *Afro-Catholic Festivals in the Americas: Performance, Representation, and the Making of Black Atlantic Tradition*, edited by Cécile Fromont. University Park: Pennsylvania State University Press, 2019. 59–74.

"The Queen [of] Sheba's Manifold Body: Creole Black Women Performing Sexuality, Cultural Identity, and Power in Seventeenth-Century Mexico City." *Afro-Hispanic Review* 35.2 (2016): 79–98.

"The Spanish Petition System, Hospital/ity, and the Formation of a Mulato Community in Sixteenth-Century Mexico." *The Americas* 78.3 (2021): 415–437.

"'That There Be No Black Brotherhood': The Failed Suppression of Afro-Mexican Confraternities, 1568–1612." *Slavery and Abolition* 42.2 (2021): 293–314.

Velázquez Gutiérrez, María Elisa. *Juan Correa: Mulato libre, maestro de pintor*. Mexico City: Conaculta, 1998.

Mujeres de origen africano en la capital novohispana, siglos XVII y XVIII. Mexico City: Instituto Nacional de Antropología e Historia and Universidad Nacional Autónoma de México, 2006.

Viana Filho, Luiz. *O negro na Bahia*, edited by Gilberto Freyre. Sao Paulo: Livraria Matins/INL, 1976.

Vieira Ribeiro, Alexandre. "The Transatlantic Slave Trade to Bahia, 1582–1851." In *Extending the Frontiers: Essays in the New Transatlantic Slave Trade Database*, edited by David Eltis and David Richardson. New Haven, CT: Yale University Press, 2008. 130–54.

Vila Vilar, Enriqueta. "The Large-Scale Introduction of Africans into Veracruz and Cartagena." *Annals of the New York Academy of Sciences* 292 (1977): 267–80.

Villa-Flores, Javier. *Dangerous Speech: A Social History of Blasphemy in Colonial Mexico*. Tucson: University of Arizona Press, 2006.

Vincent, Bernard. "Les Confréries de noirs dans la Péninsule Ibérique." In *Religiosidad y costumbres populares en Iberoamérica*, edited by David González Cruz. Huelva: University of Huelva, 2000. 17–28.

Vincent, Catherine. *Les confréries médiévales dans le royaume de France: XIIIᵉ–XVᵉ siècle*. Paris: Albin Michel, 1994.

Vinson III, Ben. *Bearing Arms for His Majesty: The Free-Colored Militia in Colonial Mexico*. Stanford, CA: Stanford University Press, 2001.

Vinson III, Ben, and Matthew Restall. *Black Mexico: Race and Society from Colonial to Modern Times*. Albuquerque: University of New Mexico Press, 2009.

Vinzent, Jutta. "In Search of Hybridity: Inculturation, Interculturation and Transculturation in Contemporary Religious Art in Britain." *Exchange*. 39.1 (2010): 29–48.

Voigt, Lisa. "Representing an African King in Brazil." In *Afro-Catholic Festivals in the Americas: Performance, Representation, and the Making of Black*

Atlantic Tradition, edited by Cécile Fromont. College Park: Pennsylvania State University Press, 2019. 75–91.

Spectacular Wealth: The Festivals of Colonial South American Mining Towns. Austin: University of Texas Press, 2016.

Walker, Tamara J. *Exquisite Slaves: Race, Clothing, and Status in Colonial Lima.* Cambridge: Cambridge University Press, 2017.

"The Queen of *los Congos*: Slavery, Gender, and Confraternity Life in Late-Colonial Lima, Peru." *Journal of Family History* 40.3 (2015): 305–22.

Walters, Wendy W. *Archives of the Black Atlantic: Reading between Literature and History.* New York: Routledge, 2013.

Warren, Calvin L. *Ontological Terror: Blackness, Nihilism, and Emancipation.* Durham, NC: Duke University Press, 2018.

Welch, Ellen R. *A Theater of Diplomacy: International Relations and the Performing Arts in Modern France.* Philadelphia: University of Pennsylvania Press, 2017.

Williams, Jerry M. *El teatro del México colonial: Época misionera.* New York: Lang, 1992.

Wheeler, Roxann. *The Complexion of Race: Categories of Difference in Eighteenth-Century British Culture.* Philadelphia: University of Pennsylvania Press, 2000.

Whitford, David M. *The Curse of Ham in the Early Modern Era: The Bible and the Justifications for Slavery.* Farnham: Ashgate, 2012.

Index

For EU product safety concerns, contact us at Calle de José Abascal, 56–1°,
28003 Madrid, Spain or eugpsr@cambridge.org.

www.ingramcontent.com/pod-product-compliance
Ingram Content Group UK Ltd.
Pitfield, Milton Keynes, MK11 3LW, UK
UKHW010250140625
459647UK00013BA/1766